THE MESSAGE IN THE RUNES

A COMPASS HOME

BY SIRROM NOEL YHTOMIT
Second Edition 2018

Published by Rune Magic, Portland Oregon
On the web at- Rune-reader.com a Tall Tim Morris company
Cover & graphics by Denis Mortenson, Mango Studios and Thompson Graphic Design.

COPY RIGHT 2018
BY SIRROM NOEL YHTOMIT
ALL RIGHTS RESERVED BY AUTHOR

TO SCOTT TULLY, MY GOTHIE, FOR
BRINGING ODIN TO LIFE IN ME.

TO MARK VOGLE, A SCALD, FOR THE GIFT
OF DISCIPLINE IN THE LORE.

TO DAVID WIELING FOR THE LOYALTY OF A
TRUE THANE.

TO MONTY MONTGOMERY FOR THE BEST
EXAMPLE OF HIGH MINDED BROTHERHOOD
AND CRAFTSMANSHIP I HAVE EVER SEEN.

TO LESA HAKALA, MY PRECIOUS SISTER,
FOR STANDING BY ME THROUGH THICK
AND THIN.

AND
TO JOHANNAN KELLY FOR BRINGING LOVE
BACK INTO MY LIFE AND TRYING SO HARD.

Thank You

OH THAT IN A THING SO
SIMPLE COULD THE
WONDERS OF THE
WORLD BE WRIT

CHAPTER INDEX

INTRODUCTION	2
PRIMARY RUNE STUDY	29
BASELINE DIAGRAMS	60
ASPECT INDEX	66
FEHU	68
URUZ	84
THURSAZ	99
ANSUZ	117
RAIDO	133
KENAZ	150
GEBO	168
WUNJO	187
HAGALAZ	207
NAUTHIZ	228
ISA	249
JERA	268
AIWAZ	288
PERTHO	309
ELHAZ	329
SOWILO	347
TIWAZ	371
BERKANO	391
EHWAZ	408
MANAZ	420
LAGUZ	437
INGWAZ	453
DAGAZ	472
OTHALAZ	486
FINAL NOTES	501
BONUS / RUNE COMPUTER	503 TO 507

INTRODUCTION AND INSTRUCTION FOR USING THIS BOOK

The Norse / Gothic Runic alphabet is the most beautiful and, until now, least understood of all the ancient mysteries.

Now, for the first time in modern history, an ancient secret is actually revealed and made of use to man.

The most wonderful and self fulfilling gift you may ever give yourself and your children will be the mastery of the information in this book.

The subject of this book is a <u>template built from clues found in Norse poetry and Folk Lore</u> that displays the many relativities of our reality using Norse Runes and Realms.

They explain in detail how everything you already know to be true is tied together in a grand design.

THE RUNES AND REALMS ARE AN ANALOGUE COMPUTER

It has been recreated here from information set aside from up to three thousand years ago.
The actual device is here for your benefit.

This computer and the ability to use it are the benefits you get from this book.

The ways in which you apply this to yourself is up to you and your situation.

In learning the first thing that you realize from this device you will affirm that it is a genuine article and a wonder of understanding.

Then you will begin to extract benefits from this resource <u>as you need them.</u>

I know infinitely more about everything in life because I am able to draw more intelligent conclusions from the same information using this tool.

The same will be true for you, regardless of your identity or description.

This is proof that ancient people knew much more about themselves than had been previously believed, and that the direction of progress may not have been driven by the ability to exploit resources and people as much as by a deeper understanding of what our actions mean to the <u>Whole Picture</u> of reality and identity.

The accumulation of wealth as a motivation, purpose, or basis for validation, as well as the dominion over others as a social qualifier of success have been misplaced and incorrectly identifies the benefits of wealth or social position.

The safety, progress and majesty of the people we live with is the greater application of wealth and, the creative, mutually beneficial result of each social interaction is the better use of social standing.

Humanity is described by our hope, not our color.

Identity is found in direction, not description.

Our common journey is toward the person we know we should be.

The majority of strife on Earth today results from a basic misunderstanding of the real power of a human being to create.

The choosing of sides on every point and issue is the result of blindness to the fact that everything is part of a pattern that has been mapped and may be referenced.

Once we make it our personal struggle and not as an enemy of others we grow to be beautiful.

Effective applications of creative power is fully demonstrated and supported by this device, thus removing most topics from argument.

At the same time we are all in this together and the way things work are not only a matter for discussion, but mastery.

We do not employ many of the tools that we could because we do not understand the fundamentals of the unintended consequences that we do create, and fear them, becoming more and more shy of direct action.

We then create ways to escape direct action.

Our methods of testing are incomplete and we do not trust them, yet they may be improved well beyond our use in the presence of this knowledge.

The world reels in response to the weight of unintended consequences that could be greatly reduced without changing any of the principles we stand by, or surrendering any of our freedom.

This tool will allow you to gain that mastery, if you choose to learn how to use it.

To those with some knowledge of the Runes.

Please note the first three Runes Fehu, the power to create, Uruz, the resistance to that power, and Thursaz, the rules that govern the interaction of Fehu and Uruz, form our reality.

All things follow and result from the interaction of our will and resistance to our will.

If you have been taught that Fehu is money or domesticated cattle, it is power you control, just as Uruz, or wild cattle are strong and resist your control.

Thursaz is the Rune of order and rules or laws.

Law may not be ignored, it is law, law does not vary or deny any thing that is in order.

This is why Thor is described as he is, immovable incorruptible, true.

Thursaz encourages orderly use of creative power and rewards it with every thing necessary to succeed.

To readers in general.

Try to keep your thinking simple as you proceed.

This is information followed by some personal observations noted in applying the lessons learned.

We have all learned at the same schools and attended the same churches and use similar media so this should be readily understood by any one in the western world and everywhere in general.

This provides discipline as well as instruction for correction in maximizing our potentials.

WHAT DO THE REALMS PROVIDE?

Everything that happens with you manifests in either a physical, moral, social, mental, familial, mortal, or educational way, or as a result of your action.
Those areas are represented by the Realms and provide a categoric self view we can focus on.

WHAT DO THE RUNES PROVIDE?

Everything we experience is made up of the base line events, effects, actions, or stations that the Runes stand for in their basic meaning.
Until now the only understanding of the Runes has been the basic meaning.
Until now no reason has ever been given for the Runes having meanings in the first place other than for divination or esoteric healing, with no explanation or foundation for those beliefs.
Those meanings are taught shortly with a clearly defined purpose.

WHAT DO YOU PROVIDE?

If you know enough facts to see an effect and the means by which it is perceived or experienced, you have enough information to set the device.
(demonstrated shortly)
Your <u>cognitive imagination</u> will then draw the relative factors of your query from the other Runes displayed around the Realm Star part of the device.
It is that simple.

DEFINITIONS/EXAMPLE

On pages 60 to 62 there are diagrams.
The Rune in the center is defined by the Runes in the eight points around the diagram.
Here is the diagram for Thursaz.

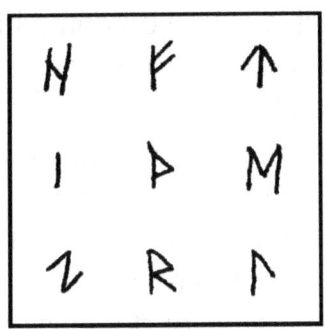

What is Thursaz, Rune of ritual, law, order?
From top left clockwise.
The balance of the elemental universe in the perfection of movement and mass are because the laws of physics are firm. [Hagalaz, balance Rune]
The power of a moral code is found in the balance of ones personal law of behavior and responsibility. [Fehu Rune]
The justice in society is only found where law encourages balance and moral strength equally for all. [Tiwaz Rune]
The ability to relate to our thoughts is found in a balanced environment where a strong moral compass and just opportunity abide. [Ehwaz Rune]
Progression of spiritual being into form is only possible when that mind is able to open to it. [Laguz Rune]

The pathway through our cycles of life is opened because the laws of Thursaz make these other things so. [Raido Rune]

Our ability to incorporate our lessons in life exists because the rules that govern all of these factors are as they need to be for it all to happen. [Aiwaz Rune]

The chance to reach a stable outcome in any of our plans or endeavors are what the rules allow. [Isa Rune]

So, what is Thursaz?

Without order none of those things would exist and our experience in life would not be possible.

Each Rune has a dynamic and full definition found in the other Runes and Realm contexts.

These are not tenets, sects or dogmas, but diagrams of reality.

This may appear to be a childishly simple device, but so is humanity when you realize in detail how we work.

It is basic, complete and does exactly what we need it to do.

It allows a full grasp of relative facts about how we operate as human beings.

The Realms are then defined by the Runes around the square relative to the whole.

The same placement may then serve unlimited data about specific interests without themselves changing.

Your interest <u>creates</u> the parameter as you direct it.

With this tool it is not a priest or public official who will serve you up the truth, but you who will know and require the truth.

You will know.

This is the one I reference just to review questions as they arise.

Even after all this time I do not think memorizing the diagrams is wise for me because I might tend to assume a relativity without seeing a connection I would see using it.

As a result I am often surprised to remember and realize an interaction.

One need not commit the whole thing to memory to use it to great affect.

Just knowing the Runes and Realms will do.

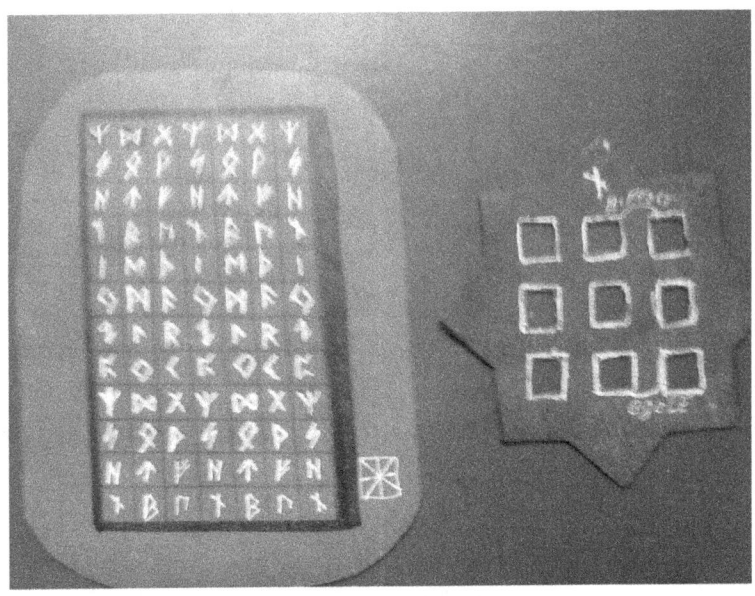

You will find this diagram following the primary Rune Study chapter.

It is simply column after column of Runes in sets of eight, repeating across the page.

The highlighted area are the central Runes.

The pattern extends two columns on each side and two rows above and below.

This is the base of the analogue computer.

THE REALMS

1	2	3
physical body	moral code	social Inter action
Vanheim	**Asgard**	**Alfheim**

SUBJECT

8	9	4
outcome	in action	your mind
Jotunheim	**Midgard**	**Muspelheim**

our learning process	transition through death	our soul history & kin
7	6	5
Svartheim	**Hel**	**Niflheim**

Using a square with nine measured holes cut, at a spacing of two Runes and laid over the Rune base you reveal the relative considerations that make up the data base.
This is a slide that moves across the base and displays the formulas.
  The soft ware is your <u>cognitive imagination.</u>

There are many kinds of Rune.

There are many books about Runes, however there are no other books on this subject matter at this time.

The **Elder Futhark** of twenty four Runes, Othalaz being the last Rune is the **Futhark** used here.

I am telling you now, these Runes are a perfect map of 'us'.

They give language and form to a fuller understanding of our selves including all of the interactive factors in situations we encounter from day to day.

You are going to learn from this book exactly how to realize the incredible and simple beauty you have always known to be true of your self.

Note:

It is said that we use ten percent of our brain.

We are able to, and do, get by on about ten percent of the available information about what we are doing most of the time.

You may now use and apply the rest.

We are very close and well directed, but limited as the details needed to shine are obscure.

Those needed details are the purpose of the Runes.

There is so much I had not put together in my word view that are very simple things for me now.

It is the absence of these relativities from our thinking that result in so many unintended consequences and so much wasted time.

For those who practice a Norse belief system.

There is a probability that many will immediately assume that this entire presentation is cut from whole cloth, so let's tie the ends on that.
BASIC FOLK LORE
You will find direction for the Realm placement in the sequence of seasonal Blots found in Norse Lore and on the common **Sun Wheel pictured here.**

1, **Vanaheim -North West, Winter Night** (where we begin each set of aspects presented in the text as number 1) is the physical form and fact of being waiting the return of life and experience, just like the Earth and Elder Gods in the Lore.

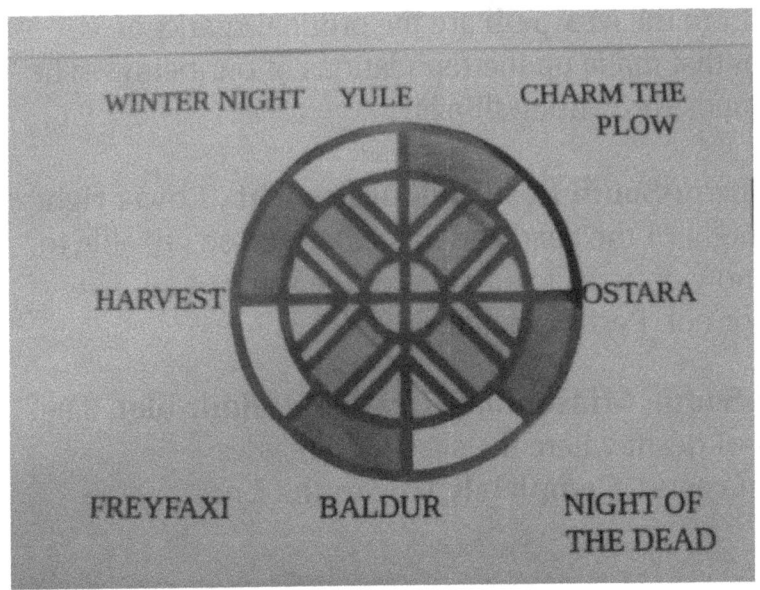

2, Asgard -North, Yule, top center. Birth of Baldur blot. a place of halls and doorways, residence to many, yet must be entered through the door of merit to hold sway, or be heard.

3, Alfheim-North-East, Disablot / Charming of the Plow, is a Frey and Freyja Blot.
Here on the Helm of Awe diagram and is the Realm of Frey's tooth gift.
 Again we see that the whole Lore is one thing put together to keep ALL of the parts from being lost or glossed over with trends or sectarian tenets over time.

4, Muspelheim-East, Ostara Blot is the coming day, season, life, or idea.
In the Lore the **Muspelli** are the original sparks of thought that make up the foundations of our beings. The East stands for coming things.

5, Niflheim-South East.Walpurgisnacht , Lower right is the night of the dead and the unborn those not able to speak now or here. The Realm of the souls of all, now living or not. Perfect match.

6, Hel-South, Midsummer Death of Baldur blot, The reality of death where the slain God resides.
Bottom center. **Completely true to the Lore.**

7, Svartenheim-South West, Frey Faxi Blot, Where Frey's steed takes his hired man on the quest for Gerd The mysterious Beauty of his vision from the High Seat and on his quest for answers.

8, Jotunheim -West, Harvest Blot, Where we reap what we have sewn in order and progress, or unintended consequences.

Each Ritual a perfect match to the Realm Star at each compass point, in reference to each seasonal purpose and each blot.

So you see in the ritual year calender, the Deities associated with those rituals are the same as the Realms that are on those compass points on the Realm Star, the ancient elementals at the four corners are also the same.

There is nothing in the history of mankind, the physical make up of the universe, the spiritual expressions of humanity or the Lore that does not line up.

This is the primal religion and college.

This is the base line political platform.

This is the primary social guide, and yet it does not tell you <u>how to pray</u>, <u>how to vote</u>, or <u>how to treat others.</u>

It tells us what is relevant so we can best decide for ourselves.

PHONETIC NAMES.

The Rune sound that begins each Realm name holds the essence of that Realm, as well as the archetype associated with the Realm.

1. Wunjo is the Rune for Vanaheim, which is our personal physical space. (W is not found in Norse, It is a V) Where our body lives.
2. Ansuz and Elhaz for Azgard, mean 'Voice of God and protection, growth and beauty. That is what our moral code is for.
3. Ansuz and Laguz for Alfheim means Voice of God and soul of man, and that Realm is our social proving ground of character.
4. Manaz and Uruz for Muspelheim means man in resistance to himself describes what the mind is.
5. Niflheim begins with Nauthiz, the Rune of need and Isa the Rune of stability and that Realm is the essence of need.
6. Hagalaz is for Hel and means balance and Ehwaz for spiritual union, which describes Hel exactly.
7. This is the Svarten Realm. Sowilo is the victory in the struggle and Wunjo is ordering of our own circumstances. This is what the mysteries are all about.
8. Jera and Othalaz are for Jotunheim and it is the Realm of harvest as Jera and Othalaz are the harvest of ourselves from our experience in life.
9. Midgard is Manaz, Isa, and Dagaz which is man in the stable place where we evolve and where we may attain our destiny when we choose and grow through the experience.

We can clearly see the phonetic values are one with the essential meanings of the characters and again the intent and purpose for the Runes and Lore are apparent.

Again let me make clear that no reasonable argument opposing the viability of this tool is possible by some one who has not learned the Runes and tested the result, so do not be swayed by nay-sayers who are ignorant of the subject, or your own misgivings.

All discussion by those who have taken the small amount of time and effort necessary to learn the values will be toward applications, not authenticity.

This is a tool for the higher development of man that can be of great importance in fine tuning the efforts of the common weal in time to come.

As with all tools, there is a learning curve and proper use is required.

It is just as it should be.

Everything in Norse mythology is a clue to this end.

Every aspect of that lore is included in the makeup.

Every poem or story displays one or more function or relativity and every character acts out the relativity involved.

This has all been before our eyes for centuries and has now been spotted.

It is real.

Good luck!

REQUIREMENTS
Put your best foot forward now and:
1. **Learn the Runes.**
2. **Use the Primary Rune Study chapter** to do that.
3. **Learn them in order,** in the simplest way that applies to people. The order is very significant. (this is really very simple)
4. **You must memorize** the **Rune** meanings and the **Realm** meanings so your mind can <u>see</u> the synchronicity of the relativities displayed.

Note:
Returning to the source pages [60 to 62] again and again to refresh yourself on the meanings or placements will be very cumbersome and other relative points will escape you if you do not recognize them straight away.

5. **Keep it simple.**

If this seems a daunting task just think about learning to navigate any new digital device like a smart phone or tablet, or even an app.
This is easier than you can imagine.
Any child can master this and those who are taught how will be infinitely better off than those who are not.

6. I suggest you make some flash card with the Rune name and base meaning on one side and Rune shape on the other.

The <u>Elder Futhark</u> of the Norse / Gothic Runes makes up one half of a template that maps the human condition.

The Runes themselves each stand for something that is a factor in the human experience such as money or balance, or the justice that governs human existence, as well as having a phonetic value for use as an alphabet.
 The phonetic value of the Runes play a small part in learning the function of this template, mainly the meaning.
 The phonetics will take you much deeper in time.
 These Rune meanings are loose and broad and require context to take on any practical meaning.

The Lore of the <u>Nine Realms of Existence</u> found in Norse mythology provide the context.

Together the Runes and the Realms make up a template with a moving graph that details the relativity of all human factors to each other.
 This book contains the template and one analogy, or allegory for each of the basic aspects it maps from the center outward around the eight pointed star, which is the symbol for the **Helm of Awe,** the significance of which is found in these templates.

The Helm of Awe represents the eight factors of all things personal.

1 Body, (the North West point, then clockwise)

2 Moral compass, North,

3 Social interaction, North East,

4 The mind, consciousness East,

5 Family, spiritual history South East,

6 Transition from life to death, South,

7 The source of learning, South West

8 The out come of our actions relative to our whole being, West.

At the center is you
The number of advanced aspect applications is virtually unlimited and are created by any question one may pose, yet there are only twenty four basic sets, one set for each Rune as it appears in the center, Midgard, or representing your total self.

Norse Lore is a wonderful puzzle.
The clues that led to the discovery of this template were found in the Rune story, creation story, the myth of Mimer, and the descriptions of the Realms themselves and seasonal rituals.

The legend of the Helm of Awe and Fafnir the Dragon found in the Song of The Volsungs and the Nibelungen hold the crucial clues to the puzzle and the building of the template.

The order of the Runes into three sets of eight or **Aetts** is also a key to the function of the device.

The columns of Runes, on the Mimers Well Page, by sets of eight are sufficient for each Rune to appear one time in each Realm, making up the base of the template.
When the Realm Star, which is the Helm of Awe, with the nine square holes cut in it is placed over the base page (Mimmers well) the Rune values in each hole display the relativity of each part of our being to the others using the basic Rune meanings.

The divisions of self are based on the Realm's historic characteristics which correspond to our being as human creatures and the placement on the Realm Star is in line with the Realms placement in the Lore, such as Asgard being to the North and Hel to the South as well as matching the seasonal Blots as displayed on the common Sun Wheel.

Advanced Search of context is possible as well as temporal reference using the **Norns.**

The Norns are, 'What is', **Urd,** 'What is becoming', **Verdandi,** and 'What should be', **Skuld,**
also known as The Fates or the Maiden, the Matron, and the Crone.

Including yet another part of Norse Mythology into the tool itself, and making it even more clear that the whole of that mythology and Lore is part of a greater message and tool for the fulfillment of the Folk as individuals and as a group.

The result is a template that explains actions, interactions, psychology and sociology in a manner so sophisticated that, so far, my research has found no circumstance that is not clearly diagrammed by the template.

A person learning to use this device in the past would learn all they needed to interact as a part of the social group, or to offer counsel. (Shaman or Spirit Warrior)

The same is true today.

The keys to our personal joy are made available here.

This knowledge has so strongly affected me that my life has been turned around and set right.

In acknowledging this I authored the book spelling my name in reverse.

What our senses tell us.

So many human perspectives are based on reflection of physical phenomenon (such as light or sound) that we habitually reverse stimuli that are not reflected as well, which leads to inverted views of those stimuli, (such as faith, intuition, pre-cognition, or deja vu).

Conscious and extra-dimensional stimuli affect us much of the time and are often interpreted the way reflected perceptions are which make no sense, leading to fear, confusion or "white noise."

This is one source of demonic possession and evil being beliefs as an unintended consequence.

Keep that in mind as you study this material and you will see very quickly that it is accurate.

As academia do not study mysticism and consciousness together, you will, sadly, find no relative research for comparison from the scientific community.

All scientific findings to date do support the assertions made here and no requirement for Divine explanations is needed.

That said; The fact that this exists is a fact that rests on reality and not religion or belief.

NOTE:
 There are no miracles discussed here beyond the existence of this wonderful tool.
 Every thing the Runes reveal conforms to the physical laws of the universe.
 So many of the things we have long believed were Divine or mystical are simply removed from our understanding by simple ignorance of some factor we have not known existed, or how we might access such information.

 Many religions have inserted magical explanations for things that are not actually mysteries, but rather have been concealed from humanity by people seeking to dominate their fellow man.
 These hopeful rulers have set the stage for the dilemma now faced by all of humanity with tales of personal endorsements from God and threats to any who deny them power or compliance.
 The result has been the denial of every one's right to know the true beauty of Divinity for themselves.
  The "Divine Mysteries" are laid bare in this book and yet proven by it as well.

 Any religion that rests upon an action that is beyond the laws of the physical universe is not rationally founded.

ODIN GAVE THE GIFT OF THE RUNES TO MAN

The Runes start by telling us what we would look like if we were in order.

Physical being.

Fehu would tell us that our ability to make things determines our standard of living.
Uruz that every time we try to do something there is resistance in the way of making it happen that must be channeled, moved, conquered, broken or paid.
Thursaz, are rules, inclusions, exceptions and consequences and is the child of the first two and its' whole existence describes the parents actions with limitation and is the cornerstone of every thing. Nothing exists outside of the rules, but explodes with potential and unlimited application when in order.
Ansuz, is our conscience and constant voice of companionship with all that is. We hear this when we are in order. Everyone speaks to everyone at this level.
Raido is the path we are able to reasonably select and which forms our identity as the person who is going where you are going and does what you do.
Kenaz is the truth about you, now that you are able to describe your self, and in that truth your place here is brought into the light.
Gebo is the gift that every thing you make is to everyone who receives from you. It is your honor and a treasure beyond price.

Wunjo is the joy of being in the space where you are standing.
It is yours and nothing is there that you have not vetted or made,
The key to being is now forged.
The first eight have shown the sequence of steps to becomes viable as a sole being.

Emotional Being.

Now the second eight show us how to interact with other people in a manner that opens possibilities for them as well as our selves, while schooling us on our own emotional presence.
Hagalaz is the act of balancing reactivity with gravity. Already people are safe from capital loss by you because you are Wunjo , you pay for and power your own life. Now the hazard of temper is not considered.
Nauthiz you employ power only according to need and then to maintain balance. The victory you seek is not in the failure of our companions.
Isa now we are solid, balanced, mindful people with honor and clear space with others testing and retesting behavior to find justice. Standing in solid support.
Jera is the harvest of all of what we experience, not just gains but the stuff of losses that now are life lived.
Once able to harvest from all that we do, we are viable universally and are joined with the Cosmic.

Aiwaz is joining with the rest of the universe in harmony.
Pertho is all possible possibilities, now yours in concert with all your endeavors.
Elhaz because now safe and growing you may reach your true beauty and majesty.
Sowilo champion now over self fear, doubt, acceptance and struggle.
Those who love you pay no price for it, suffer no ills from it, have no reason to regret.

Spiritual being.

Tiwaz
We are now able to see justice and decide sacrifice as they really are and take steps toward them.
Berkano
We are now able to care for others in the way that best serves them.
Ehwaz
We are capable and welcomed partners at any part of life's journey. We are a part of the whole and one with ourselves in body and spirit.
Manaz
We are now able to see ourselves in a light of completion and potential, whole and viable.
What it means to be 'as we should be.'
Laguz
We are now able to understand the span of our physical existence and relationship to the grand scheme of things.

Ingwaz
We are able to relate to the chain of beings that make our access to life and an avenue for others to come.
Dagaz
The nature of change, death and development are now clear.
Othalaz
We are now able to find a home in ourselves that is unique and precious to us alone and to all at the same time.

Note:
The definitions and observations given by the author are cursory and as simple as can be made and still assure that the reader have enough to work with in moving forward.
The Runes and Realms themselves will grow in scope and value as the reader learns to apply them.
When you realize that you know something deeper, try not to limit that knowledge with the authors own observations and descriptions.
They are the authors.
What you gain will not be a dogma, but a data base in reference to yourself and your experience.

This goes so deep you will be amazed for years to come.
You will be able to see how every bad action comes to be and how to correct them without hurting anyone.

PRIMARY RUNE STUDY

To understand this work, we must first recognize the characters and their basic meaning.
The meaning and extent of reasonable comparison of situations to Rune values expands as we get to know them, but the scope of activities narrows with experience so that the seeming complexity of the Rune is reduced with the seeming complexity of the world around us.
The world as a random collection of factors that exist independently may appear very complex.
The world as an ordered forum for a specific type of action and interaction does not.
We learn a little, then we learn a lot.
This is not cursory. You must recognize the Rune, the basic meaning, and what that brings you personally to recognize the significance of the relativity displayed in the Realm aspects that make up this work.
They are very easy to learn and because they are in the order of human development, it is even easier.
This part should take from a very few hours to a couple of days.
                    Let's begin.

This is education.

It is quite entertaining, even exciting and fun, but once learned, this can change your life as much as learning to read. This is learning to read on a Cosmic level.

But try to have fun.

The First Eight
Corporeal Man.

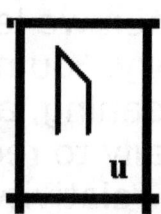

Fehu **Wealth, cattle, personal power and influence. Your creative power.** This is the creative force that causes all things to become. The personal power you can control.

Uruz is **resistance** to creative power.
All energy and gravity is an aspect of this Rune.
Understanding this gives us access to material manipulation and channeling of natural forces that we do not control.
This gives us scope.

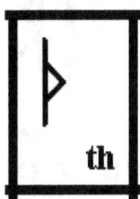

Thursaz Giant, **law** - This is the action of bringing order out of chaos by using personal power or channeling natural energy. Education. Training. This action is the basis of ritual, form, religion, and right action.

The **rules** that govern the first two Runes. This is "what we do." Done well, this gives us authority.

Ansuz This is the **voice of God** that we know as our conscience.

On a grand scale, this is the group conscience. On a Cosmic scale, this is the consciousness of the universes - the God mind.

This gives us the enthusiasm of acting in concert with what we know is right.

 We plug into this by using our power in an ordered way, by the rules.

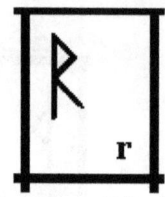

Raido **Journey your path in life** .
A rambling and chaotic journey is not Raido.
A disciplined direction in life is Raido.
All travel of Cosmic Bodies in their orbits is Raido.
 The result is conscience driven creation.
 This gives us identity, direction and destiny.

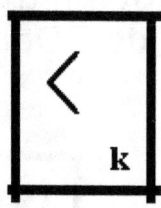

 Kenaz
 Light / the **torch - The truth**, about you, the world, the Gods, your peers, everything created in the sequence of the first five Runes is the truth.
 Living in the truth gives you strength.
Small truth first, then big truth, real strength that will not lie.
This is our reality.

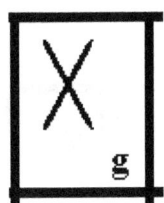

Gebo
The **gift - Fair exchange, fair play,** the absolute refusal to cheat! This simple tool is the essence of honor, your honor!

Wunjo **Personal space, joy**
This is the real physical state of being that exists when we apply the first seven Runes to our life.

This gives you your personal space and control of your life.

This is simply living as a discipline and the key to true social acceptance.

This is not dogma, this is you.

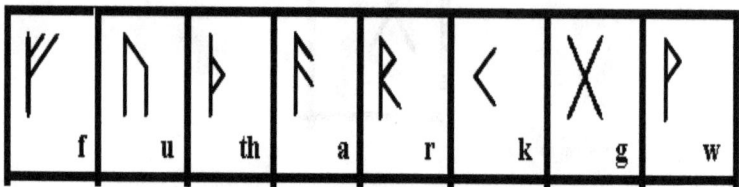

This first set of eight Runes are the steps taken to get you to joy.
 Wunjo .
The person who pays his way, realizes the resistance to their actions, follows rules and gets an education, follows his conscience, stays on course, tells the truth, and plays fair is a better person than those who do not.
This is all about being better men and women.
Simple common sense, but, you can't fake it. It must be true.
 You have to really apply them in order.
 This person is the key to all success and is in order.
That is their truth and may not be denied.
 When any of the steps are rationalized away the result is not Wunjo and the benefits of Wunjo are lost.
 When looking at the Wunjo diagram you will see that the doorway to social acceptance is found in being Wunjo.
  Wunjo is the key.

The Second Eight
Temporal Man - Emotion

[Hagalaz rune image]

Hagalaz **Hail** – Imbalance, **balance, duality** of + - forces.

Embracing balance as a desired point of reaction to emotional stimulation gives you control of the parameters of your thoughts and thereby your actions.

To control emotion and not be controlled by emotion allows you take responsibility in difficult situations.

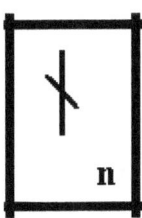

Nathiz
Need - the irresistible urge to take the next breath. **To be.** Everything in the universe shares this common part of being. Knowing that all desire and addictions are responses to this urge, we become dependable and centered,. We control our need!

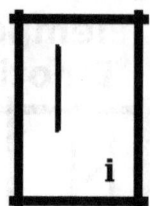

Isa, Ice — **stasis, stability,** support.
Under-standing duality, controlling need. Maintaining a stability of reaction and using a system of behavior or discipline make us viable and necessary.
 We become the support for positive things.
 Knowledge and Lore are **Isa**, Holding things up.

Jera, **Harvest,** year.
 What we get from our lives and what the Cosmos gets from us.
 This gives us a clock and calendar and a plan.
Negative < or, positive > both taken from experience and used to grow.
 This is the place we were aiming for and the ability to manifest our will in the world is the harvest of the Runes to this point.

We are now halfway through the Runes.

Up to now we have applied the Runes to ourselves. Now we begin to apply and join ourselves to the universe, while finding completion and wholeness in ourselves.

Aiwaz, Backbone, **joining,** bow the **hook.** This is the tool that **joins** us to another tool. Systems, layouts, appointed helpers, social tools. This idea moves us along our path, adding essentials as we grow and go. This is what/who we use and how we use them. Properly done, this encourages others to offer their service, or provide tools (very important). **Joining and being joined.**
The clubs, groups and projects we join are Aiwaz and the person you have become in reaching Aiwaz will be a boon to any of these connections.

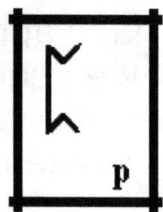

Pertho is **all possible possibility.**
Note: The description here graduates.
By high minded moral presentation of self in tune with the Runes so far, our chance of success also graduates from **potential** to **possibility** to act of will or **promise.**
This gives us what may seem to be mystic powers, but are simply human.

Elhaz, Elk **protection, Progress, majesty.** Guarding what you have gained, growing into a stronger, more virtuous person to a point where form and grace become majesty, like the elk, lord of the forest.
This demonstrates our growth, advancement and beauty.

Sowilo, **sun victory** .This person has soundly beaten himself in the wars of imagination vs. emotion. This person has balance, self-control, stability, experience, connections, opportunity, and form with grace.
 This person can be loved, without corroding the ones who love him/her, with their' toxin.

 Putting these eight Runes in practice gives us a truth about ourselves that we and our companions can deal with, respect, and love without pretense, excuse, or ill consequence.
 Face it, we put up with people who, often are hung up on stuff and don't deal responsibly with themselves or others.
We are never taught how.
This is how!
This works.
These Runes apply outside ourselves in reference, but it is ourselves we apply to the world and the Runes, when applied to ourselves, make that possible.

We know much of this from common sense, but here we have **order, continuity**, and **names** that we can use!
Use them! Say the names.
Put these names to the things in life.

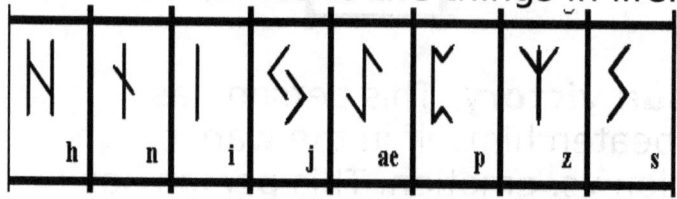

Balanced emotion, managed need, stability, use of both negative and positive returns, a full offering of self to each endeavor, all possible choices, growth, majesty of self that is real, and victory over self defeat and rejection.

This is what a complete person would ideally encompass.

This is what the Runes help us to create of our selves.

There is no dogma and there are no tenets. Just some steps toward our desired self.

This is what the Runes offer, and it is huge.
The Runes are exactly what we each need to reach our potential.

The Third Eight / Spiritual

Tiwaz, **Divine justice**, sacrifice of personal power to the creation of what is right.
 The primary need of the social group is justice and honor.
The person who applied the first sixteen concepts to themselves is the only person with the integrity to judge what is out of order in other lives. This is just true.
This is our awareness of the weight of Divine responsibility.
Think about it.

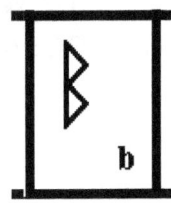

Berkano, **Nurturing,** birth, birch tree, mother, Goddess.
 This Rune stands for taking care of every living thing that is not you — everything!

The Great Mother gives us all life equally and man alone on earth is able to systematically care for things other than man.

This is how we pay our dues. We don't have to argue with fools if we don't want to, we can still fight for right this way. This is the feminine way, but applies to us all!

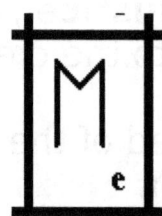

Ehwaz, horse, **partnership, marriage, joint journey.**

This person is finally whole enough to be a mate, Equal beings holding firm. This is where we find our mate.

We carry each other, or other things, but not because of slavery or weak character, but because circumstances allow or require it and we wish to do so.

These people know Spirit because of the Spiritual Oneness they share. These people observe, correct and nurture each other so that success can continue, not to hold control.

This gives us social correctness, tradition, and wonder.

Manaz, **spirit warrior, man.**
This Rune is **man as he should be.**
This person can reach the physical, emotional or spiritual troubles of his fellow man and offer what is necessary to heal their wounds and restore unity or purpose.
This gives us purpose, fellowship and love.
NOTE: This is also the last Rune that is about us as individuals.

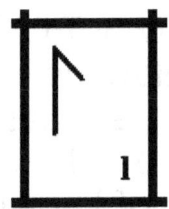

Laguz, the lake, **Soul, spirit,** primal waters of the subconscious.
This is the part of us all that connects us all to each other and to the Goddess.
We share this as humanity and add to it daily.
This brings us dreams and the places where they happen. This is our essential self.

We are all a part of the Lake of Souls.
We are all one in the group of one.
We are Gods' Parents and children at once.

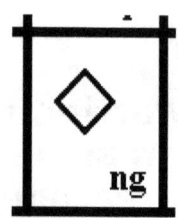

Ingwaz, Kin, **Door, window,** The God Frey / Freyja, the physical door to this life (our mother)and the conceptual door to all things.
This is looking into our other parts, using the third eye.
The Mystic Doorway To All things.
Knowing your relatives in truth.
History, heroes, tests passed, tests failed.
 The experience of all our Folk, ever.
 This is the book of knowledge of what is, of who is.
 When the Runes lead you to this place you are able to enter, to see into and to apply all that you are and see.
 Everyone has the pieces, and simply knowing there is an order lets us put our pieces in order and come to this understanding.

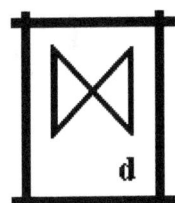

Dagaz, day, **evolution change,** cycles, life times

This is the turning of the macroverse, and the pulse of the microverse , the generator of illusion, life death —day night - on off.

These cycles are real and as immutable as only they themselves can reference.

This is our motivation to participate in what would otherwise be eternity in paradise.

The laws of the physical universe dictate that all things are in a state of change at all times, with no exception.

To exist physically we accepted this and the death that comes with it.

This is not the end of you, it is the change of your experience as the person you are now and you will have to re-form the primal relationship (spirit to ego) with the person you will be when next you take form, creating new ways to find victory in the Divine Struggle that is life.

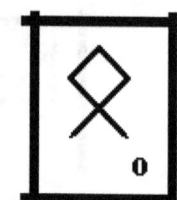

Othalaz, home, **whole being,** ancestral home, body.

The goal - to be at home in this time, this place, this life, this body. To find in what we have, the thing we want.

Like no other place we can be.

Our eternal destination and hope, for just like all of you, I want to feel at home!

Learn these Runes and get an idea of what they mean.

Make some flash cards if you have a hard time.

Try to be moderately prepared for the rest of this book.

This Rune has been misinterpreted to mean some country or sacred home land.

It stands for your body and spirit in one time and place. Your body is your home and you are your ancestor.

Knowing this, the care of this planet and your future home take on a new meaning.

As you continue please remember I am writing this with love and in good faith for the purpose of sharing this evolutionary wonder and because it shows a lot of conventions as harmful behaviors, please remember,
I know that the fear, guilt and hatred that we all wrestle with could be aroused by many of the things written here, were they taken out of context, or not as a part of the whole presentation.

All of the claims about being able to understand true Divinity are not the crux of this tool, but the threshold. All reference to Divinity, God, or any higher being are directed toward the same wonderful, Divine personal compass we all share, by whatever name we know them.

I know that in reading the book and learning to use the tool every one of us can be a good deal happier about their lives.
To reach that point will require your patience with my inexperience as a writer and my sadly terse and direct grammar.

The Rune computer taught me the most useful way to be the man I am supposed to be and in that I am not the font of this tool, but the finder.

So stick with it until you see what it is.
You will be so glad you did.

SYMBOL FOR THE HELM OF AWE

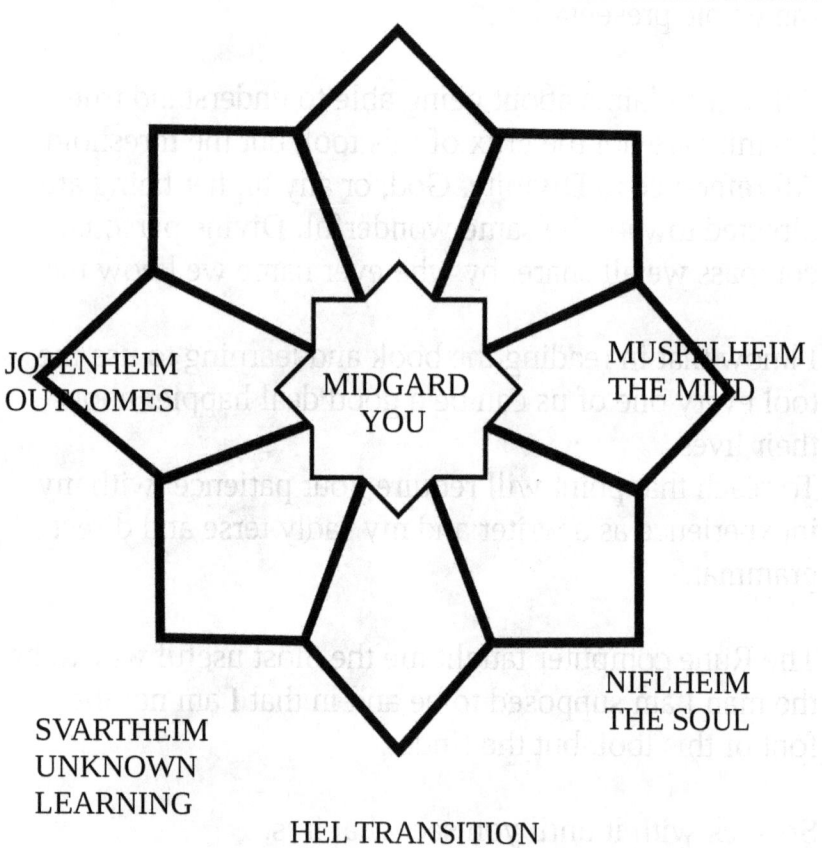

THE REALMS

1	**2**	**3**
physical body	moral code	social action
Vanheim	**Asgard**	**Alfheim**

	SUBJECT	
8	**9**	**4**
outcome	in action	your mind
Jotunheim	**Midgard**	**Muspelheim**

our learning process	transition through death	our soul history & kin
7	**6**	**5**
Svartheim	**Hel**	**Niflheim**

When you place a Rune at one of the Realm points it creates a concept.

Physical stability is a concept and differs from the concept of a stable outcome yet each concept is considered in concept form when the Isa Rune is placed in the Physical Realm, Vanaheim, or the Realm of outcomes, Jotunheim.

The other relative concepts are just as varied yet rely on many of the same Runes in many different ways when represented in different Realm context.

This creates a language of concepts rather than words and allows for an encompassing view rather than an itemized one.

The 'subject matter' categories of the Realms removes questions of focus from constant review as to context and allows a more detailed study of the significance of information.

This is clearly designed to work this way and does so perfectly, opening the doorways to our many facets with poetic harmony and grace.

YOU AND I AND THE HELM OF AWE

HOW IT WORKS.

A supposition is entered using the Rune meaning found in the question, and placed at the position (Realm) that most closely defines the part of our self from which the question arises. -use of personal power socially would be Fehu at the upper right corner, #3, Alfheim-

The meanings of the Runes found in the other positions define the whole meaning of the otherwise singular supposition of spending money or ability socially or publicly, creating a totality of understanding of the most simple or complex of problems, struggles, or relativities.

BENEFIT:
The most important tie-ins of social or political actions and events is exposed and may no longer shield corruption, manipulation or deceit.

The definitions for the Runes is refined by the Realms.
The definitions of the Realms is found in the Runes.

EXAMPLE

Fehu
If you want to understand personal power relative to any part of your self, place Fehu in the numbered square that represents your interest and review the Runes in the other positions to see what factors provide you with the best use or requirement for applying that power.

Uruz
To study the manner in which resistance to your will appears place Uruz in the focus Realm.

Thursaz
If you want to know the rules about a Realm, put Thursaz in that Realm square and the other squares will explain the rules of the Realm you are in.

Ansuz
To see how spiritual guidance will manifest or 'speak' so we may interpret our conscience correctly.

Raido
Will explain the many facets of our journey and identity when in focus Realm.

Kenaz
Will help you see into the depth of the truth as it relates to our whole being, part by part.

Gebo
Honor is a great mystery that is easy to understand using this tool to judge what an honorable outcome would look like.

Wunjo
Shows what being correct in form both looks like and offers, as well as lessons on how to achieve Wunjo.

Hagalaz
Shows how to bring balance to ourselves in our many parts.

Nauthiz
Helps us to find what we actually need to reach our fulfillment. (This will involve the people you know, the things you use, the work you do and the dreams you pursue, not a dogma outside of yourself or tenets towards which you aspire)

Isa
Taking a stable stand or securing a viable personal platform for action is made possible here. What stability looks like may be a mystery undefined.

Jera
What we may expect to harvest from our many parts is revealed here. (at present most people only know how to accumulate things in order to reach these deep needs where things are only relative to physical form, leaving us unfulfilled in most of our being)

Aiwaz
What it means to join with other concepts as well as people and things is detailed so we can develop our entire being and reach our potential more fully.

Pertho
These wonderful possibilities are, for the most part, unrealized in todays world because this tool has not been available, but show us potentials that reveal a paradise before our eyes such as the best imaginations have long written.

Elhaz
Our safety development and beauty have been denied in most potentials and the way to find our real beauty is opened to us here.

Sowilo
The definition of success is so difficult to understand because of the materialism prevalent in the world today.
These are such helpful points when choosing to act.

Tiwaz
Justice and sacrifice are the most beautiful of human concepts, but it has been unclear as to what that is.
No longer true when detailed here.

Berkano
The care of physical bodies is just one aspect of nurturing and may be wasted effort when all parts of a person are not considered.

Ehwaz
Both defines and refines relationships, making true and complete interaction possible from each point of being.

Manaz
Both the picture of and the means of becoming the person we are capable of being is mapped here, making it possible to actually work on ourselves to our own benefit.

Laguz
What an eternal spiritual being is and how one is present in ourselves is explained in a way that we recognize as personal and true.

Ingwaz
If you want to know how best to access a Realm put Ingwaz in the square and you will see how to master access there.

Dagaz
The way that change takes place as we evolve through self understanding and action is defined in these aspects. This makes change understood and welcomed as well as allowing us to direct and incorporate our self development.

Othalaz
Explains how to accept ourselves as transient and eternal beings at once and fully employ our time and opportunities in life.

Odin cast a spell on the severed head of Mimer that he might speak his wisdom even after the Vana Gods returned the head to him in a sack.

The following three pages feature diagrams of the first, second and third aetts, or sets of eight Runes as they will appear in the chapters of analogies later in the book.

When you learn to recognize the placements as the Realm section describes them and the Rune meanings, you are able to 'work' the device.'

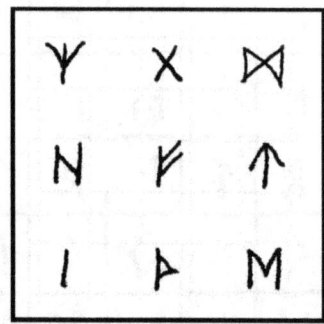

The Rune placements here for instance display how being physically safe, progressing and becoming majestic would be the result of your use of your wealth, creativity, or influence (Fehu; wealth, at the center relative to Elhaz; safety, growth and majesty at upper left, in your physical form)

This, of course is commonly known, but what the other Runes positions tell us goes much deeper into our use of wealth and power.

By 'reading' what is relative to the top left Rune in the other positions you would see what it means to be truly majestic in form.

How to honor your higher moral code in reading the Runes relative to the top center.

How to evolve socially (top right)

How to do justice to your intellect (center right)

How to manage your relationship with your ancestry and progeny (lower right)

The factors that apply at death (bottom center), in this case the rules that govern death are within our personal power to control and how that is done. (the potential applications to you are endless)

How all these factor into your learning process (bottom left)

And what the balanced out come of your actions means to the other relative concepts, in this case the use of power you can control, Fehu, at the center.

You may also reference any position with a Rune meaning in order to find how best to accomplish what that Rune stands for through your control of the other aspects of your self, for instance reaching balance in the out come of your work, as here, or make an actual question.

Note: Hypothetical questions have no relative factors to observe, do not serve beyond general descriptions, and are not viable here. They are abstract.

When something is amiss in a story or situation we know it and with this computer we can explore the event or telling and find the reason for the misgiving or the truth, depending on what you NEED TO KNOW.

Our learning process is need driven, as you will learn in mastering this simple device.

In reading the analogies you will see how deep this can take you into the wonderful mysteries of life.

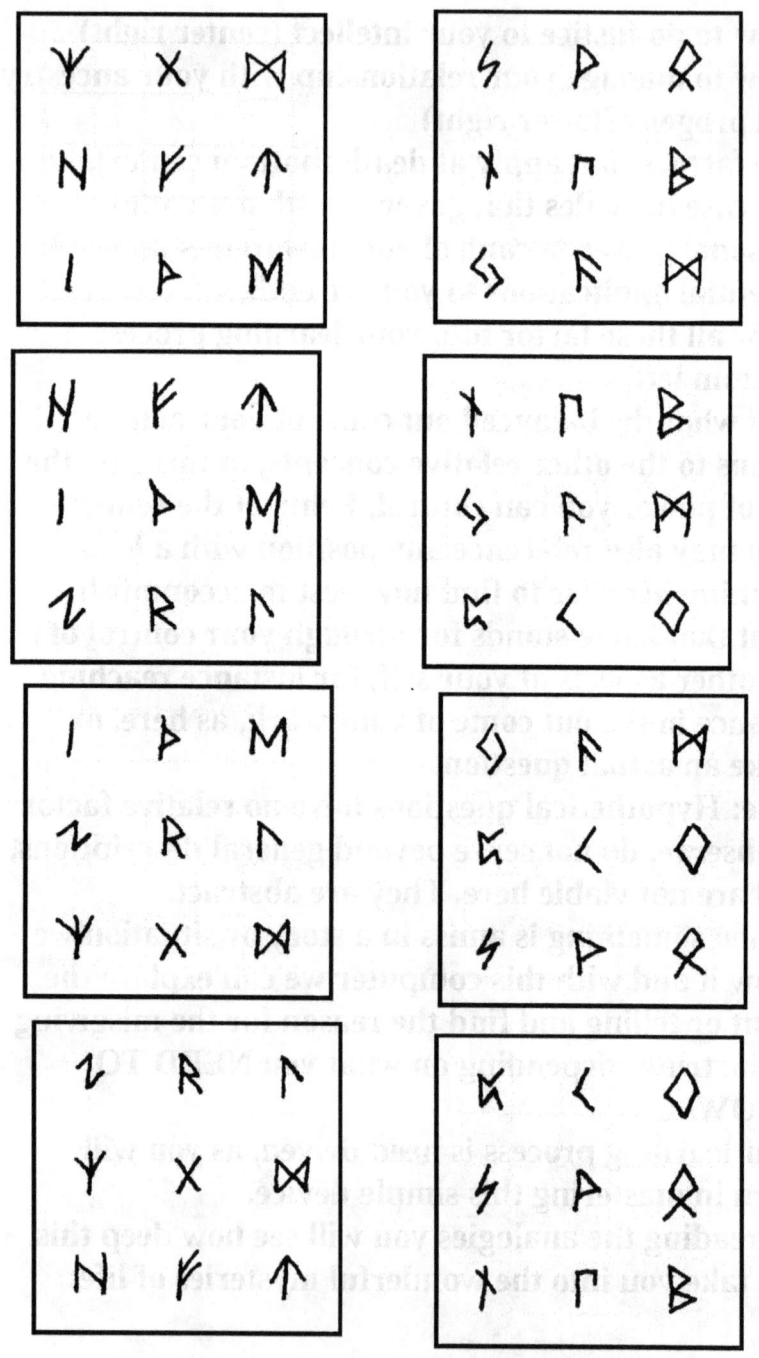

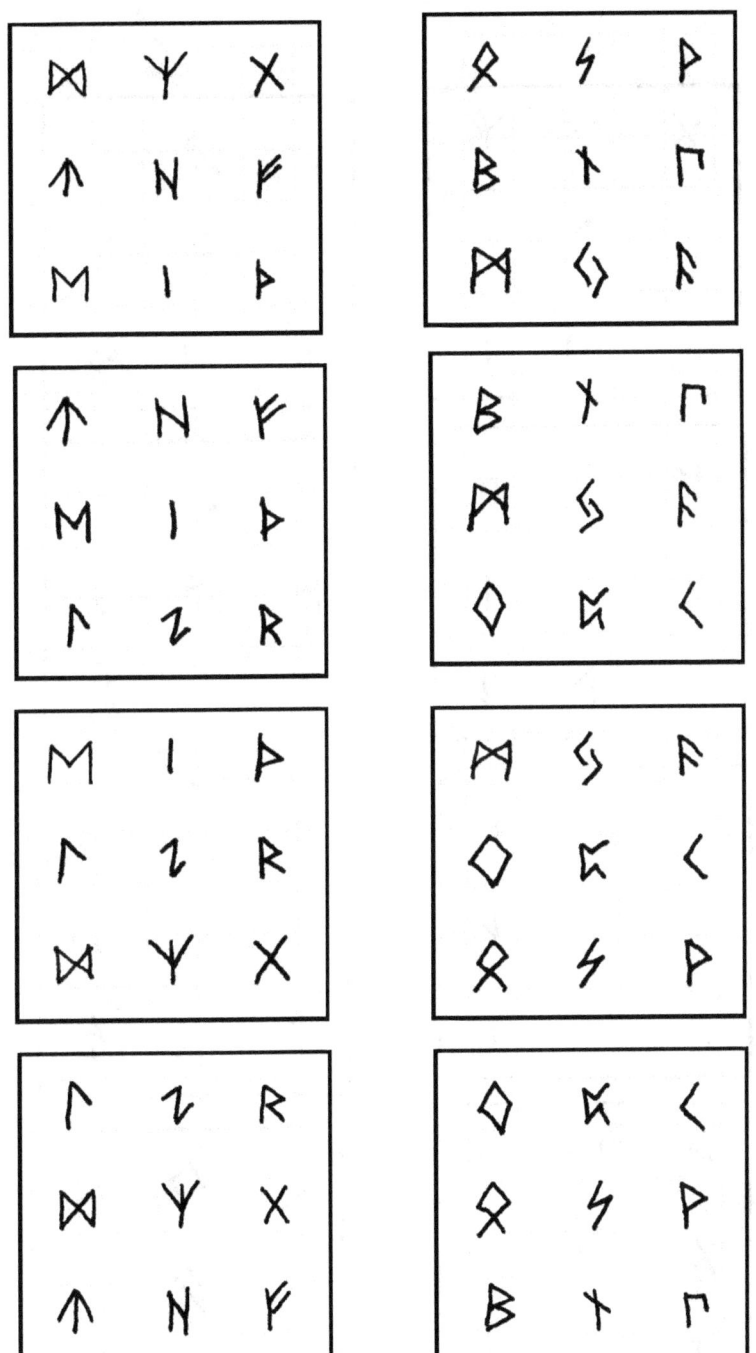

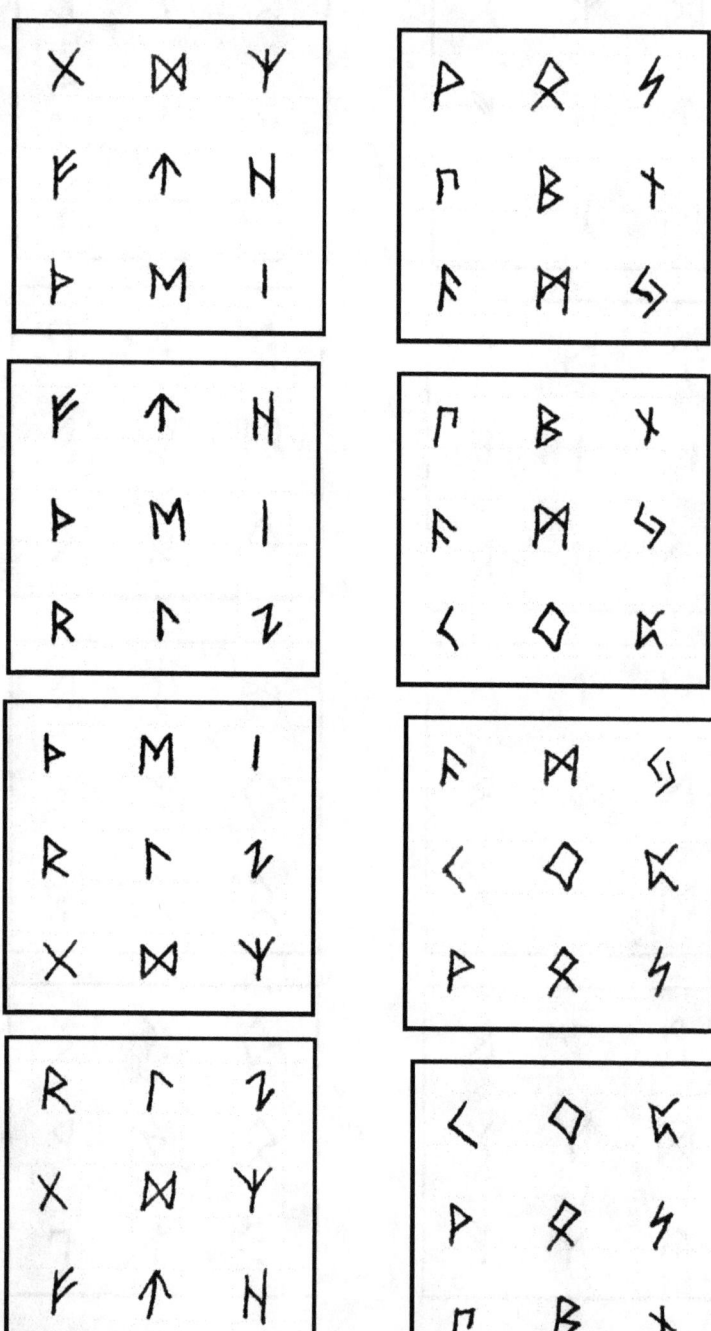

ADMONISHMENT

IF YOU PROCEED TO THE FOLLOWING CHAPTERS WITHOUT LEARNING TO USE THE RUNE / REALM COMPUTER THE TEXT WILL APPEAR TO CONTAIN WILD ASSERTIONS AND INCREDIBLE CLAIMS THAT COULD NOT POSSIBLY BE JUSTIFIED BY ANY RATIONAL PERSON.

IF YOU HAVE LEARNED TO USE THE DEVICE THEY WILL APPEAR AS THEY ARE, WHICH ARE BASE LINE APPLICATIONS IN THE SIMPLEST FORM TO HONE YOUR OWN USES.

NO PERSON IN THE AUTHORS EXPERIENCE IS ABLE TO GRASP THE DEPTH OF HUMAN POTENTIAL IN THE ABSENCE OF THIS DEVICE. <u>NO ASPERSION IS INTENDED HERE.</u>

THE LORE SAYS ODIN (THE HIGH GOD) GAVE THE RUNES TO MAN AND THAT ODIN ARMS MAN AGAINST HIS ENEMIES.
IF A GOD WERE TO GIVE AN AIDE TO MAN THAT WOULD SERVE IN ANY CASE, THIS WOULD BE THE ONE.

HONOR YOUR SELF, AND LEARN THE RUNES AND REALMS AS QUCKLY AS YOU CAN.

The following chapters contain lectures on the first observation made in proofing the device in 1999 and 2000.

literary and technical errors appear in the text.

The religious, political and social difficulty noted by the author reveal the mindset and world view of the author and have grown over time to a much deeper and more settled one.

The originals are presented because it is believed that they will most closely mirror the average person seeing this tool used for the first time.

If a bird did not know that it could fly, it would not fly even though it is a bird.

The author does not see us as broken, only in need of information.

None of us needs to change, only to be able to develop to our potentials.

In that, change will come because people are beautiful and perfect when in possession of the truth and the facts.

The facts are yours.

A way to find some truth is here.

As the author I am trying to become the man I am capable of being by helping you to apply it to your own benefit.

Again, GOOD LUCK!

Aspect content

An observation for each Rune aspect as relative to the center or Midgard is indexed here by page.
The aspects as relative to the other Realms would entail the details of everyones personal life and, of course could not be recorded on any number of pages.
Your own life story will be one that you will write or tell yourself in much more poetic a tone through the use of the Runes.

Do enjoy the journey, and call me if you want to chat.
I am actually easy to get hold of.

	VAN	ASG	ALF	MUS	NIF	HEL	SVA	JOT
Fehu	409	101	255	216	340	180	481	387
Uruz	422	119	274	237	358	200	495	404
Thursaz	438	135	293	258	218	77	384	417
Ansuz	454	152	314	276	239	95	402	433
Raido	473	172	336	296	259	110	416	451
Kenaz	487	191	353	317	279	127	432	470
Gebo	372	70	214	338	298	143	449	482
Wunjo	391	88	234	356	319	160	467	497

	VAN	ASG	ALF	MUS	NIF	HEL	SVA	JOT
Hagalaz	99	253	412	377	479	342	182	81
Nauthiz	118	272	425	396	492	362	202	97
Isa	134	291	441	413	379	221	80	113
Jera	151	312	459	426	398	242	96	131
Aiwaz	169	332	476	433	414	262	112	147
Pertho	189	350	489	460	428	281	129	165
Elhaz	69	211	375	478	445	300	145	184
Sowilo	86	232	394	491	462	321	161	204

	VAN	ASG	ALF	MUS	NIF	HEL	SVA	JOT
Tiwaz	250	410	102	74	178	480	343	226
Birkano	270	424	121	92	198	493	364	246
Ehwaz	289	439	137	105	75	382	224	285
Manaz	310	456	155	123	93	400	244	285
Laguz	331	474	174	138	108	415	264	305
Ingwaz	349	488	192	157	126	429	283	325
Dagaz	209	373	72	176	141	446	303	345
Othalaz	230	392	89	196	159	465	323	367

Remember;

Each of these numbered aspects stands alone, as they are written relative to the center.

This is not a novel.

Some aspects flow directly from the last, but this does not read like a story so much as like a reference book.

The aspect index will direct you to specific aspects.

It may be better to pause after each one before reading the next.

Take the time to find each one in itself.

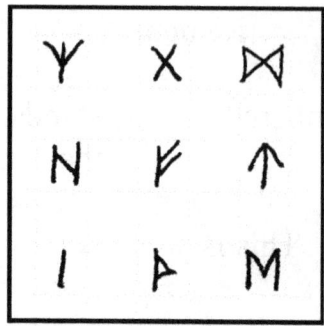

Here we aspect the Rune of wealth.
This is true wealth, actual sheep, cattle, gold, silver, land.
This is not the wealth of illusion, or mortgaged property.
This is the Rune of personal power, so it goes to influence, as well as goods.
As we presented the primary Rune study knowledge, this Rune (Fehu) is the Freedom you really have.
Having self determination is a very real circumstance.
The world is full of people who do not want the masses to enjoy this ability.
They will go to great lengths to deny you.
The most base method is force.
The most cunning is finance.
When you owe wealth, you have no wealth.
We can sell our freedom for credit.

Let's see what happens when you control
your own wealth
(no matter how slight it may seem).
ᛉ
Elhaz in Vanheim, the elemental.
This is the Rune of progress and protection in
the physical universe where you live.
When this is in your control you are free in
the physical world.
When someone else controls your wealth,
your progress and protection depend on
their allowing it to 'be'.
Now we've all heard of the magnanimous
master who provides for his subjects' well-
being as they never could.
Have you ever seen it?
Have you seen anyone with control over
people act to make their lives better in ways
they would not handle much better by
themselves?
Of course not.
People do not have control by accident, or
for the benefit of those they control.
When we are in some ones power, that is
"where" we are. We do not progress.
Sure, our basic needs may be covered and
some luxury to boot, but progress is not ours
to determine.

We fall with the master, but we do not rise with him.
Build your power, don't spend it.
You decide.
You may appear less well off than those with big credit and mortgaged property, but your progress will be real.
Guard this power.
You need it and you will always need it.
This Lore is for those who want to master their lives.
Those who choose to master their life and be the joy of creation, continue, progress, protect, and find majesty in true paradise.
You must guard your power.
You must make it grow.

2
The Rune of exchange and gifts / fair play / in the Heavenly Realm.
Gebo in Asgard.
Here we have our moral code.
Our freedom to determine our actions allows us to give a fair exchange of effort to the moral Realm in return for the strength of character that our moral code provides.

Just as we must be free to determine our progress and protect ourselves, we must be free to give a fair exchange here.
For instance, your company may be a polluter.
Do you compromise your moral code? Risk your job?
Is your mortgage holder a slum lord?
Do you serve someone who causes you to understate or violate your moral code?
Have you noticed that people in control seem to insist that we prove ourselves by denying our moral code?
Could that be what control is all about?
Do those who seek to control others take these things into account?
We are able to give fairly to our moral responsibility when we function under our own power, and pay our own way.
People get pressed for money and get dirty.
Why is it that we have to soil ourselves to stave off the wolf?
Money problems are not money problems, they turn into moral problems right away.
This is important stuff.
Think!

3
Dagaz in Alfheim the social Realm.
Here we see that the evolution of the social Realm is bound to our personal freedom and control of wealth.
(I feel that the cycle of social evolution so visible up into the 1970s was interrupted by a legal shift in the currency in the United States.
The excellent educational development of the young and technical direction of invention was toward a new and better social parameter.
That all ceased and an older, more violent social policing and harvest of private wealth began through the price of durable goods and energy.
Those who stood to lose future profits through the development of alternative energy sources invested not in research, but in politics to prevent the evolution of a less dependent social structure.)
The social cycle will eventually step toward more advanced use of resources, but here we see the value of this aspect.
An advanced society produces more opportunities for the people. Not just for the few, but the many.

When we use our wealth and influence toward this rather than to inhibit, we meet our place socially.
Society evolves toward the ideal we all essentially know.
These Runes tell us this is not random, but by design.
The influence part of Fehu is how we work to guide this ideal into form.
A little thought reveals that those with a clear understanding of these principles can skillfully guide others toward or away from our desired goal.
Understanding this aspect will help you to resist and clearly identify the efforts to divert the positive social Realm's evolution that our children will benefit by so much.
Speak out about use of authority and resources that does not evolve with the society they are supposed to serve.
Take your power or surely someone will take it from you.
Help society evolve.
The heavy-handed control of the old Empires is not the tool to rule the world in an age of light and knowledge.
The light must be dimmed, the knowledge hidden, as it always was before.

We must grow out of that now or we will die.
Now we can put that old nonsense behind us through communication.
The social cycle is on time.
Be a part of it.
Invest in the positive evolution of society.

4
The Rune of justice in the Realm of the mind.
Tiwaz in Muspelheim.
The Realm of Muspelheim is a place of incredible power.
The forces here are beyond measure, unconfined, and fluid.
The instant circuitry of the mental process can access and control these forces in a manner unbound to form.
Such is the mind.
With contact to the actual Cosmic intellect and a personal point of view and intent, we can discern any solutions with a real awareness that we are correct.
Knowing that you can do this is the gift we have.
We owe justice to this remarkable capability.

If we are seeking a career because it pays more, and for no other reason, think about the three aspects we have just been over.
Of course it matters what you are paid, but the mind is there to be challenged.
Do something you want to understand and master.
Do something you can improve and modify to be a real victory of thought.
If you have to do something outside of your work to bring justice to your mind, do it.
Your mental health and ability depend on it.
Honor and justice are partners.
One exists because of the other.
This, it appears, is a long known and real part of the truth about you.

5

The Rune of partnership in the Realm of time. Ehwaz in Niflheim.
This is a coming and going aspect that we are all familiar with.
This has to do with wealth and influence passed from ancestors to progeny.
Of course we all have a genetic partnership with our ancestors, and some of us benefit from the passing of wealth to the family.
This is an instruction for such an action.
Those whose families traditionally preserve wealth to provide for future generations

have the potential for greater success, stronger family ideals, more social contribution, and political influence.
It is important to use our influence and wealth in a way that makes that partnership more than just a flowery idea.
We are not strangers to our family, though some people feel they are or act like they are.
We can do a lot of good in setting up a legacy for our children.
We see here that the lessons of Rune aspected relativity is not all unknown information.
All of these things are known in themselves. It is the relationship to other things that sometimes seems something we have not considered.
Common sense is what helps us to realize the benefit of these relationships.
It becomes personal power (wealth, knowledge) that can be passed along.

6
The Rune of ritual and change in the Realm of Death.
Thursaz in Hel.
Here we have the action Rune in a place where action is not a factor.
Thursaz represents the action of using the power we can control to channel the power we cannot control to create a manifestation of our will in form.
This represents the act of changing.
We change a wooded lot into a field of grain.
We change ourselves into better people through the rites of hard challenges faced and education.
Later we will see more aspects of the Realm of Hel that will make clear this first aspect, which simply put, is changing the mortal self into the immortal self.
What is most clear is the overview this gives us of the whole living process as revealed by the Runes.
Everything that will be in your story of life will be something you have done.
From start to finish, this really is your life.
That there is a pattern has always been known.

What the pattern is has always been a mystery.
As we have seen in the Realm of society (Dagaz in Alfheim) the cycle of social progress has now reached the time for this mystery to come under the light.
This must be true or it would not be happening.
Seeing the pattern will free us from the colossal mess that seems to be inescapable in the world today.
The pattern you will find here will cause the mess to seem petty and open wonderful new horizons for life.
We will see here the pattern itself.
No prophecy, a visible map!
These are not rules for living, just concepts to consider.
You must take those rules into yourself. You'll learn how.
You will see what things need to be addressed in relation to the nine aspects of everything we deal with in life.
When we resolve conflict between the relative aspect and our action harmoniously and then do whatever it is we intend to do, we become in tune with the pattern, which is charged with the power of the Cosmos.

We "do" this life individually, but we are not in it alone.
Every success gives us more strength, more access.
Every correct use of power gives more power.
Every application of order with our life to the pattern gives us experience for the next, which makes our efforts more manageable, though the tasks may become more difficult. Unlike the typical modern person who is forever facing the same problems over and over (generally problems about wealth and personal power) without the guidelines of this Rune Lore our lives become full and the meaning of our lives becomes clear as we apply ourselves with an understanding of the order of the universe, the Cosmos, the self.
Thursaz in Hel here represents the coming to life in the whole world that before we only suspected to exist.
It all starts with using your wealth and power in concert with the rest of the universe.
Keep this in mind as you proceed.
Being born does not make you alive, you must bring yourself to life intentionally.

You must want to know, and want to be.
Fear not! This is beautiful, real, and complete Lore.

7
The Rune of stasis in the Realm of Darkness.
Isa in Svartheim.
This aspect tells us that the things hidden in the darkness may indeed be a danger to the unsuspecting.
Do not move in the unknown.
Do not accept that you must rely on trust or faith and walk in the dark.
We will aspect the Manaz Rune later in this book, where you will find that a state of being exists, and you will reach it, where light and truth are found in the Realm of darkness.
We will learn to use the mysteries without entering the darkness before that chapter. The mysteries have a viable place in every part of life, but our lives never focus on the darkness in day-to-day life.
When anything requires that we accept in darkness or operates from a position of secrecy, there is no place for us there.
The Rune of truth is the Rune of light, not mystery.

In this way our wealth and influence will bring stability to the Realm of mystery, and the powers there will not bring imbalance to our lives.
When you walk through your living room in the dark it is your knowledge of the truth about where the furniture is that keeps you from stubbing your toe, as long as no one has moved the furniture.
Just as no true man will ask you to believe. This Lore does not ask to be believed.
Test the darkness.
Make it stable.
Know what you are paying for.

8
The Rune of balance in the Realm of help and strength.
Hagalaz in Jotunheim.
This is the Realm of strength outside ourselves.
This is the army, the search party, the fire department,
the A.C.L.U. Your friends, neighbors, family.
When the policies of these groups are not balanced, the help they offer is exclusive.

Use your wealth and influence to bring balance to these things.
Resist negative uses of power outside yourself.
Assist in positive acts of strength to help others.
In this way when we need strength we do not have, it is there for us.
We have but to reach out.
Will the neighbors rush to put out the fire at the neighborhood cheapskate's house?
The guy who never bought cookies from the Girl Scouts or gave his neighbor a jump start.
We need to have help in a lot of things by design.
Help from outside ourselves.
Sometimes we need the big hand to lift us up.
Sometimes we are a part of the big hand.
It's all a question of balance.
How rich is a wealthy guy who gets no help from the people he's too good to talk to?
This Realm is not social, this is the Big Being of which we are a part.
Jotan is the Cosmic being.
Sometimes a hand, sometimes a foot, sometimes a dollar.

Be a part! Bring balance to this Being, this giant.
Do not allow your creative power to be wasted in dealing with the unintended consequences and products of your efforts.

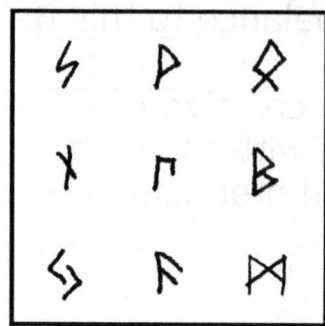

Uruz
Universal Power, Cosmic Force, Life Force
This is the one power of which all natural factors of force or power is a part.
This force is identifiable in its manifest finality, that is to say, the force promotes the circumstance where life will exist.
Science studies the manifestations of force independently, noting that a magnetic field surrounds an electric charge or a gravity well, but never the certainty of all three in every instance.
Science tends toward a view of billions of random factors making up the universe, rather than that of a self-correcting universe with no random factors.

The latter would yield a different standard of information, and many useful truths.
The Uruz Rune represents the one power that contains all power as a part of itself.
The power that charges thought.
The power that charges life.
The power that charges the ethereal connections of all spiritual beings, and, yes, the power that lights a light bulb.
When we realize the one power is, the pattern becomes much more clear.
This truth gives us the universe as a whole thing with many parts rather than many things with similar traits.
In the sphere of sentient life, this is the moral imperative.
The idea that we know the right and wrong of a thing in all acts of life, bind us to this power in a way that cannot be denied or escaped.
Resistance to will is Uruz.

1
The Rune of victory, Sowilo, in the elemental Realm.
Here we see that the manifestation of the Cosmic energy in Midgard (our lives, in this place) *is* the victory of the elemental universe.
This is where the Cosmic being, All Father, universal self, God, if you will, is putting the pieces together into sentient form (you).
This writer knows that, at best, our religions have taught us that we are God's pet animals gone astray, and at worst, that our existence is a product of evil.
So it is difficult to grasp that this may not be true, and a greater leap to presume that our lives are the point of the entire universal existence.
Victory in the Realm of base mass and physical law would be the joining of base material and pure energy to create form and forum for the truth of reality to become real.
On a scientific level the fact of reality bears this all out as true.
Everything is part of the Cosmic dance from quarks to granite boulders zipping through space.
The mass energy cycle that is self-perpetrating is hard evidence that the

universe is a being, not a place.
That everything comes together here in the form of man, facing the challenge of right action in the face of base fear, is further proof.
That each of us knows this in our daily struggle with right and wrong is final proof.
The power of Uruz in Midgard is victory over the void.
The very thing we fear, that we will become part of the void, is laid away here.
There is no void.

2
The Rune of joy in the Realm of higher moral ideal.
Wunjo in Asgard.
Here we see the presence of the primal power in Midgard is the joy of God.
The void is vanquished, the power of life is centered and has taken root and grown to sentient form.
God is being born in the perfect contrast of human choice.
Here the proof will ring true.
Is God a ridiculous vanity of cynical chaotic power?
Is God an unimaginable wonder of primal power balance and justice?
Can God be both?
Here, we will find out. Here it can be known.
Just as the edge of the knife is nearly invisible in the fineness of the steel, the magnitude of the universe comes to the pinpoint of Midgard in the focus of becoming.
The true power of the universe and Cosmos is the essence of the God Dream made real.
This power is the very will of the Cosmos.

We can know this if we choose.
We are here.
The perfect set of ethical questions beset us daily.
Yet some of us pretend it is somehow by chance.
To grasp this truth is to bring joy to the House of our higher moral code.
The Divine Power is what makes us work.
Embrace this and see the Cosmic joy become personal.
God and you run on the same power and much more.

3

The Rune of ancestral home in the Realm of society.
Othalaz in Alfheim.
Here we see the home we find in the social Realm is a product of the primal power centered in Midgard (you).
This tells us that the monastery or the nirvana of stillness is not the peaceful place we should go to seek the primal power in our lives.
It is in our social interactions and our willingness to be a part of something more than the individual that will bring us the greater access to the Cosmic power.
We are social by creation.

The social forum is necessary for the quest of becoming to play out.
It is the primal power that charges the social Realm with all the stimulus that our choices are based on.
Remember, this Rune represents something that "is," and vicariously, circumstances or ways in which other things exist, or are affected by it.
Uruz may not be said to "do" anything. Yet anything that is done must in some way use Uruz to happen.
The energy building block at the center of our social home is Uruz.
It is not our wealth or power that gives us a place in society to play out our part of the Cosmic experience.
The Cosmos puts us "in play" in society.
It is by rebellion that we refuse to be a part and face our quest, not by station.
It is also by rebellion that we outcast those with a social ideal we do not embrace.
The majority be damned!
The Home we make in the social Realm is ours, but the social Realm is Divine of itself.

The creation of the forum cannot be claimed by nations or governments, as they have only served themselves and never mankind. It is mankind, who are part of society, and the institutions they build are the test of the quest.
The power for this comes from the Cosmic. We each must have a place where the strength of our efforts will tell the truth of our intent and the power of our resolve.
This is why no creed or government has ever been sovereign in the hearts of men.
Only heroes, be they king or common, win men's hearts at home.
Only those whose actions prove the Divine is the power they revere, and not themselves stand above.
This power men cannot control.
We can only channel this power in the shaping of the social mores.
Be a part of this!
This is the power of Odin in the home of Men.

4
The Mother Rune in the Realm of the mind.
Berkano in Muspelheim.
This aspect simply describes the power that charges the function of thought as Uruz.
Thought can exist in a magnetic field or gravity well, or electromagnetic field.
Direct voltage can alter a brain's function, but the mind is effected only insomuch as the brain is injured.
Your personality will not change because of the presence of energy.
Imagine being subject to energy fields.
The mind is so strong, and powered by an energy source so sophisticated, that nothing in nature can short it out.
You will remain yourself throughout life with a continuity of existence that teaches itself.
It is the nature of the Divine power to care for us in this way.
The very essence of the Cosmic power preserves our mind so that our quest can be made.
We must be able to enjoy continuity of reason to display virtue.
Uruz, the Cosmic power, is the fullness of the God mind.

It protects and nurtures us when we enter the Realm of endless possibility and no reality.
Such is the mind, and the life force that cares for and protects the mind is a universal constant.

5
The Rune of man in the Realm of time.
Manaz in Niflheim.
Here we find the Rune of man in the fullness of time.
The Realm of those who lived before you, and those who will come behind.
The wholeness of the one power (Uruz) is the power of spiritual life as well as physical life.
Our spiritual being is also man.
We do not descend from an alien being and take on flesh.
We are man. Always man.
As you will see in the next aspect, the lower Realms are not "Bad," but simply reflect the receptive polarity of the physically creative, and morally challenging middle and upper Realms.
Just as Uruz is always the one power, we are always men.

We did not become men, so much as to say we have always been and always will be "becoming" men.
This may appear to change over time, but what will not change is this: We are. We are becoming. We are becoming what should be.
The Norns are true.
Of course, the end will never be reached. When we discuss the ego function later, this becomes crystal clear, but think about it as you progress so your own view will be a teaching tool for you.
The principle here is eternal.
This would be pointless unless you were eternal also.
Time is irrelevant to all but man.
We fear time because it will run out on us while we race to finish our life work, or refuse to begin because there is not enough time, or do a poor job trying to get more done.
Get over it!
This is the beginning of some really good news that is not news at all.
This aspect tells us that man exists in all of times.
So get busy doing the hard jobs.
You have time.

6
The Rune of Cosmic consciousness in the Realm of death. Ansuz in Hel.
Remember the last aspect (Manaz in Niflheim) as you read on.
This aspect tells us that death is a conscious state.
Our conscience, and consciousness are powered by the Cosmic energy that powers everything, existing where physical life has stopped.
Remember you are man, have always been man, have always been aware, and real, and part of the God mind, before you were born, after you die.
We are part of the whole.
We are a part that cannot be dispensed with.
Our conscience is powered by the one power and that truth is a big part of the victory over the void (Sowilo Vanheim) that begins this Rune's aspects.
It is the application of the whole power that brings the God mind alive.
The God mind is the consciousness of which your mind is a part.
You know this is true because it speaks to you everyday.

The one power charges the God mind, so they would appear to be two parts of a single whole.
As we learn more about the message in the Runes, we will see that the Cosmos is a single beautiful Being.
We are also a single being, but part of the Cosmic being.
Our consciousness is not subject to the circumstance of physical death, but is still powered by the one power, always.

7
The Harvest Rune in the Realm of Darkness and Mystery. Jera in Svartheim.
This aspect is fairly simple.
The dark Realm holds the mysteries and occult wonders that intrigue and frighten man.
The key to unlocking the mysteries begins with the knowledge that all occult phenomena are charged by the one power, and is primary in the analytical process of understanding.
Because man is charged by the one power and can learn to channel it quite easily, we can "feel" the way the particular phenomenon is charged.

We all do this regularly when we "sense" someone's intent.
We can feel how they are channeling the one power, or if they are hurt or sad, by the way they retreat from their usual energy level.
So you see we already do this a lot, and it's simple self-growth to pay more attention to how it works, and do more.
Healing is the act of channeling Uruz power to another person to cause a correction of the Uruz power in them.
This power holds things in proper form, but emotional distress or trauma can cause us to become "out of sequence" so to speak (emotional or physical shock).
The harmony of organic systems then breaks down and the strain injures the organs, or causes rogue healing (cancer).
There are many such mysteries that can be harvested through the Uruz power.

8
The need Rune in the Realm of Giants.
Nathiz in Jotunheim.
The enormous Giants of sun, planet, sea, and stone need the one power to

hold their form, their orbit, their ebb and flow.
The Lore speaks of a giant from whom the earth and sky were made.
When we think about it that is true in a sense.
The Jotan strength outside ourselves gets its power from the Realm of the individual man (Midgard).
Just as all things receive their power from Uruz directly or indirectly, the Jotan power, or the power of the great hand of God comes through the Realm of human existence.
The hand of God needs us to have strength to help us.
As in all things large and small, the power of God must come from somewhere.
The well must fill before we can draw from it. Our actions as we will study next fill the well we draw from.
If we do not put in, we cannot take out.
Because nature's laws are evidence of the Divine plan, we know the strength of the Jotan/Wotan or the God made whole must follow those laws also. This is important to know when we are planning important work or hard right action.
We can empower the Giant and the Giant can help us.

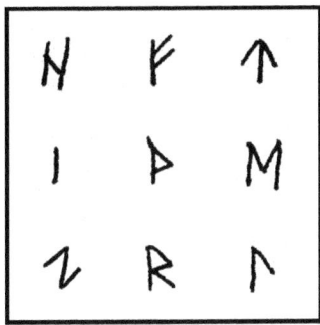

The Rune Thursaz, Thor's Rune, is in the physical plane, the Rune of law.
In the emotional self it is the form of intent that we act upon.
In the spiritual Cosmos it is the ritual dance of movement, change, and life fire.
Aspecting this Rune should be done with all three in mind, as much as possible.

1
Hagalaz in Vanheim.
Here we see the balance of the elemental universe is held by the law of Thursaz.
We see that our balance in the physical world is also held by our actions to make it so.
And finally we see the Ritual that is the Cosmic Balance is centered in Midgard, in us.
Thursaz is our act of creation.

Thursaz is both the parent and the child of the Cosmic self. The action of all is Thursaz. Every physical event, every personal act, the content of movement of the universe is Thursaz.

"What is becoming," on every level, in every life, is Thursaz.

This is the hinge that every door turns upon, and that is the law upon which everything rests.

Thursaz is the authority that determines what is right and what is wrong.

This is the only Rune in the Futhark that is so charged.

This is the Rune of Thor, the strongest god, the god of action, natural law, just conflict, vigor.

Right action brings balance to the chaotic explosion of motion in the universe.

Just as right action brings balance to the chaos of our personal life.

2
The Rune of personal power, wealth in the Realm of Gods.
Fehu in Asgard.
It is the concept of right action on a grand scale that gives us the archetypal God figure.
Here we are shown that right action in Midgard (men's lives) is the wealth and power of the Gods.
This is the chicken or the egg theory for man.
Because there are good men, there are Gods.
Because there are Gods, there are good men.
Both sentences are true.
This is why those who do not promote right action can say there is no god.
Those who are committed to right action say God is strong.
Those with no strong commitment say God is weak.
They are each correct as far as they are concerned, and in truth.
When we ritualize our personal program toward right action, we empower the Gods.
When we look to the Gods for power, we see it there.

Our moral code begins, and with it, the
moral power of the Gods.
As in the macroverse, so in the microverse.
This is the natural law portion of Thursaz
plus the creative right action.
The higher moral code becomes wealth we
can use.
Our use of it makes it greater.
Just as Thor lusts for battle with the foes of
Asgard and of men, we begin to hunger for
opportunity for right action.
With each act we become stronger, and
more hungry for the physical, emotional, and
spiritual wholeness of true development.
Just like Thor we expand our universe day by
day.
The ritualization of daily life gives us the
feeling of reality that lifts us from a rut to a
program, bringing wellness to ourselves and
the Cosmos.

3
The Rune of justice in the Realm of society.
Tiwaz in Alfheim.
Here we have the Realm of society, and the
idea of co-operative existence that man
demands through the ages.
We are social by design.

The social Realm is the proving ground for all theoretical right action.
Yes, we know right from wrong.
Yes, we abhor the evil deeds of villains.
Yet we tend to step away from action when we encounter villainy in society, or watch the savage actions of the cruel with no thought of acting ourselves.
We view our social institutions in decline and wonder why somebody doesn't do something.
Do we not realize that our ticket to live was purchased in the hope that we would act to create justice in the social Realm while overcoming fear?
Why is it so hard to see that this is why we are constantly choosing between something hard but beneficial and something easy and self-serving?
Justice does not come to society.
We must create justice by our right action.
All of the stories of heroes are the same.
We love to hear about it.
We watch it on TV.
We hear countless stories about the man who stood up for what was right.
But, we teach each other to stand by and let bad things happen to others so we won't get hurt.

We accept the lies about abuse and corruption in our social institutions.
We accept degradation and abuse from public servants.
The police focus on everyone but the violent criminal. Why?
Because of fear!
Fear is our meter that tells us how important it is to act at any given time.
Oh, we have lots of explanations about being civilized and letting the authorities handle trouble.
This aspect tells us that we bring justice to society through our actions.
Our right action.
We do not need to commit to wrong action.
The level of conflict will be decided by the party in the wrong.
Wrong action is not empowered by Cosmic power but by petty personal drives, no matter how high the actor has reached.
Right action is empowered by the Cosmic power when justice is the intent.
This aspect goes a long way in revealing the nature of our struggle.
Be like Thor.
Take joy in the struggle.

We all see in the hero a person not much different from ourselves.
That first step is the difference.
The Runes say we should take the step.
What should I do? Step up. Do something.

4
The Rune of partnership in the Realm of the mind.
Ehwaz in Muspelheim.
This is the aspect of self-validation.
It is here that we try our ideas and plans out in real life.
So often we let others do the planning, set the agenda, and make the rules for our lives.
That is a very destructive practice that is in full flower in the world today.
The necessary social institutions must be managed and paid for by the public.
That is the purpose of government.
Setting the agenda and standards for the behavior of the people are far beyond such a mean organization.
In fact governments often set standards and make rules that they themselves are unable to live by.
This cannot be overcome by the making of more or better rules or plans.

Man cannot be governed into wholeness.
We must become partners with our own intellect.
We must find education and put it to work in our own lives to find the power of our own minds.
Let government help the schools to excel and expand.
Let the minds of the teachers share what is learned.
Let each person prove the lessons in their own life.
Prove them in your own life.
Validate your ability to plan, act, and realize your own goals.
This is a natural aspect and one cannot truly blame their leaders for using authority to serve their own ends.
The idea is to give yourself authority, through a process of reason, to decide your own life.
There is nothing stronger than a person who knows they are right.
When we use our mind to its potential we will find a lot of programs exist to invalidate the individual.
Other people create those programs for a purpose.

It does not matter how many people accept them.
There is no power that transcends our freedom of mental process that is not part of our own fear, guilt, or hatred.
Here is where education plays such a pivotal role.
Do we learn how to think, or what to think?
Do we seek knowledge or reasons to believe?
This aspect makes clear that from the first moment you decide to become alive in a Cosmic and real way, there will be something to believe in.
That something is you. Believe in yourself.
If you just ride along with the powers that be, or never make a stand on right action, there won't be much to believe in.
That is as it should be.
When you use your mind,to bring justice to your social circle, empower your god, and balance your actions with the Cosmic dance, there is much to believe in for you and those who depend on you.
If you are smart enough to read this, you are smart enough to do it.

No matter what our station in life, we can each be true through right action, and thinking.

5
The Rune of spirit / soul in the Realm of spirit / soul.
Laguz in Niflheim.
Here we have a Rune placed in a Realm that is its natural domain.
The Realm of the Folk Soul, the Rune of the Folk Soul.
What is important here again is the idea of right thought and right action.
The message is that through right thought and right action, the soul is as it should be.
There is no Rune of prayer.
There is no Rune of faith.
There is no Rune of salvation.
There is no kneeling, no begging.
The soul will not be as it should be through the gifts of faith or forgiveness.
All of the other aspects of Laguz presume the Folk Soul as it should be.
This first aspect of Laguz tells us how to make this so.
Norse Lore speaks of things coming out of the mist to become real and be seen.

Our piece of the Folk Soul is, of course, there from birth, but that means nothing by itself.
We act to gain our soul.
With Thursaz we break up what is there and build what we need.
We take life as given and build life as it should be.
Our wholeness calls for the union of body and soul.
In today's world, that may seem unnecessary, and for a good number of people today, who have no redeeming qualities or virtues, the soul is superfluous at best.
Those who wish to be real, and do real things, have need of the soul and the communication of detail from other peoples' souls that goes with it.
The sensationalism of the young is a poor substitute for true adventure in right action.
Making things right about ourselves and our Folk and the world are true adventures.
Here we bring ourselves out of the mist and into the real world.
This aspect opens the frontier of time and wholeness.

It is through ritual that we embrace and further the soul in the physical body, bringing ourselves out of the mist of confusion and spiritual alienation.

Welcome home.

6
The Rune of journey in the Realm of death. Raido in Hel.
This is one of the most powerful statements made in aspecting the Rune stone with the Helm of Awe.
Here we see that right action to bring balance to the physical reality of our existence plus right action to empower a higher moral code plus right action to bring justice to society plus right action to partner with our true intellect plus right action to join with our spiritual self allows right action to make death a part of our immortal journey on the tree of life.
This is a large statement, yet which of us does not know it rings true?
We seek religion because we know eternity is a part of our being, and religions promise eternity in exchange for the bended knee. We see that the bended knee is not a part of right action.

Steadfast strength in opposition to what is not as it should be cannot be of use in the kneeling position.
The awesome power of the universal and Cosmic wonder of the All Father must be revered.
The awesome responsibility of the sentient being to bring order, progress, justice, and truth to this life does not allow for the central actor to fall down in the face of the power that allows us to be.
We can do it by ourselves, though "by ourselves" is not a circumstance that ever really exists.
The power that charges our minds and the Folk Soul is not exclusive.
We are never outside the living being that is both God and men.
We have the option of acting as if we are, or of right action.
How dare we take such a grandiose position?
In the world we live in it is we that own the hands and feet, the eyes and voices.
All in life we must "do."
Our death also is along that path.
Later we will find many more aspects which describe the relationship of the Realm of the dead, as we have thus far.

Never does death appear as a finality.
Always this Realm shows purpose,
conscience, and continuity with the cycle of life.

7
The joining Rune in the Realm of mystery.
Aiwaz in Svartheim.
We are describing the aspects of the Runes, one after another, not because they follow in that way, but for the simple reason that this is the only way to put this into language.
The Runes, as aspected, demonstrate an overall relativity of all things human, Divine, and base.
Thursaz is the "action" Rune, and is a bit different than the others in that way.
Because it appears third in the Futhark, the quantum effects of the actions indicated may not be easy to see.
The writer suggests you return to the Thursaz aspects often as you realize the importance of the other aspects you read about.
In this way you will become clear on just what these particular forms of "right action" will bring to your life.

For many of you, what follows in this book are things hidden in the mysteries (Svartheim), in the darkness.
This aspect tells us that as we learn of the mysteries we should add that knowledge to ourselves through application (right action). Appropriately, the instruction from the action Rune Thursaz tells us what to "do" with the mysteries.
Fear not, there is plenty of information about the Realm of Darkness and the mysteries there to make sense of this instruction.
For now it is enough that we are instructed to figure things out, and use the knowledge to make a better world.

8
The Rune of stasis in the Realm of Giants. Isa in Jotunheim.
This is the Realm of strength outside ourselves.
Viewed in the negative, this is your child out of control, the neighborhood out of control, the city out of control, the mob in riot, the government without a firm agenda and method.
Insurgent armies killing those in their way.

This is the bully taking from those willing to act weak.
No matter what we do, this giant well of potential strength will exist.
We have seen how "wrong action" can set events in motion that destroy everything in its path.
This is the Giant, Jotan.
This aspect is the sum of all right action.
Here we bring stability to the enormous power of the giant.
We can do this through a series of right action as we have just studied.
In applying the indicated principals to our actions we gain true authority to guide the Jotan strength toward what should be.
There is a difference between true authority and false authority which is clear.
Right actions grant authority that cannot be challenged.
You can ask questions of a true man and find that he has the authority, on a Cosmic level, to guide others.
False authority can make nothing clear.
No clear plan, no clear answer, no clear view.
No clear reason for its action.
This brings instability to the world.

It does not matter if authority is legal, or lawful, f it is not true authority, it causes chaos.
Right action stops chaos.
What is very important to note is that anyone can see true authority and right action.
Anyone.
Virtually all of those who lead do not practice right action as a form of living.
Those in power will usually act in concert to destroy the oddball who practices some form of right action.
The steps to true authority have been hidden for as long as the Runes have been suppressed or ignored.
The Runes are back.
The world is waiting for true leaders to bring stability to the child, the neighborhood, the city, the future.
Finally the time has come when we can define what should be in a way that has no negative side of itself.
Only the actions of men brought into the light.
Right action does not strip away freedom, but challenges us to find a right way to do what we will.
This makes us better people.

It is not the salvation of God or the damnation of men by God that gets things done here.
It is people stepping up and being true.
This work should pretty much show you how to do that.
It is your application of the action Rune, Thursaz, that will tell.

So get busy.

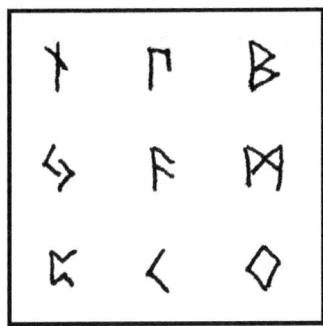

Ansuz, the Rune of conscience and consciousness.
As we have seen in our primary Rune study, our conscience is a part of our physical existence.
Everything we do is subject to the acceptance or rejection of our conscience.
We know when our thought process becomes action whether or not right action is our intent.
Because consciousness is bound to action, the Ansuz Rune is part of the physical aett (eight).
Aspecting consciousness in the nine Realms shows great yet simple truths.
The binding of conscience to consciousness is the giant step that modern psychology must take to aid in the recovery of those with crisis of conscience or level of

consciousness that prevent joy or inhibit belonging and purpose. As we have just studied, right action is purpose, no matter one's station in life.
We will learn how to use the conscience, and how the Realms relate to consciousness.

1
The Rune of need in the elemental Realm.
Nauthiz in Vanheim.
The elemental universe needs consciousness.
How important is that statement?
When a baby is born, it needs to do something it has never done before.
This is something physically difficult, completely alien, and very frightening.
The child needs to breathe.
So important is this compulsion that the entire life span of each person shares this as a starting point.
As in the microverse, so in the macroverse.
What we see when need is placed in the physical universe is consciousness at the Cosmic center.
A need for consciousness so strong as to cause the Big Bang.

The beginning of the "I am," or of the physical circumstance that would allow for the actualization of the God self.
How important is that statement now?
Consciousness is.
As surely as stone and ice, the aware is!
If not the stone itself, then the whole of which it is a part.
The chicken or the egg to the farthest degree, but still true.
This tells us a lot about the elemental universe and about the primal consciousness.
Wrap your mind around this as we continue.
2
The Rune of natural energy and power in the Realm of God's home.
Uruz in Asgard.
Here we see the power of the Gods is a product of both conscience and consciousness.
This is where the joining of the two forms an understandable essence.
For instance: A man denies the existence of God.
For that man, there is no God.
For that man there is no energy to manifest a higher code of right action.

Simple rationality will guide his life, but there can be no power of right action to give power to the voice of conscience.
Why?
He cannot allow it.
He has declared himself God in a Godless universe.
He has declared his microverse subject to different laws than the macroverse, and he is powerless to challenge anything.
He has done this based on a rationalization that shows a dissociative view of all that is from himself.
The power of the conscience and consciousness is so great that one may become frightened of the concept and terrified of the fact.
Here lay many phobias and fears.
Here also lies the explanation for the greatness of many people.
Empathy, teaching, healing, leading, all require a grasp of the scope of power adherent to conscience and consciousness.
Power comes from consciousness.
God's power comes to us through the conscience.
Our moral code holds our source of Cosmic power.

3
The Mother Rune in the social Realm.
Berkano in Alfheim.
Here one must note the fact that society is an amalgam of each person's idea of just what society is.
Society exists for each person, and so can not rightly deny anyone a place, based in large part, on that person's idea of what he or she has a place in.
This fairly well slams the idea of compulsory moral standards.
The mores can only be raised by the individual, not law.
It is through conscious nurturing that the social mores are improved.
The back side is forming social institutions that work to develop the conscience and consciousness of the people.
In this way the idea of society is more common and people see their place in similar parameters.
Failing to teach this lesson results in a pre-molded, stagnant and repressive society where no forum for advancement in standards and expression can be tolerated.
To make the best use of the natural forum of the social Realm, we should nurture the foundations and institutions that further the

opportunities for the individual, while regulating the entities and corporations which function most profitably in a non-evolving society, and which do the most to cast the pre-mold for the people to be forced to conform to.

Non-conscious entities should have no authority in a Realm that exists only as a mass perception of idea.

They may be worked, but must never control.

Make sure your social interaction is based on plans your conscience approves of.

Make sure the social institutions you inspire or support promote a free realization of social responsibility rather than a forced one.

Make sure your idea of society is not based on the profitability of non-living entities, but on the living people who thrive or suffer because of that idea.

Because we grow up in society, we never have sight of the fact of its existence. We do not stop to realize society is a magical construct of the group mind.

That is why some of us feel dispossessed or alienated.
That is also why some of us simply ignore the limits perceived to exist on the success of certain groups or classes of people, and succeed anyway, while some of us condemn ourselves based on a perception.
When an individual or group see themselves as alien to the social mind, they will behave that way, for good or ill intention.
The mores, manners, and customs are society.
Our manners and behavior either nurture and advance the mores, or they do not.
The care and nurturing of the social Realm is our conscious effort, and a matter of conscience.

4
The Rune of man in the Realm of the mind.
Manaz in Muspelheim.
Manaz the Rune of noble completion, signifying the sum of Rune Lore in the individual.
If man is not automatically complete just because he lives, then what is he if he is not noble man?

Throughout religious history, we hear of evil beings.
The demon Araman and his greedy minions.
The dragon Fafanir and his gold.
Mostly the evil we can trace all goes back to people living in ignorance of their potential, and in service to a dogma or an ideology that denies the possibility of noble man.
The "born of sin" doctrine.
This Rune Lore has been available for millennia and is a guide to our potential of being noble.
It is our conscience alone that will allow us to name ourselves man and not animal.
This aspect is our first notice that we are a God mind in an animal body.
When we act like animals, terrible things happen.
We must keep ourselves aware of what is noble.
We must use our conscience to think like a man and not an animal. We must use this Lore.
The dilemma arises when dealing with people who choose to act like animals.

We must secure ourselves in advance of such trouble through policies of restrained interaction with those of a base nature or ideology.
If we run with dogs, we must act like dogs or be bitten ourselves.
The risk of being named racist, protectionist, or paranoid is irrelevant to the value of being free of base persons no matter their complaint or condition.
This is not a game.
Young people are beginning to join the army because it is fun to kill. Our leaders tell them this.
Conflict exists with the most closed minded repressive ideology in history when every contact should have been controlled and abuse of commerce refrained from.
The errant man does not profit from the animals' abuses, he joins the animal by taking profit.
Noble man teaching the way to success and completion shares the greatest gain of all in raising human to man.
This is Godlike, and will happen if we do it.
Everyone must raise himself up.
One cannot raise another.

We can only show the way to do it by doing it.
We can make true man of our mind and have a true view of our potential on every level of endeavor.
This begins with mental discipline guided by conscience.
The God mind will manifest in you with the power of God through your mental process rather than through paranormal physical events.
Remember, nature's laws remain true also.
As we proceed, the Runes make it more clear that this is an advantage to applied thought rather than a denial of the Divine.

5
The Rune of sight and inspiration in the Realm of time.
Ingwaz in Niflheim.
Here we see consciousness as the doorway to the past through the group memory of the Folk Soul, and a window to the future generations through action led by conscience.
This is where we see the value of the "golden rule" idea bear fruit.

The inverted aspect of Ingwaz in Midgard places the Cosmic consciousness in the elemental universe.
Here we bring that consciousness to reality in the application of the lessons of our fathers plus our own actions to bring our children a world they can understand and prosper in.
The doorway to being is in you, here, now. Again we see the importance of setting store in the living man and not the non-living entity that succeeds best when man is trapped in static social or economic circumstances.
Empires can neither live nor die.
Corporations likewise.
It is to those who share the Cosmic that we are kin.

6
The Rune of truth and light in the Realm of the Dead. Kenaz in Hel.
Here we see that consciousness penetrates the circumstance of physical death.
As we will discuss in detail later, the ego, which is in control of the physical and sensory application of self in the physical world, is at rest in sleep.

The subconscious does not sleep, neither does it die when the physical body expires. This is explained in detail in the discussion of the spiritual Runes.
Here the pattern simply states that the truth about the Realm of death is consciousness. This inspires us to apply a conscious constraint on free identification of self through ego.
So many ideologies talk about breaking down the ego.
Well, this is why.
Our subconscious has all the ability to create an ego as a tool. It is fragile, but you are not. The ego is like a data process actuator of function.
It is not you. It is yours.
Keep it simple. Make it serve its function.
Do not follow where ego leads; it dies, you do not.
Lead ego with conscience, fearlessly endlessly.
You may seem more simple, but you will be more able to focus on human goals.
You and I are simple. Wonderful, eternal.

The subconscious can not create an ego greater than itself.
When we perceive this truth, we may feel inferior.
Do not do so.
Do not let the ego machine take over and color the truth of life.
7
The Rune of chance in the Realm of mystery.
Pertho in Svartheim.
We are taught that schemes and machinations are the avenues to success, and that those whose schemes are the most refined will have the most success.
This aspect tells us the reverse.
Here we see all possible things in the Realm of dark mystery come through the presence of conscience in our lives.
Schemes and machinations are tools of the fearful.
People who don't think they deserve to succeed, and people who think success is alien to man in a true state of being.
Nice guys only finish last in useless competition.
Right action never results in loss.

Injury or death do not change the fact of right action.
They just expose what and who is not true.
It is not the perceptions of others that opens doors or brings opportunity.
It is going through doors by choice with clear conscience.
Our pretensions are just that only our truth is real.
Our conscience is our strength.
Nothing is stronger than a man who knows he is right.
All of these statements are used endlessly in our lives, but they mean nothing until we realize that all of our steps forward are all taken in the Realm of dark mystery.
There will be apprehension about all, and trying to tilt the playing field so we will win stops right action and prevents movement guided by conscience.
Do not be afraid, and do not believe the fearful.
Let conscience be your guide.

8
The Harvest Rune in the Realm of strength and help.
Jera in Jotunheim.
Here we see the manifest power of the God self as it helps us in our lives.
People pray for God to help them, knowing that it "feels right."
How can God reach down and help you?
This aspect appears on the same plane of existence as our physical life, but it truly is a manifestation of God.
The power of God to help us in this life is created by man's conscious efforts as a whole to make that help available.
In following the Runes of this set of aspects for the Ansuz Rune, we see the building blocks for the highway to Divine help or supreme right action.
Make no mistake. This statement says that this is how God works.
The Ansuz Rune is the voice of God and this is what it is saying.
If God is not working for you, then you are not doing right action and applying conscience to your Realms of
existence.
When we do apply conscience and right action to our Realms of existence, we

open the avenue to receive Divine strength through the Jotan.
The Jotan / Wotan is God on earth made real by noble man.
The greatest Giant (Jotan) is Wotan.

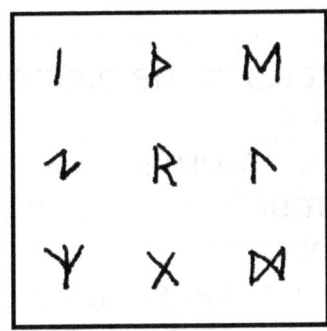

Raido
This is the Rune of the Journey.
Each individual journey, each social step, each life.
This is the Cosmic journey, the journey of God and the Gods.
Many of us feel that our path is a random set of circumstances that we have no control over.
We often choose jobs that put us at the whim of our employer as to relocation, advancement, or supervision.
Our belief systems are subject to politically correct decisions by the clergy, which often excuse or embrace immoral practices or dangerous people in positions of guidance.
Here are the guidelines for securing a path in life that will lead to joy and also the final Norn, Skuld, What should be.

1
The Rune of stasis in the elemental Realm.
Isa in Vanheim.
Remember that nature's laws are true constants, as much as anything can be, in a universe in motion.
As in the macroverse, so in the microverse. Here we see the static natural law that holds everything from the sub-atomic level outward in form.
The message here is twofold.
First, that the stability of the elemental universe and natural law make our journey in life possible.
Next, that our journey should be tuned toward natural law and the stability of the macroverse.
Such as the destruction of the ecosystem in our journey toward wealth and power, as opposed to reliance on the stability of natural law to guide us on our path and promoting stability and natural law as we journey.
If you would do "anything" to reach your goal, perhaps you should rethink your goal.
When the rich and powerful purchase legislation which denies natural law or threatens the stability of the elemental

universe (physical existence), then the path they travel is not in harmony with the Cosmic order.
Service to such is service to the path they travel.
Use your freedom, scope, education, and conscience to walk a path that preserves stasis and stability in the elemental Realm of your existence.

2
The Rune of law in the Realm of higher moral code.
Thursaz in Asgard.
This aspect is one of the few that actually tells us "what" to do.
We see here the Rune of ritual, rites, and law, in God's home.
Our higher moral code should be practiced in definite form, for a definite purpose, that is, our righteous authority.
We should have clear personal law about what we will and will not do, and a way to express this to ourselves.
These things must journey with us so that our path does not change with popular belief, or failure to follow a discipline in our moral code.

By religiously declaring and following a moral discipline, our resolve will remain strong when our path is difficult.
It is from individuals that group morals are realized.
In times when the group may falter for lack of moral discipline, it is important for the individual to stay strong.
It is by degrees that we fall away from our moral standard.
A discipline or moral self rule that sees each degree as failure will not find us bound by guilt, hatred, or fear of what the failure adds up to in our whole being.
Rigid or flexible are terms often used to describe a moral standard.
Those are poor terms for the companions our moral code and conscience are to us through life.
Build a steadfast moral companion with rites and discipline to share your journey in life.
Cosmic law does not vary in time.

3
The Rune of partnership in the Realm of society.
Ehwaz in Alfheim.
The message here goes to the nature of relationships.
Our quest is to be able to be "what should be."
Our forum is society.
It is sad that so many of those believed to be the most successful achieve their success based on plans, partnerships, and alliances that are secret.
On one hand we should not regulate society so that people get in trouble just for being "normal," or a bit outside of "normal."
On the other hand we should not succeed because of plans and partners that shun the light of day.
We are to join with the social as ourselves and build truth about ourselves into our social institutions.
When we criminalize a common activity, it drives a wedge between meaningful social intercourse and whoever practices that activity.
It is odd that these days immoral behavior is protected, which drives a wedge between the moral citizen and society, while

recreational activities are illegal, which drives a wedge between those practicing them and society.
Divide and conquer.
These wedges are not accidentally placed, but the product of secret plans and secret partners who have gained our trust and would turn your journey in life to service to their wealth and position.
We are to join with the social Realm in our own right.
A true partnership. In the open. Honest and unafraid.

4
The Rune of primal being in the Realm of the mind.
Laguz in Muspelheim.
Our journey in life here shows the investigation of our spiritual origins using our mental process and not our naked emotions.
The existence of our Folk Soul is something that is much better known and understood than simply believed.
What we are seeing here indicates a reality so far superior to current and common beliefs about man's existence as to create a new being.

The whole business of this book is to show us that our Divinity is provable.
The relativity of spirit to form is understandable.
The ability to realize the incredible potential of the being we have always suspected we were, is drawn out so simply and so perfectly that even a simple man such as this writer can make it work.
When we get an invitation to investigate the wonder of the ages rather than an admonition to believe without question,
it is like having God give his address and 24-hour phone number.
We are supposed to know all about it, beyond question.
We don't have to believe anything because it's all self-proving.
Here our life journey takes us to the only place where spiritual realization makes any difference: our own mind.
Knowing that most of our true realizations take place in the deep subconscious level of our being and not through its tool, the ego, we escape the turmoil of self-doubt as we assemble our whole view of past, present, and necessity.

The Laguz Rune represents all the knowledge of every being in the Folk Soul up to the moment, yet we often fail to act because we don't know "what to do."
The ego by creation requires certain proofs before it will operate the body.
This is a self-protecting trait of ego.
This is why we don't venture into the abyss to find truth.
We venture into the mind.

Journey to the center of your mind.

We are all there with everything that has been learned.
When we sleep, the Folk Soul puts its data together with our days' or weeks' queries and when we are awake, we "come to realize" what we have learned.
Knowing this, we can access the process, bridging subconscious and ego conscious function to become about a thousand times smarter.
This is not about getting you to "believe" there is a Folk Soul.
This is about taking life in a direction that uses the vast wealth of knowledge found in the genetic link and Folk memory of every man, woman, and child, and every one we

are related to.
Misunderstanding the power and purpose of the Folk Soul is the largest source of hate on earth today.
We are who we are, we are what we are.

5
The Rune of cycles in the Realm of time.
Dagaz in Niflheim.
Here we see our journey of life taking us to and from the timelessness of the Realm of spirit.
There are nine expressions of the cycles of Cosmic and human things.
None of the nine involves a single occurrence.
As we progress through this Rune study, it becomes clear that we are eternal and that our eternal self is readily known to us, but only when we take hold of it with sure knowledge of what we are doing and a moral interest that is in tune with the truth about what is, what we are becoming, and what should be.
The stuff we need to do all this has been available for ages, but has been set aside through the machinations of ignorance and just plain laziness.
The tools have fortunately been preserved in

the Runes, the Helm of Awe, and the myths of the nine Realms.
Once again we can function in tune with Cosmic design through the natural order of our existence.
The cycle of civilization is an evaluation of Divine design.
Our individual life journey is made up of past and future manifestations, as well as present.
Make those a part of your life journey. They are a part of who you are.
We don't quit our jobs and leave our families to spend an hour in the park.
That would be foolish, there is. too much at stake.
The same is true of our eternal being.
Why on earth would we deny our true existence to please a passing urge of our ego to seem better than our peers, or equal to a pretense?
Decadence is an act against our self, not against the poor or the weak, just as greed or sloth are.
The ego is relative to a single cycle of life. It serves you now.
We must not injure our being to serve our non—directed emotion.
We don't have to be pious or stodgy, just

because we know how great life really is.
By actively including our history in our identity, we become so much more.
Who would throw that away for a moment's play?
It's a long trip in many parts. Journey well.

6
The gift Rune in the Realm of death. Gebo in HeL.
All of our lives we are told that death is the curse of the creator on the crimes of the first men.
What a cruel and painful burden that is.
People live their whole life in dread of the end.
This aspect tells us that death is a gift.
How can that be?
We have just studied Ansuz, the Rune of consciousness, in nine of its aspects.
The Rune of cycles - Dagaz - was not part of the pattern.
That is because Folk consciousness does not cycle.
Knowing this, we become confused as we grow older and experience our body wearing down while in our mind we remain the same person as in our youth.
"Rage against the dying of the light!"

The Ansuz Rune showed us light in death.
The Rune of journey shows us a gift.
This is gross existence. Weight, resistance, matter, gravity.
We wear out the body.
To continue in a decaying form would make right action impossible in a true struggle after a few years.
What better gift than renewal?
When we embrace truth and set out on our true journey, the resistance to our continuation toward the God Self realized is equal to the assistance we give to the God Self realization.
(Karma) + E = mc2 = next cycle.
In this Rune study, the concept is not an iffy philosophical suggestion, but a real and demonstrated part of our eternal existence.
The reason why this knowledge was allowed to slip away does not matter. It is here for you now.
The absurdity of the dogmas and doctrines which replaced it is clear.
Doom, destruction, and death prophecy serve no benefit.
The realization of human susceptibility to fears guilt, and hatred, and toward violence and deceit which is almost always founded there, is a sharper tool when one has a clear

path in life.
Whatever field we choose, the knowledge of what a life journey really is gives us so much advantage that it cannot be measured.
The distractions and detours of ordinary life disappear.
The frustration and hopelessness also disappear.
The way we live will not injure our selves when the time comes to surrender the body and start a new cycle.

7
The Rune of warding in the Realm of mystery. Elhaz in Svartheim.
Here we move directly from the last aspect. We see here that when our journey through the particular dark mystery of rebirth occurs, those who offer a fair exchange of life in the realization of the God self are protected and advanced.
This is as close to a promise as we get.
The choices are all ours. Be a good person!
We can waste a lot of time on faith and belief if that's what it takes to make us risk a good hard look at how things would be if they were real.

Most of us don't think any of this is real because our idea of the Divine is impossible according to the things we know for sure.
If we don't believe in God, we can't believe in ourselves, so we don't believe we could understand if we did know.
Yes, that is crazy. But it's true.
It's time to take important steps.
This writer suggests you learn this material and live according to the best your conscience can guide you.
Progress means change to something better.
The entire journey of the Cosmos is about changing to something better as events, choices, and natural law allow.
Each victory over fear, guilt, hatred, and death is a step along the way.
Each cycle brings more opportunities for right action.
Each exchange of life vehicles brings new strength.
Each risk taken in pursuit of the wonderful mystery brings more progress and protection.
The Elhaz Rune also means majesty and we find majesty in the honor of this quest for the realization of the God Dream.

We get to meet the challenge of living a life in true virtue.
It is all in the way we do things, and why we do things.

8
The Rune of joining in the Realm of Giants.
Aiwaz in Jotunheim.
This is the Realm of Giant strength and power.
The writer is going out on a limb here and has high hope that the reader will overcome the dogmas of upbringing and realize this beautiful bit of truth.
As we have looked at the aspects of the Rune of life's journey, we have seen material stability of the physical laws, the ritualization of moral practice, the union of self to society, the investigation of the soul, the cycles of time, the price of continued existence, the expansion of self through the mysteries, and we now come to the hook.
Aiwaz is the bow that joins the hunter to his arrow.
The backbone that joins the brain to the legs.

Here, it is the hook that joins our successes in right action to the actual being of God.
The great strength outside of ourselves, the Giant is God.
This Rune study shows the "hand of God" is a creation of men.
We are a creation of the Cosmos which is the whole God mind / God body /everything.
We found the need Rune in the physical universe when we studied Ansuz, the Rune of conscience.
These things all come together in man.
Our challenges are so very real that our failure is the failure of creation to commit right action if given a choice.
Our success is the realization of creation as a living work of right action by choice.
This is the realization of the God self in form.
Will this ever be complete?
Are we ever finished with life ourselves?
Are we not always becoming more?
As in the microverse so in the macroverse.
Not only can we accept a God who is also becoming through time and experience, we can more readily relate to such a being as the creating force of the universe.
A God that has a personal stake in the outcome.
As this writer has stated before, there is a

perfect order to the truth about all things human and Divine.
That order and the pattern it creates is displayed in the Runes, as well as every thing that exists.
As with the journey of man, so with the journey of God.
This is the Gift of Odin, Wotan, Jotan.
Use the gift.
Join your journey to the Jotan journey.

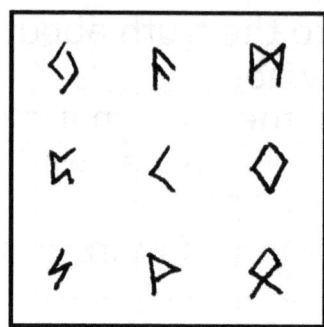

Kenaz, the Rune of light.
This Rune is one of the most difficult to grasp because what it represents is one of the most difficult things for us to do.
This Rune stands for the naked truth.
The very idea of embracing the whole truth about ourselves can be the most frightening and difficult thing we ever face.
As we begin to look at what the Runes tell us about truth, remember that there are two sides to each of these aspects.
What manner of relationship is there to the Realms of being and the Realm of conscious action?
Can the truth be rigid in a universe where nothing else is?
Can the truth be flexible when so many important things depend on whether or not people know the truth?

If the answer is "no" to both questions, then the truth can be neither rigid or flexible.
What is left?
The same thing that is always left after the rationalization and explanation is finished.
The truth.
As we progress through this Rune study, we learn that we are more than we may have believed ourselves to be, and less in need of rationalization and explanation: also known as excuses.

1
The Harvest Rune in the elemental universe.
Jera in Vanheim.
This is a cold clear truth.
There are positive and negative sides to every choice we make in the Realm of conscious action.
When we harvest the positive, we have the positive in our basket.
When we harvest the negative, it is not the positive in our basket.
When we harvest based on belief in what we do not know to be true, then the elemental harvest from which we build everything is a gamble.
Luck is created by acting in ignorance.

Good luck, bad luck.
When we observe the truth in the elemental universe and then act contrary to that truth, the negative effect may not be immediate.
A delayed effect does not change a negative to a positive, it just visits the next generation, or moment.
The same with positive action.
The effect may not come in the form of profit, and may be delayed by generations, but is still positive and will benefit the Folk.
The knowledge of continuing existence makes it a lot easier to act responsibly where the elemental universe is concerned.
After all, we do have to live here.
Would you choose dead forever or alive forever? Rich for twenty years and a slave for ten generations?

2
The Rune of conscience in the higher moral Realm.
Ansuz in Asgard.
Here again is a simple truth.
Using light and truth as the base of your moral compass is a matter of conscience.

We can twist any semblance of truth to suit any desired end.
The sky does not open up and smite us.
We alone know how we are twisting the truth to get what we think we should not have, or to get some thing of justice that somehow is not possible through the truth. (Which is often the case.)
Does the conscience condone or condemn our use of the truth?
Once the deed is done, it is no longer a matter of conscience, but has become part of the truth.
Does the truth condemn us?
We are able to embrace the truth in its entirety because that becomes the truth about us.
Then how will we stand compared to the group?
Do you want power, authority?
Those with power have a tenuous grip on it because of the absence of truth.
You can take it with the truth, as a matter of conscience.
Will you do it so that you can get a high price for it?
Will your price be met?
Every one in power who uses not the truth has found their price.

This aspect says a lot about the direction of our journey, and a lot about the nature of right action from under the heel of tyranny and corruption.

How can we build for our children and leave in place a system that will rob and abuse them?

The enthusiasm we gain when we choose to be a partner with our conscience is lost if we cannot act with truth in the forefront.

This is the building block of courage.

When we truly embrace our conscience and a higher moral code of Divine and Folk consciousness, the light will make conscience choices clear. We see truth.

Be prepared for some disappointment when you realize how few people even care at all about the truth.

If you want to lie, you let people lie to you. Pretty much everything is a lie now days, which calls for quite a bit of courage to get it going straight again.

Who will believe that you can see the truth? Proof of truth may be easy to recognize, but hard to find.

The conscience will be true.

3
The Rune of Man in the Realm of society.
Manaz in Alfheim.
Here we find the truth about man is revealed in our social action.
It matters little what we profess or know as far as our worth as a human being is measured.
What we create in society or support are the true mark of a man.
The Manaz Rune is man as he "should be."
Active, interactive, reactive, in tune with the Norns.
If you want to be real, do it in the open.
The reverse of this is that the truth about social conditions and demands empowers the ordinary Joe to the Manaz level of wholeness.
We can all look good if we keep the clique small or exclusive enough.
It is in the home of greed and corruption that activism has its purpose.
Win there.
Use the truth to get things done in the social Realm.
So few people do, that your results may be dramatic or unpredictable, but stay the course and realization of a superior order of being will be yours.

This is a major building block to personal power.
Again, be sure to remember that this is real.
If you start to live by this Lore and then decide to rejoin the cattle of raw humanity, you may find yourself in a hole.
If you want to equal your potential, the truth will light your way.
We all seem small when we first start the Asa path.
That is because we are starting as teens or adults.
Give these truths to social institutions and our children won't have a problem of self awareness or self esteem.
But, we have to do it in society, in the open. This is strength in responsibility.
When we think this through, we see the lack of truth that is pervasive in society. We see plenty of room for action.
You are needed now to restore the social Realm to the living, and to future generations.
There are a million and one illusions to distract us.

4
The doorway Rune in the Realm of the mind.
Ingwaz in Muspelheim.
This aspect is a plain statement.
With truth we can see what is really in our mind.
The Realm of Muspelheim is a timeless, spaceless Realm of incredible powers and no hard surfaces.
The imagination is totally unbound.
The mind can embrace any manner of idea, conceive of any number of solutions, and arrive at a correct and usable answer, if the truth is used in the process.
We can close the access to real answers through fear, guilt, hatred, or deception.
Often people have no intention of beginning with the truth or embracing it when it is found, and so have no real expectation of success.
Unfortunately, such people often make a great to-do about their failure, blaming other people for prejudice or hate and intolerance.
This has become the standard.
It is all right to be intolerant of what is not true. It is all right to deny filthy or disgusting behavior,or the idea that such things are subject to prejudice and not truth.
To find true answers is one thing.

To go forward in truth once you see truth requires a whole mind.

Dealing with a system that embraces false ideas and forces acceptance is not strongly founded and will break under the weight of truth.

Our minds must prevail against many efforts to draw us into participation in immoral behavior.

Remember the power of the mind is not a part of such sinister plans.

They are cheaply made and transparent, and their authors abstain from the practice they teach.

With truth, the power of the mind is available, but we have to surrender to truth first.

This is the only thing the Asa-Folk need ever surrender to.

The true picture may appear bleak at first look, but what is real, bleak or not, is far better clay than illusion.

From a true perspective we can build real character.

With honest disclosure we can build real trust and friendship.

We must first see and accept ourselves as we really are.

When we excuse weakness and flaws of character in ourselves, whatever we build will rest on the excuse, not the demonstrated will we use to correct or compensate for the shortcoming.
Knowing such things about ourselves will, in the positive, give us more determined action, and, in the negative, keep us out of the way of those who are building on real character.
Know thy self.

5
The Rune of home in the Realm of time.
Othalaz in Niflheim.
Do we know our home?
Home here is shown in the Realm of the primal waters of our genetic code.
We are our parents' children.
We are history's children.
We are the children of the laws of nature through hundreds of centuries of nurturing and development.
Our home is in the truth of the product of that development.
There is an attack in progress upon the Asa-Folk from without that home.
The illusion that the product of natural law, nurturing and development is not

Divine proof of itself has spread to every corner of the world.
Here we see the truth about our timelessness resides in our spiritual home.
Our home in time depends on the truth in the Realm of conscious action.
This writer will not be ashamed of being part of the Asa-Folk, nor will he contribute to the breaking of the natural law that nurtured and developed him.
This is not hate, this is love and respect.
Respect that is not sought outside of the home, but brought into it.
Love that is not offered outside of the home, but brought in.
This truth is universal, and denied as a matter of course.

6
The Rune of joy in the Realm of death. Wunjo in Hel.
This is the simplest aspect in all the Runes.
It is our human ego that keeps all the pain of disappointment and betrayal from the course of our life.
It is our ego that must be tamed through the trial of conscious action to serve as a tool of our eternal quest.

Those who have done this the best hurt the most.
There is joy in the victories, yet the failure of one truly loved rides with us to the end.
So much for the heart.
Our bodies are not fragile, but at a certain point the breakdown begins and we just wear out.
The greatest gift of all, our lives, is not jerked away.
The ache of heart and body pass away with ego, not the life.
The life returns fresh to again strive for right action in the Realm of conscious being.
And so death brings joy.

7
The Rune of victory in the Realm of mystery.
Sowilo in Svartheim.
The Realm of dark mystery is a vast and unimaginable well of danger and defeat.
OR
The Realm of dark mystery is a perfect learning place for the application of will and the power of truth.
Every tool, scheme, or machination that has an effect on you, which you do not know or understand, is a product of the dark Realm.

The dark Realm is real.
Part of this Realm is created by men who believe they must act in secret to reach their ends.
The negative side of the dark Realm is powered by fear, guilt, and hatred.
Ignorance, hubris, and greed are the ideals.
All of this seems to say that this is an evil Realm, but the truth says something else.
All of the force of will that is collective in the dark Realm forms a sort of battery from which a true man or woman can power acts of will that may appear to be magical.
The confusion of the uninitiated is the fuel for the plans that hurt them.

Learn the Runes!

This aspect is the best example of the benefit of understanding the order displayed by the Runes.
The best made plans to take advantage of the Folk came from those with an understanding of that order.
This knowledge has been secured and guarded for centuries.
Now it is ours again to use.

The plans and machinations that deprive the Folk of the power over their own lives are applied according to that order.
Because we don't know, we languish under the heel of secret groups of people set on controlling the nations and the world.
The proof is in the pudding.
The manipulation of currency that has no value, and economic structures that require you to spend your wealth as fast as you get it so the value does not diminish.
Organized control of invention so that energy and medicine are only developed by the controlling group.
Proscription and prohibition that prevent personal control over education and ritual application of knowledge, and legislation that does not serve the private living being.
Political correctness that denies the reality of ethnicity and the pursuit of its truth.
The removal of truth as a governing factor in social and political affairs.
The production of worthless goods and the sale of them through the fears and doubts of target demographics.

The legislated prohibition of proprietary control over private businesses, institutions and dwellings.

The first eight Runes of physical, corporeal living when distorted, equals the social dilemma of the Folk in the world today.

The applied knowledge of truth plus the order of human things represented through the Runes, breaks up the intrigues that shun the light of day.

The great secret groups of wealthy and powerful people take on the aura of crafty and mean-spirited children, they can now be managed.

The machinations of the most Machiavellian schemes become as transparent as glass the instant truth is brought to bear. Now they are held accountable.

The truth can be found in the order of the thing.

Where the order serves the real interest of the Folk in a traceable and relevant way, the truth will be evident.

When the thing deprives or denies the well-being of the Folk, the order of things will expose the scheme.

This is not a religious dogma, but can guide us in forming a discipline of ritual life.
This is not a political platform, but can guide us in the administration of social programs, policies, and the social institutions, and the making of law.
In this way, truth shines a light into the dark Realm, giving us mastery of the things unknown and unknowable.
The light of truth truly is a sword to bring victory over the mysteries.
This is the only way to find victory there.
Even the father of lies will fall to this sword.

8
The Rune of possibility in the Realm of giant strength.
Pertho in Jotunheim.
This is the Realm of strength outside ourselves and the outcome.
Each positive union of right action and multiple people adds to the strength in Jotunheim.
Such unions become part of "what is," and give power to the "high power" we can access. (The God that answers prayer.)

As we progress through the Runes, the nature and strength of Jotan becomes clear. Pertho is all possibilities.
Here we see that it is truth that gives us access to the incredible power that every right action has added to, for every possible reason.
How does the Hero get the strength of will to defeat the mighty?
Why in myth and story do we know the hero alone has access to the Divine power, while the villain never does?
The Cosmic consciousness tells us this in the very core of our being.
It is our acceptance of a lesser description of our reality that lets us see ourselves as not being able to do the right thing because it is too hard and we are too weak. (The Hodur archetype)
It is here again we see the wonderful gift of Rune Lore.
The order of the Runes allows us to become secure in our being so that acting on the truth, no matter what the situation, is possible.
Here we have a promise, for Pertho really is a Rune of promise.

That promise is that when we move forward in truth, all of the strength we need to succeed will be there for us.
When we accept that the struggle never ends, but is in fact the essence of reality, we can embrace our role as the realization of God in form, and live what becomes "extreme life."
No sport or entertainment can compare to destiny.
Imagine yourself prevailing in the struggle that every day finds us misleading our loved ones or making excuses for no reason, abetting or allowing deceptions in the companies where we work, accepting failure from our government, or backing down from tyranny.
Just standing tall is too hard for most of us because we don't know how, or can't find help.
Imagine standing tall, being respected by your wife and children, your husband.
Knowing yourself to be a powerful force and one trusted with the power to effect change and make things right.
The truth makes it all so.

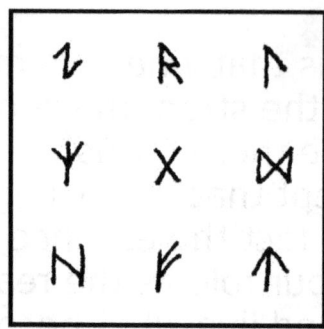

Gebo, the Rune of the gift, exchange, karma, fair play.
What does fair play get you?
Why give away anything?
What can you do about karma, if it is even real?
How can we trust some Divine being to give us a fair shake, when all of their preachers are so intent on taking us for as much money as they can scare us into paying for "salvation"?
This is the Rune of Honor.
This Rune is in play whenever we deal with other people, but it is not about them; it is about the individual.
This Rune is as personal as life gets.
Our respect for this concept is the content of our true character.
It may take a while to get in the habit of seeing this simple concept as the powerful force it represents, but just

remember when as a child you learned that someone did not play fair.
All the shine went out of your view of that person.
As adults, we are more jaded to this and even expect people to fail in matters of fair play.
There is no clear difference between right and loophole.
But there is.
We all know there is.
Let's see what it brings us to see exchange as a gift.

1
The tool Rune, Backbone, Bow, in the elemental Realm.
Aiwaz in Vanheim.
This is one of the reassuring aspects of Rune Lore.
Aiwaz, the Bow, the Backbone, that joins the brain to the body, the archer to his prey, is seen here to join man to his elemental universe.
This is no mean feat.
Man has always wondered what our place in the Cosmic scheme is.
Are we an anomaly?
Are we a quirk of nature?
Are we a pastime of a Great Deity?

Are we the failing of the creative perfection of God?
What is our status?
This Rune aspect serves us with two vital answers.
One is that, indeed, we can join with the elemental universe as a part.
Two, we control that connection through our quality of interaction in the Realm of conscious action.
There is no magic spell that will join us to the Cosmic.
There is no trick that will give us footing in the grand scheme.
No prayer, no price, no sacrifice will acquire the much sought place at the table.
Giving fairly, charging fairly, playing fairly, judging fairly, living fairly pays the price of a place in the main show.
This gives us more information in the negative.
Those who do not play fairly are not charged with the power of the elemental universe.
Remember all of the stories about the lowly heroes with only right on their side defeating incredible odds.
These mythical heroes always had some weapon, something that joined them to

the Great Power and brought them victory.
Something simple and true.
While the villains always had the might, sorcery, or minions to enforce their will, they are always viewed as separate from the Cosmic.
Myth and imagination reach the truths that, sometimes, there are not enough facts to find.
Here we find written in the ancient pattern the means to our attachment with the Cosmic.
This is so simple a child could understand, which, of course, must be so.
Even if you're the only one who knows you're being fair.
Even if you're the only one who is being fair.
To be a part of the Cosmic, one must join the Cosmic.
The only time the joining Rune appears in the elemental Realm is in the Gebo aspect.
This is how it is done.
Your conscience, your journey, your truth, become part of the Cosmic through your honor, your gift.
You, and everybody else.

This cannot be faked, forced, or purchased.
Join the Cosmic.
Gebo is the cradle of honor, the anchor of life.

2
The journey Rune in the Realm of moral being. Raido in Asgard.
Here we find a rather unforgiving truth, as well as a big relief.
It does not matter what we profess to be, only what we are.
When we give too little and take too much, our visit to church does not make it right.
Whether we know a lot of Lore or not, our moral journey rests directly on our give and take.
The reality of our journey through the moral Realm is the reality of our honor.
The cloak of righteousness will not warm a cheat.
A man who plays fair may not be seen to be the Great man, while the biggest despoiler and cheat may appear to be the best man.
Honor cannot be legislated.
Honor is easily portrayed, and only men of honor can nay-say the practice.

Where is the outcry?
Who is not billing what cannot be paid in today's loose and over-tolerant venue?
You are there!
You are not alone, and honor is not dead.
Here is a piece of ancient good news.
Our higher moral code is reached through the gift of fair play.
The Gebo Rune is the gift Rune because it brings a gift, not because it represents one.
The gifts that Gebo brings are revealed in these Rune aspects.
This is the aspect of walking with God.
This is not restricted to a few prophets or picked men.
We all can take our journey on a higher level, just by being fair.
If we had to be special, then it would not be a fair deal, and that is what Gebo is all about.
We can be fair!
Will we be fair?
The demons and deities are far removed from reality.
The truth must be a picture we can all fit into.

3
The Rune of Spirit in the Realm of society. Laguz in Alfheim.
The task of all ministries is to bring Spirituality to the common weal.
It is important to recognize that the Spiritual being is a natural, not a supernatural being.
Presenting the Spirit as supernatural is divisive, not conjunctive.
One God then wars with another in the social structure, preventing a unity of purpose in the design of social institutions.
The flaw is in the presentation of the "separate Spirit" idea.
The avenue is in the evenhanded development of social institutions that serve the whole person.
Advanced developments in healing are made at facilities that treat the whole person.
This same idea must apply to education and law in an even-handed way.
Criminal behavior is often a symptom of Spiritual disassociation from self and, through that, antisocial behavior.
Could it be that many antisocial people simply reject a society without a Spiritual anchor as false?

Are they antisocial, or are the institutions they rebel against anti-human?
By giving fairly to the needs of the social institutions with a true view of man's reality, we can bring the human Spirit alive en mass, and create a society with more than power to punish.
When only a small percentage of the people feel that society is about them, then a retrograde move is in effect.
The people cannot be corrected.
The foundation of the society is the people.
The institutions must be corrected.
This is not a question.
There is no room for leadership that stumbles about.
Only those that play fair in their personal lives are suited to bring forth the power of the common Spirit through social planning.
Think about taking a role.
Think about removing those you do not trust.
Political savvy does not make up for treachery.
We don't need crafty leaders, we need honest ones.

We need a Spiritually aware society that springs from fundamental fairness.

4
The Rune of cycles in the Realm of the mind. Dagaz in Muspelheim.
This aspect is one of great importance to our personal growth and experience. Just suppose you have a new idea that takes your life in a new direction, opens new doors, or opportunities.
You cannot put the idea to work because you are in dishonor on a debt, and that is that.
Or: You meet someone who can help you do what you have always wanted to do. Someone else comes along and reveals the fact of your prior lies and abuses, and that is that.
Or: You are in fear of discovery about cheating in one way or another and cannot use your mind to evolve and develop through new experiences, and, of course, that is that.
We get in those spots by taking more than our circumstance has to offer, or thinking that way.

Life is a series of experiences that each lends to the next in the form of knowledge plus whatever is gained.
Waiting for that one big break, or trying to make an ordinary experience into more than it is, denies the natural order of human personal development.
What happens when we find the ivory tower?
Gebo means that everybody gets their due through our interaction.
We make sure of it.
Honorably.
We get ours and we move on.
Such is life.
If we take more, we don't move on, and life becomes static.
Does that matter to you?
How many marriages die because one partner becomes static?
How many parents cannot teach their children because they are exposed in dishonor?
How many dreams are not realized because we cannot move on?
The answer is, most.
We will change over time, as we all do. These can always be forward or lateral changes and need not signal the end of anything, because we take knowledge

and experience through the cycles of the mind.
Trust, truth, and fair play will bring a marriage through even extreme evolution, and any worthwhile thing we wish to keep.
Love too will evolve.
In order to have enduring relationships, we need to realize this aspect.

5
The Rune of justice in the Realm of time.
Tiwaz in Niflheim.
Again the reminder that each Rune appears only one time in each Realm.
This is the one avenue for bringing justice to the efforts of millennia by our ancestors to build the civilization that can survive itself.
Do we get it, or are we stupid and selfish above all things?
This is not a harsh question, but a necessary one.
We can say that things are different now.
We can say that its our time, and it is.
We can do whatever we want, just as everyone before us could.
What do we want?
A breath of fresh air?
A drink of clean water?

A voice in the plan of nations?
A chance to earn a living?
We are not starting from scratch here, we have language, math, and science, livestock, and centuries of experience to draw on.
The business of "self-made men" is naked hubris.
The "Great Men" whose ruthlessness and greed mark the passage of history did not build our place here.
It was the steady hand of honest men that saw us to this time of opportunity.
It is that same steady forward pressure that will give our children a fair chance to realize their destiny.
The idea of rewriting reason to make it politically correct denies justice to the ages.
The idea of non-living business organizations in control of the evolution of being is so stupid that it is nearly incomprehensible.
Yet that is our path.
We are all in debt to companies that are poisoning our children, or planning for their slavery.
We buy from those that endorse ethnic suicide.

We listen to those who embrace moral vulgarity in the most extreme form.
We do this because we are in dishonor and fear to rock the boat, lest we lose what we do not own.
By playing fair we gain the kind of strength needed to bring justice to time.
Our parents' time.
Our children's time.
Our time.
There is only one way.
As far as the masses are concerned, this seems hopeless.
It is not hopeless.
Bring justice to your parents, and your children.
Make a good example of it if you can.
Taking advantage of opportunity is smart.
Taking unfair advantage is not.
We must be strong, not tolerant, in securing justice.

6
Fehu in Hel.
The Rune of personal wealth, control, and power in the Realm of Death.
This aspect clears up a lot of conjecture about an afterlife, judgement, and karma.

Again, a child can understand this, and I have yet to meet one who did not.
What happens when we die is fully explained in this book.
Look at all twenty-four Runes as they appear in the Realm of Hel.
Look at the Rune that appears in Midgard, and you will know what awaits you. The pattern is clear.
This aspect tells us how to take control of the process.
That is what we want.
That is what we know we need to do.
If only there was a way. Blah, blah, blah.
Well, here it is.

PLAY FAIR!

As we progress through the message in the Runes, the whole business of being here takes on wonderful depth and promise.
To be powerless here is failure of our destiny.
That is truly the saddest thing man can contemplate.
It is not easy to be fair, but we see here that it is so important our sentient eternity rides upon it.

Let's surprise ourselves, let's take control of the scariest thing we will ever do. Take power over your death.

7
The Rune of Balance in the Realm of the mysteries.
Hagalaz in Svartheim.
This gift of great value is one we don't think much about because it deals with "what we do not know."
In describing the gift the clarity comes. People are often overwhelmed by things they do not expect or understand.
This aspect tells us that the action of fairness in our lives will create a formula for our exposure to things outside our ken that we can balance with our reality. Or more simply, our challenges will come in a way we can deal with.
Most often, the unknown fails us through unexpected expenditures, back payments, under-budgeting, waste. Sometimes through the refusal of others to support us in some endeavor because of our unfairness to them in the past (unexpectedly), or their unfairness now. The tendency is toward alienation and non-personal programming of our

activities, rather than correcting our behavior, keeps it in the negative.
We stop dealing with people rather than deal with them fairly.
Life becomes stagnant.
We don't enter the mysteries at all.
We don't learn to understand things we don't know.
We are supposed to explore the mysteries and expand our temporal universe, becoming more and better through our handling of new and unknown things.
This proves the Divinity of creation as the perfect struggle.
Why do any of us settle for a life with no mystery?
It is through the mysteries that we marvel at life, not the mundane.
This Realm is critical to our wholeness and is itself the greatest mystery because through this Realm the Joten joins the positive action to become the Wotan.
The unformed Giant plus right action by choice equals the manifestation of the God self.
This is a bold statement.
This is also a true statement.

Ask yourself, "How would creation be if it were real, using the universe as it really is?"
How could God exist, with no history, when all that does exist is so clearly the creation of God through natural means?
Creation is not flawed!
Creation is perfect!
The product of this Balance of Mysteries is a God made by right action in free will.
How else could God be real?
This way there is a history of every choice by every person that furthered the reality of "what should be."
So get it straight.
Get off your chair and square away your program.
It is through fair play in all things that the power of the mysteries are balanced, and can be used.
They help us, they do not destroy us.

8
The Rune of Progress and Protection in the Realm of Giants.
Elhaz in Jotunheim.
This aspect plays directly off of the last.

This is how we protect the purpose of creation and progress toward the reality of God.
It is not easy to act fairly.
Every reason imaginable to guard against failure fills our minds with every step.
Yes we have to make it a part of every decision to admit and explore our fears and means of action.
This conscious self-examination, as we live, empowers the manifestation, outside ourselves, of the Giant strength that is the source of Help in times of need.
The aspect is reciprocal in that our progress and protection from outside ourselves comes through fair play.
We have so much power to shape the Cosmic that only a long close look and proof by trial convince us.
We are the guardians of creation, not the victims.
We are able to create.
Nothing else we know of can create, but the idea of God.
Our application of the Gebo Rune is what will make God's creation Paradise or Hell.

It doesn't happen later, it is happening now.
Let's do it right on purpose.
Prove that man can take care of our parent,
Every child knows this is true.

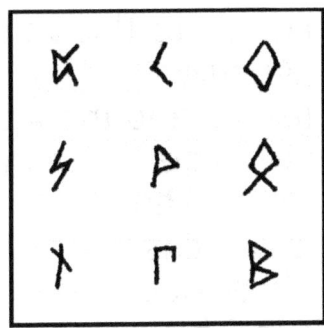

Wunjo.
This is the Rune of joy.
Joy here is not an emotion..
This is the joy found in the character of those who have chosen to live the discipline of the Runes of the first Aett (eight).
This person has standing among his peers - Wunjo.
This person deals on a level of honor - Gebo.
This person relies on the truth to sustain his/her plans - Kenaz.
This person has chosen a path from which to access life - Raido.

This person listens to the voice of conscience - Ansuz.

This person learns and incorporates new knowledge and experience into life on a continuing basis – Thursaz.

This person is not cast upon the rocks of a reality that cannot be controlled or survived – Uruz. This person is free of the financial control of others -Fehu.

We can understand now why this joy is real, and not subject to the whim or power of others.

To protect this joy, it is our responsibility to protect our personal space and time from trivial pursuits and trivial persons. This is not fear, guilt, or hatred, but reality.

This is your life and should not be subject to the fancies or troubles brought by those less concerned about the integrity of their lives.

1
The Rune of all, possible possibilities in the elemental Realm.
Pertho in Vanheim.
This aspect of Wunjo is one reason why Pertho is also known as the Rune of promise.
Here we have an ordered life in the Realm of conscious action - Wunjo in Midgard.
This person keeps disciplined application of the first eight Runes.
Why?
The Pertho Rune in the elemental Realm (Vanheim), tells us that for this person anything is possible in the physical universe.
There is no level of human material accomplishment that this person cannot strive toward.
Being born to privilege, wealth, or position does not open these doors, they break them.

True, greed and corruption can secure many things, but those who apply the discipline of the first aett or eight Runes can achieve the elemental universe.
The reason for this is a resonance and harmony with natural law and humanity as "it should be."
We find it in our power to perform creation of the Goddess of the future, Skuld.
This aspect tells us that a grand destiny awaits those who choose to take responsibility for what they are, who they are, and who they should be.
Those who choose to abandon themselves to another, no matter how lofty, are abandoned. (The physical demon.) They no longer have themselves
So what has been saved?

2
The Rune of truth in the Realm of higher moral being.
Kenaz in Asgard.
Here we continue to extol the reality of joy in Wunjo.
Without an ordered discipline, our higher moral code is subject to the predictable and expected breakdown in the areas represented by the first seven Runes.
People really are forced into a moral breach by financial problems.
People are broken by failing to accord the forces of natural law and intelligent recognition.
People fail because of inadequate training or living without the stability of a ritual system.
People develop doubts about their failings of conscience.
People wander without a path, and fall prey to deception without the truth.
People struggle against the inevitable without honor.
Or, they do not!
Here we see that the preservation of self through Wunjo allows us to have the truth to guide our moral code.
Exposure is not a problem and so the truth is our ally and a Holy state through

which God can really be found.
Desperation and condemnation are not states of mind conducive to higher spiritual communion.
Wunjo is strength, standing, will, direction, decency.
When the truth about us is Wunjo, the truth about God is clear to see.
With Wunjo the truth is a good thing.

3
The Rune of view/doorway, in the Realm of Society.
Ingwaz in Alfheim.
Here Ingwaz represents the portal or doorway into a Realm.
The Realm of society is the arena for the struggle.
The idea that the struggle of right action goes on in ourselves is an error, or at best an understatement.
What success does the Cosmic gain because one of us "realizes" something? None!
The Cosmic gains when each of us, or only one of us, "does something" toward "what should be," in the forum of right action: society.
Wunjo is a statement about what someone is.

This positive content is the key to entering fully into the Realm of society, where the reality of Wunjo cannot be denied.
Again we note that each Rune appears in each Realm only one time.
In this case, Wunjo, being a physical state of ability and will applied, enters the interaction as a viable entity.
The only true entry into society is by one exemplifying Wunjo.
The physical being, the physical act of taking ones place in society, is reserved for this entity.
This is the reason social problems are unchecked.
Many social engineers are not even qualified to interact without supervision, let alone design the forum we grow in.
In today's world one reaches their majority in age and with some degree sets out in life without ever reaching Wunjo.
The result is social error and failure to achieve the potential of humanity.
The cure is to know what Wunjo is and refuse to support anyone for leadership who does not bring the fact of Wunjo to office with him.
We will not be perfect, but we can be

Wunjo.
We can try to create.
We can teach.
We cannot, however, claim superiority without a base of Wunjo.
From Wunjo the world is the steps we take, the space we hold, the truth we tell.
This is our first magical step, through Ingwaz into society, rather than through ignorance or illusion.
For Wunjo society holds the potential of paradise.
Wunjo is our key to real power and opportunity, and it cannot be faked.
You don't have to believe it, you can see it.
This is the quality of the person we bring to society.
This is the Realm of society as a positive, not a chaotic, place.
We control that by the fact of self-discipline.
We only experience the truth about society through a discipline.
Social intercourse is not a discipline, yet we use it for one.
This diminishes the qualities of the individual to the lower levels of mental stimulation as a standard demographic.

This is where Realm understanding is such a benefit.
When we realize that society is the place where right action proves out, and that an ordered individual can access the true heart of society, the process of interaction takes on an importance unfelt by a random participant who is motivated by style's fads, fears, or dogmas.
Our success is then not qualified by the restraints of the norm.
This allows for real accomplishment, and mastery of our social interaction.
Realization of purpose and belonging is a result.
Form is the Cosmic dream.
Form is, for us, possibility, but we must take form deliberately in order to enjoy the possibilities of society, for it is in society that the Cosmic takes form.

4

The Rune of home in the Realm of the mind. Othalaz in Muspelheim.

Here we will see why the ordered person is able to make such large steps.

The mind can be a maze or a wonderland, depending on what we know about ourselves and our circumstance.

Some people excel at business, but are socially inept. Some learn at incredible levels, but have no sense of humanity or business.

Many smart people are criminally anti-social.

Few are good at everything, and that is a shame.

This aspect tells us that by striving for Wunjo and being true to form (which is not a test of intelligence), we can be at home in the wholeness of the mind.

From this point our mental frontiers become clear and we can use our mind for our own growth and potential.

It is really good news that these potentials are not dependent on great knowledge or spirituality.

Usually great success comes from a basic understanding of some of these principles, which are, unfortunately, not common.
This book is a good example of how the playing field can change with a little sharing of knowledge.
People who understand these principles will cease to be sales targets and change their world for the better without fear or blame.
We need not be confused or afraid to think the scary stuff through.
If a good man can't figure out what's being said, then someone is lying.
Also, from this relaxed place of mind, we can observe those we interact with and know why they say what they say, why they do what they do, and what we can do, if anything, to achieve a positive result. We can read each other.
Putting our base existence into order so that we are not directed in our thinking by our interactive partners brings peace to the mind.
So we see that being at home in our own thoughts is not the ordinary state of man, though common sense says it should be.
It is through ordering our base self that

the real use of our mental ability can begin and become.
The reason for this is the ability to recognize what is not in order.
The mind works best with simple elimination reasoning, so here we get the mind at its best, working from the inside (the best place).

5
The mother Rune in the Realm of the lake and time.
Berkano in Niflheim.
We have long known the Holy place our ancestors hold in the truth of the Asa-Lore.
Every religious ideal teaches reverence to parents, but few give details as to how one can best do this.
Again we see the simple power of the message in the Runes.
The way to honor our parents is to order our lives.
This aspect says more.
The order man can bring to the world of conscious action also creates a meaningful and useful Realm of time.
Often we feel that time is our enemy; life is too short, there are not enough hours in the day to do our work, let

alone pay attention to our parents' legacy or our children's needs.
The hours in the day are sufficient.
The message here is that an ordered physical existence will give us the ability to nurture the Realm of time.
The person who maintains Wunjo is able to avoid situations created by cash flow problems through the Gebo and Fehu aspects of their life.
Crisis of action through the Thursaz, Ansuz, and Raido aspects of their lives, and misunderstanding through the Kenaz aspect of truth in their lives.
Nurturing our place in time, the reasons we come to it, and what will follow is possible because of Wunjo.
Wunjo means joy!
Being in control means joy.
Being free, safe, educated, aware, moving in your own direction, truthful, and honest, means joy.
Take away any of these and one will be busy just making up for it.
This is not easy, but it's not that hard.

The benefits so outweigh the cost that it is not a question.
The question lies elsewhere.
The dogmas and dictates of men have left us confused and lost about our place in time. The power structures of those dogmas interrupt man in his building of Wunjo.
The wonders of the universe make themselves known through the Runes, but to use the information we need to build a tool that can do so.
That tool is us.
Wunjo is all you need to be of use to yourself, and with that comes profound joy.

6
The Rune of power in the Realm of death. Uruz in Hel.
Remember the last aspect as we visit Hel.
Uruz is power we cannot control, that is true.
We can, however, channel Uruz to service our needs.
Uruz is more than can be simply said, because it is the "one power" that charges the Cosmic.
We don't need to be a genius to reach

Wunjo, and Wunjo brings the Cosmic power to our death.
That's right. Let it sink in.
Uruz is life.
The "one power" is also the power of life.
Cosmic life, human life, God life.
Later on we will discuss the cycle of life and death, but for now just be aware that we gain the power to affect the circumstance of death through the act of will exercised in ordering our life.
Each of us is different.
Each of us has different problems, people and circumstances to deal with, so the way we put our lives into order is unique to each.
The Runes allow that all of those things are true.
You will be who you are, but you will arrive at the stations in your life in a manner that allows you to deal with what you find there.
The goal of all this, as we will study in the next Aett is victory, and the fulfillment of our human destiny.
Power in death is part of that destiny.

7
The Rune of need in the Realm of mystery. Nathiz in Svartheim.
Science has theorized that a great original action gave form to all that is in a single moment.
The Big Bang. The Nathiz Rune is representative of the driving force behind that action. The invisible need that causes a baby to draw its first breath and every breath thereafter is irresistible.
Here we see the Realm of the unknown. Magic, mystery, darkness.
These mysteries are the subject matter of the human struggle.
What would be pure magic two centuries ago, is common place today, yet the deeper mysteries are still veiled because of their very nature, and the means by which other mysteries are solved.
Science itself seems to deny the Divine, when the Divine needs science most.
The mysteries cry out to be known, to draw a breath as knowledge, and be a part of the great Cosmic becoming.
This work is the business of the ordered person, for one learns quickly that the truth of things is found in the order of its

existence.
Especially when one finds the benefit of putting themselves in order.
The unique aspects of each person unlocks another mystery of Cosmic reality when life takes charge of itself in the form of our design.
As we will see later on, it is the Cosmic being itself that sets the pattern, and a pattern does exist, by which those with the hands, minds, and unique perspectives of you and I will do work that is beyond Divine.
As we come to realize what this means, the whole idea of the meaning of life becomes clear.
The creator awaits its first breath.
All has to come in order, and remain in order by free choice to reach the final mystery.
The breathing God is the Cosmic idea. Our child.
We are the means to the realization of the Divine in form.
Surely a dogma will come forward, and a bureaucracy to attempt to manage mankind yet again, but the ordered life of Wunjo puts us above that.
Kinship, fellowship, and harmony of purpose allow group efforts where

hierarchy does not.
If mankind were not ready for this mystery to be revealed, then this work would not be written.
If the need were not dire, then the same would be true. We are turning, as a people, away from the battles of dogma, but where do we turn to?
This evolution is a wonder beyond the horror of a final conflict.
This is the kind of mystery to be addressed by the ordered persona.
Wunjo is all of this and more.
8
The Rune of victory in the Realm of giants (mutation). Sowilo in Jotunheim.
This is the end game of the ordered life.
This Realm is strength outside ourselves.
This can be an invading army burning our homes, or a search party finding our lost child.
Very bad, or very good.
It all depends on what we put into it.
Do we make war over wealth, ritual, land, truth, behavior, betrayal?
Do we watch the world spin out of control while we struggle with credit card debt or marriage?
Do we stand powerless while everyone

lies about everything and destroys our world?
This aspect tells us that Wunjo can transform the power outside ourselves into victory.
The very meaning of a "grassroots movement" is that it starts with the individual.
Are we a bunch of morons who would stand by and watch our own destruction, or are we people who put our lives in order?
Realize that much of the power over us comes from our being out of order in specific ways, so the movement toward destruction will be stopped by our movement toward Wunjo.
The power outside of us is reflective of the life we are living.
This message is simple.
The bad goes away, the good is victorious through Wunjo.
This is not prayer.
This is personal commitment to make ourselves whole.
This seemingly simple process will complete the making of a strength outside ourselves that is positive, not parasitic.
Creating interactive, homogeneous

government and group action.
Success-oriented self-description.
The creation of the great helping hand,
rather than the great smashing fist.
The real manifestation of Divine power
on a plane of human action.
Does anyone not know what that adds
up to?
Wunjo brings all these things.
Things we all want but do not know how
to get.
This message is so important.
If you do it just to be more comfortable
in your home, it doesn't matter.
Wunjo is as good as man can expect to
be, but still only common sense.
Wunjo will make the world healthy
again.
Put it in order.

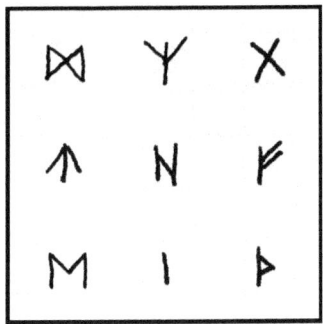

Hagalaz - the Rune of destruction and chaos / the Rune of perfect balance and harmony. So which Rune is it, chaos or harmony?

As we progress through the aspects of the emotional aett we see the fact of duality so clearly that the faces of the 'powers that be' become clear in the mist.

This is a Rune of great power from either view, and is the fulcrum of the Cosmos. The way to find the greater perspective, is to use the lesser.

As before, remember that all things, primarily mankind, are reflected in the pattern demonstrated by the Runes. Universal balance is the wonder of all things, even though often only one phase or side is viewable at any given time.

Some of the great complexities of thought center here, in this simple truth. The enthusiasm of believers often veil this important reality, which is described by the thing itself.
This is the inescapable fact of contrast in singularity.
The idea of people thinking they are powerless is so far from the truth it is frightening.
Man has power in contrast.
Choice.
Only man can change reality through the use of the power he controls, wealth, influence, will.
These changes must be made with the end in mind.
If the end is just, the use of destructive power is no different than the use of influence or wealth or creative powers.
The scope of this is enormous.
At this point in the study of Rune structure, the individual messages in the pattern begin to gain dimension.

We have seen how the Runes are established by the Rune preceding each. Here we form statements from the rows in the Aetts.

It is in the second Aett that the catalyst of substance and thought become reality; reality being the condition of the result.

For instance, peace with heavily armed troops and curfews may not be peace at all, but public prison, or a marriage without trust, or a business without enthusiasm.

Real success in the business of life is a many-faceted truth, but each is relative and makes sense if we know what we are about.

Remember that even though you are different than Bob or Jane, or me, we are all part of the same whole and the pattern fits us, not the reversed.

1
The Rune of days/cycles, in the Realm of elemental form. Dagaz in Vanheim.
Here we see that on a level the very turning of the universe is seen in the principle of duality.

The cycles of positive and negative, yin yang; male female is the axis, not a mere aspect of observation, but the substance of the whole.
Sorting chaos to find order, changing the old order, with chaos, to a new order.
On a personal level this tells us that we must be aware of our point of balance and control ourself to maintain that balance.
The best way to do this is to consciously apply the first eight Runes as a discipline.
Be right when you act with intensity according to your discipline, rather than the nature of your emotion.
Failing this could change the physical structure of our lives to the very base level.
The fact of our existence is an expression of duality that we can embrace and master, or, deny and suffer from.
The very idea that we can escape by accepting some belief system that

attaches blame for this reality on some group or other is silly.
The idea of laying the "burden" of dealing with duality on the name of a savior may also be not quite what the lesson intended.
Why we presume failure as the only possibility is one of the deeper questions in life.
This Rune is the key to the other possibility: Success!
By tuning Hagalaz into our thinking, we stabilize and balance the cycle of change in our physical existence to our ability to deal with it.
Here it is just something to do, and we have a way to do it that is not a full-time job.
Agrarian schedules do it for the weather.
Just like the weather, everything cycles but the mind.
Give this some thought.

2
The Rune of progress and protection in the home of God.
Elhaz in Asgard.
This is such a promising aspect.

We become stronger in our moral code through our control of our reaction and interaction.

Our balance of wealth, power, influence, and dissent, used to a just purpose, protects and advances our moral truth.

This means it gets easier as time goes by.

Soon our higher development takes on wings and a truly superior life opens up.

People will act out duality if they don't control it.

We can use the lessons of the moment to demonstrate the power of destruction or of evolution of being represented here, but only if we are not part of the evil, or the rapture.

We see here that the will of Heaven is to protect and promote balance, and balance promotes and protects the higher moral code.

The Elhaz Rune also represents majesty of form.

The King of the natural plane.

This balance of beauty and strength is what proves the truth of a higher moral code.

One without the other lacks majesty.
We are conditioned to accept that majesty is only for the anointed, or descendants of those chosen by God. Here we see an equal opportunity for moral majesty through emotional balance.
It may be that limits need be set on emotion while we gain experience. The aspects of Wunjo make that fairly clear.
As we grow, our ability to explore the power of emotion will grow too.
The patience required for this is a good training tool for that growth.
Rest assured there is a reason why we are constantly beset with hard choices about things which arise just when that moral lesson is the focus of our moral quest.
The reason includes the chance for success in reaching majesty, progress, and protection of the higher moral ideal. Our lives are all about something!

3
The gift Rune in the Realm of society.
Gebo (X) in Alfheim.
Here we see the source of great success or great trouble in society.
There is no one way to be.
There is no average Joe.
The whole business of right brain, left brain function comes into play in our social behavior.
Rational, linear, or artistic emotional logic.
Male. Female.
The key to social success is in avoiding the creation or management of social programs or institutions while motivated by high emotion, be it the desperation of the educational system to succeed despite being sandbagged by the illusion that everyone learns the same, or sadness and anger at a public display of terror that leads to war with people who did not do the deed.
Society is an idea shared by all, yet for each the idea is different, a little or a lot different.

It is our gift to society to bring a balance of nurturing and strength to the table. Yes, the strong can overpower the caregivers, so the caregivers hone their strength and abandon the nurturing until things are "more ordered."
Society becomes a training camp for battle.
Creativity dwindles. Caring dwindles.
Religion battles academia when both must be whole.
Male battles female when both must be strong.
Nature battles industry when both must be strong.
When all the parts of the social whole are strong, the purpose of society is fulfilled.
When leaders prey on these divisions to find support, they should be removed. Only the individual can decide who will lead, not those who wish to lead, whether they are true or not, because the act of campaigning leads to singular focus and denies the gift society requires.

A leader must be strong and nurturing, yet free from the need to defend on a personal level.
Our grasp of the duality of Hagalaz and Gebo in the social aspect will help us to decide how best to make our social institutions work, and who best to support as leaders and managers.
These are some of the hardest choices to make and the most important.

4
The Rune of wealth and personal power in the Realm of the mind.
Fehu in Muspelheim.
This is an aspect of powerful promise.
Our mind is where we give ourselves the chance to live our destiny.
Here we see that in applying the truth of duality to the process of intellect, the process itself is empowered.
The choice is not so much the relative factor as being aware that there is a choice.
Even the simplest thing has a counterpoint, another meaning, or

an alternate possibility or application. Every such truth, when recognized, lends power to the reasoning process. The examples are too numerous to list. The ability to truly reach "what should be" is so much greater as to change the concept from "trying to figure things out," to one of "intelligent selection of correct and contributing value."

Right and wrong are at primary to those without a declared intent.

Once a rational person has determined that life must be lived with meaning and purpose, they have chosen "right over wrong."

If we then become locked into a continuing struggle about a choice already made by adopting a program of belief that focuses only on this first step in the mastery of duality, our need for power in our mental process is nothing. It is through the empowering of the mental process that we achieve human growth.

We need not be confused or unable to see the depth of a situation.

This comes from application and experience.
Once free of the fear that we may be wrong, the way becomes smooth.
When we see both sides of issues and devise a path toward solution, our will becomes the shape of reality.
The personal freedom Fehu represents in the personal Rune application, becomes freedom of creativity in the great pattern.
This is the source of the intelligence that gave form to a perfect, healthy environment.
Knowing this, we can act to give form to our highest possible being.

5
The Rune of ritual, right action, law, in the Realm of time.
Thursaz in Niflheim.
Here we bring value to history, and leave value as history through determined, right action.
When we adopt ritual means of accomplishing right action and deal with

the law of resistance as a matter of course, we create.
This is not an idea or concept, but actual creation.
It is the duality of truth in time that can make change within the truth that is also a lie.
To create from the failures of the past that are also victories.
We are charged to maintain the balance of action upon those works begun by our parents, as well as to develop working uses of law that endure through time.
This is the way to empower ourselves through the ritual year.
We do the rites to maintain the right to do the things.
Whether we are joining for a solstice blot or wording a trust for an orphaned child, the ritual in time is an act of right action intended to exceed our span of years or at least the present time.
The defeat of the past cannot be victory in the past, but the lessons learned and applied can bring victory in time.
The nature of Hagalaz, which is a double thing, is not a chance fact, but the reality upon which all lasting principles are based.
It is a rock that is also the sea, the sky

that is also a field, always.
This is why the Realm of spirit and time is a Realm and not an idea.
It is real!
As real as anything in your life, and as capable of being formed as the wood you carve, or the bread you bake.
The duality of the chaos Rune must then be creation in time.
Firm ritualized intended creation, based on natural and fashioned law, and resulting in what should be, in time.
So the most mysterious Rune turns out to be in our grasp through the clearest, simplest Rune and the tool of creation: time.
This is a non-dogmatic, scientifically viable, whole scale creation model, without stupid conditions of probability attached by wires of superstition, and fully within our reach.

6
The Rune of stasis in the Realm of death.
Isa in Hel.
Here we find the dual principle of chaos and order, in the Realm of life's end, stable and continuous.
It is important to remember that man's interaction in time is found in Niflheim, not in Hel.
The bridge between time and death (Gjole) is the return to the Folk Soul of our being - subconscious - true self.
The Realm of death is timeless, yet is the point of transition from the Realm of conscious action (Midgard -life) to the Cosmic soul energy.
There the true self, our part of the Folk Soul, is a tattered, battered, mostly ignored remnant of our life's experience, or, is the essence of our being, filled with the truth of right action and victory over the anti-virtues of a good life lived. Victory over illusion.
Remember that the mind can consciously deal with base duality through the Lore, or, the true self will

force the tests to the front of our experience.
We will choose to live true, or we will not.
We will not avoid choosing to be tested. The message here is that in our ego conscious control of our life, we can avoid the struggle in any number of ways but then our subconscious will make us deal with the dual struggle and all manner of symptoms of emotional distress and general chaos will ensue. By standing up and dealing with the hard questions in life, we control the chaos balance to the point where a stable soul condition is present at death. Thus we rejoin the whole Folk's soul as the able doer that so truly faced life.
We don't have to face shock or fear, terror or judgement, but stability and Lore, of which we are a part.
This is such a great aspect of the message in the Runes.
Not oblivion, fire, or eternal suffering. Just more life, continued conscious being, and belonging in the great pattern.

There are those who choose to bypass the daily challenge of mastering the balance by dedicating themselves to a criminal life, a sexual life, a life of religious seclusion or suicide.
Sadly, that can be understood.
When we realize life is an endless parade of hard choices and we have no weapons or tools to help us succeed, when we are alienated by ruthlessness, greed, and hate, it is hard to find logic.
The Isa Rune represents this Rune Lore among the forms of stasis and stability.
This Rune Lore is a tool for just this purpose.
With this tool, the appearance of difficulty is no surprise.
The constancy of the struggle is no burden, but a meaning for life.
Self-validation from this truth and companions in the knowledge bring belonging to a higher purpose.
In accepting this struggle, we control the way our challenges reveal themselves and success is probable if we stand on true ground and stand tall.

7
The Rune of partnership in the Realm of mystery / magic.
Ehwaz in Svartheim.
Here is the Realm of unknown forces, magic and, potentially, very dark behavior.
"Dark elves" does not refer to dark skin, but to dark hearts and minds.
In our Rune study, we have seen that the truth – Kenaz gives us victory over the dark powers, and people with dark purpose.
We will study the way in which Manaz - the true man - can see into the truth about the dark mysteries.
Here we see that a balance of forces can create a partnership with the power of dark mystery.
It is through a real understanding of the necessary part the negative plays in the wholeness of reality.
This is not fantasy.
There is bad stuff in the real world.
The Realm of dark powers is not "the bad place" any more than the Realm of light elves is "the good place."

Mostly it's a dog-eat-dog pinball game of joy and sadness.
Just as our life journey mates us to the social Realm, the balance Rune lets us mate with the source of mystery.
The basic fear of the unknown and the real fear of the manifestations of evil intent in people we interact with teach us to withdraw from the mysteries.
Our understanding of the duality of existence and willingness to strive toward keeping a balance so that creativity can flourish joins us to the very womb of mystery and magic.
This is the myth of Guldvig, the Norns and Freyja Becoming.
This is a far cry from the things we have been raised to believe.
We have come to accept that we can get an excuse from our debt for life from the mercy of a saint.
Even under that premise, standing by, or worse, helping to destroy your mother (earth) and deny your father (free will) because of a professed belief, would surely judge one in the negative.

Bullies don't stop.
They must be stopped.
Greed does not stop.
Good people need not accept whatever comes out of the darkness. We can be a part of the darkness where evil comes from and refuse to let it come among men.
The power that charges evil is not evil.
It is intent that is evil if we choose.
The dark energy has no intent, only men do.
This is the power that can truly magically change substance.
Add this power to your life and you become more.
Balance, duality, wholeness.

8
The Rune of justice in the Realm of Giants.
Tiwaz in Jotunheim.
This is the Realm of both angels and demons.
The Jotan is hard, cold, strong, and wild.
He is the product of blind resistance, desperate struggle victory through deceit and betrayal.
This is outside ourselves.
Here also is the Realm of great strength,

hope, and the mutation of chaos to order.
The manifestation of God in form that comes from action in virtue.
Our grasp of the concept of balance and dual nature gives us the power to bring justice here.
Only when evil takes form is it subject to justice.
Education, will, character, and virtue prevent evil from taking form, while giving form to God.
Denying the true nature of our experience does nothing to help further justice.
At this point our contribution is complete., deceit, destruction, and waste comes.
The myth of Thor's Hammer meting out justice to Giants is shown here.
At this point the payoff for imbalance, deceit, destruction, and waste comes home. Giants, demons. At this point the payoff for courage, constancy, sacrifice, and progress comes home. Wotan!
Looking back to the first aspect of the Hagalaz Rune we find Dagaz , the Rune of cycles.
Here we meet justice, then the cycle starts again. Perfect!

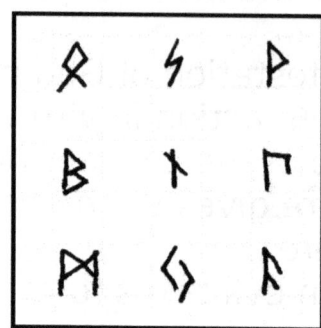

Nathiz, the Rune of need.
Here we examine the aspects of one of the most important Runes.
Our personal grasp of this idea is what gives us the power over distraction, addiction, and emotional desperation.
Our habits, relationships, and employment hinge on our ability to deal with need, as well as our financial stability.
How we do these things varies from person to person, but this outline of fundamental need will help us to focus in a way that allows for success.
There are several disciplines that are demonstrated in history where personal excellence are achieved, but none of them deal with this basic concept.
The idea of needs are by and large never addressed as a whole concept.

A man's needs, or a woman's needs, are discussed in terms of inconveniences and concessions.
The fundamental nature of need is largely overlooked, which leads to a state of hopelessness at ever finding peace in our hearts.
It is from the state of peace in ourselves that real emotional growth begins and endures.
Some of these aspects require acceptance, some require work.
All require that we maintain control of our emotions, even our extreme emotions, which will continue and may even intensify.
The sentient mind converts emotion, based on perceived need, into right action, or chaotic action.

1
The Rune of home/ancestral home in the elemental Realm. home in the material universe.
Othalaz in Vanheim.
This aspect is one of the hardest to accept, especially by those of us raised to believe that the earth, the universe, and mankind are transient things created singularly by God, who is himself outside of creation itself.
This widespread belief, and the accompanying dogma and doctrine, promise horrible consequences to any who question it.
The result is, unfortunately, a disregard for the environment and/or those yet to live here, and a sense of homelessness that stays with us throughout life.
We may feel strong in our faith that we are to return to the arms of the Creator. But who among us ever chose to leave the arms of our Creator to suffer alone on this rock?
Why would He cast us out and make us fear for our safe return?

Why would he risk our failure and eternal death in this transient and corrupt world?
Those questions have no place in the message in the Runes.
We don't need to know why we are where we don't belong, because it is a fiction that we do not belong here.
This aspect tells us we need to be at home in the elemental universe.
Here in the matter and energy cycle of life where we are, where the air is, where the water is, where the food is.
Why would we choose to believe that we are not here to deal with the stuff that is happening here for its own sake?
Why would our "spirit" long to leave the body and abandon touch, taste, sight, and sound?
Why is form seen as a curse?
Because we are taught that form is not our natural state, we are not at home in form, that we are really just a soul.
This aspect of the message in the Runes tells us we are at home in the physical elemental universe.

Just as modern physics has learned the physical and spiritual universe are joined in a way that science has not yet explained, but that is, nonetheless, certain.
Once we get past the idea of being strangers in a strange land, we can go forward without fantasy, fear, or illusion. This is an old message that is more important today than ever.
The idea is not that this is not our natural form, but that we have taken form, and "need" to deal with what that means.
We need to do that in the material universe, not our imagination.
We need to settle into our lives and live them.
Do this life.

2
The Rune of victory in the Realm of God's home.
Sowilo in Asgard.
This deals with the reality of our morality.

It is unfortunate that morality exists in degrees and is, often as not, governed by visibility or circumstance.
This is a charge for us to live up to.
Morality is seen by some to be "the way others say we should live."
When we decide we're in this life alone - about age twenty, we disregard the overview of others as a waste of time.
Along with this we often discard our moral structure, especially when or if we step away from our parents' church.
This is one of the horrors of the times.
When we do not find a spiritual answer to our spiritual outcry, the greatest disappointment is not staggering, but just another in a series of great disappointments that brings us to adulthood feeling that life is falsified.
We decide the level of our morality based on the moral code we "see" in action.
Sadly, most of us display a moral standard that we are ashamed of because those around us may reject us if we act "better than they are."
That is moral defeat.

Many people will loudly defend base behavior.
We need victory in our higher moral code and it is personal!
Spiritual awakening is not on sale.
A higher moral code is not built in.
Our conscience is built in and we need to use it to build a true moral structure that we are not ashamed of.
Then we need to stick with it!
This is not about commandments, this is about character.
We need this!
Just as the victory of creation needs us to succeed, in form, over base values and behavior.
Our moral structure is the defining aspect of our intent.
What do we intend?
Bringing morality to action is victory!

3
The Rune of joy in the Realm of society.
Wunjo in Alfheim.
Society has become a burden.
Society has become a non-stop sales pitch.

Government takes way too much in taxes.
Business takes way too much in profit.
Entertainment is too commercialized.
But wait!
Is that required?
Schools spend way too much time grooming minds, and not enough teaching material.
What can you do?
Wunjo shows us an ordered being, true, fair, and honorable.
Remember that society is an amalgam of ideas.
Most of the stuff represented in the blind chaos of greed and deception in modern society cannot compete with anything true. Just as factional religion cannot compete with truth.
The message here is to bring yourself to society.
If the truth about you seems to deny you a place in society, then the model is wrong.
By bringing our Wunjo self to society, the inappropriate aspects will fade.
The model will change.

It is important to realize again that the model is theoretical, based on the intent of the social planners.
Wunjo is not theoretical, but a real strength of action and character.
Wunjo is joy.
Real joy.
How long has it been since being a part of society has been a real joy?
Political correctness is not joy.
Intolerable corruption is not joy.
Nurturing, belonging, and purpose are joy.
Molding ourselves to fit society is not joy.
Molding society to fit us, is joy.
Good people are not outdated.
They are hiding inside of us, afraid to be crushed in the dog-eat-dog world.
Take courage and sally forth into the social Realm, secure in the knowledge of your Wunjo self.
We need Wunjo to do this.
A half-hearted stab at being a "good person" is not enough, but taking the steps to Wunjo is plenty.

You will still be yourself, only you will be better.
It's like writing with a sharp pencil, it's nice, but you have to keep it sharp.
Life is real.
Staying sharp is a little harder, but it's worth it.

4
The Rune of elemental power in the Realm of the mind.
Uruz in Muspelheim.
This aspect takes us to a higher level of being.
It is presumed that intelligence can be measured.
Perhaps so, but is intelligence fixed according to that measure?
The message in the Runes tells us that the entire exercise that is our lives is toward attaining right action through free will under adverse circumstance.
It stands to reason that the very power of the universe is available to our use in finding ways to do that.
This aspect tells us just that.

Unlimited power for the mind to use in creating "what should be."
This is power!
Not the concept of power.
Not the suggestion of power, but power.
This power is natural.
The mind operates on this power, as does everything else.
Psychokinesis is not extraordinary behavior or beyond anyone's ability.
The Uruz power is there in every mind.
This is how we convert raw emotional reaction into a constructive thought process.
We need to pay attention to this process in other than an abstract way.
When we know about it, we can apply it. This goes toward using Uruz as a healing power to bring failing systems into true forms which is health; to bring misconception into understanding, and to bring confusion into strength of will.
Helplessness is a condition of ignorance about this Power.
We need to know this and use it to reach our potential.

This is the most important tool of the mind.
Study it.
Use it.
When we need to find an answer now, we hesitate to open up to this power, even though having it described makes perfect sense.
Some of us are better at this and we can get better at it by just putting the idea in place.

5
The Rune of conscience/consciousness, in the Realm of time.
Ansuz in Niflheim.
This is a two-sided aspect in more ways than most.
How many times have we said, "I don't know how I know, but I just do"?
The Folk consciousness **is.**
Our consciousness is a part of Cosmic totality, while at the same time all of that.
Our ancestry and ourselves contribute all of our experience to the Folk Soul, and we are the Folk.

The Folk Soul needs our experience because that is what it is.
The experience of the Folk Soul is why we are not the same as people one or two or three thousand years ago.
Theoretically we are the same, but it is those experiences in time that make living now completely different than at any other time.
The Folk Soul will not benefit from our X-box victories, only form our efforts in society.
It's not what we know, it's what we do.
We need to embrace the past as "what is" to get a sound footing in reality.
This is the purpose of tradition.
To disregard history is to struggle with no insight and become apart from reality instead of a part of reality.
<u>The Folk consciousness is the continuity of humanity.</u>
Otherwise time would be a barrier.
"The time barrier."
How do we breach the time barrier?
Deny it!
Take from your eternal self, leave to your eternal self.

Do not deny your ancestry, do not deny yourself.
Do not embrace what is passing as anymore than what it is, and do not hide from the fact that just because you don't know where you learned something, you don't "just know" what it is about.
Open yourself to this wealth of information, and take the leg-up that it gives you.
The amount of time we save in our own day-to-day lives more than makes this worthwhile.
The knowledge of the Folk Soul does not come from a "dead" source.
The Folk Soul is eternal.
You **were** a part of it.
You **are** a part of it.
You **will be** a part of it.
What kind of part should that be?
Give yourself and everyone else something to work with down the line.

6
The Rune of Harvest in the Realm of death.
Jera in Hel.
Here again we get instruction on the passing of life.
Death is the subject of horror and revulsion.
The Runes tell us clearly that death is neither.
Once again the problems of many religious upbringings come to the forefront of our thinking, and once again we are re-assured.
In harvesting the fact of death into the whole of our existence, we gain an enthusiasm toward our day-to-day actions.
Death will come.
We need to take it as part of the whole and not avoid the hard choices because we fear it.
We may put off dealing with issues that define our character and values.
This reflects on the Wunjo aspect in the social Realm and emphasizes the importance of maintaining an ordered personal makeup.
This is all by choice.
It is not by faith or belief that we do

these things, but through the certain realization that it makes us better.
As we enter the Realm of death, our last act of will in this life of right action is to harvest our self.
We need to do this or it will not be done.
This is your life.
You have as much life as anyone else does, and as we see in the Realm of the mind [Uruz in Muspelheim] the very power of the Cosmic to use in preserving that life through death.
This is not God's job.
God's part in this is done.
The Folk consciousness [Ansuz in Niflheim] says that the God mind is eternal, timeless, and our' part of that need not diminish.
Here it says that **we** must do the harvest.
If you haven't figured out yet that this is whole Lore, this should help.
The whole map of human reality is here.
This is not prophecy.
This is not promise.
<u>This is a technical manual of the makeup of the human Situation.</u>

7
The Rune of man in the Realm of magic/mystery.
Manaz in Svartheim.
As we touched on in the last aspect, this Rune Lore is a tool to accomplish this task.
Here we are instructed to find the mystery, or more specifically, the dark mysteries of man.
We need to try to find out why we make choices we know are wrong, and correct ourselves there, making right choices.
Many such choices are easy when the information here is applied, and reflect simple ignorance.
But some men choose to kill for gain, hurt for spite, hate for envy.
There are horrors upon horrors in the potentiality of human experience.
We also need to explore the bright mystery of men.

Why do fathers sacrifice so much to get their kids through college?
Why do we choose as we do?
Why do we love?
The examples of the mysteries of man are too numerous to explore here and may detract from the many ways each reader would apply this aspect.
Just apply yourselves to the learning of the wonder of man and especially Manaz.
For here is a different kind of man.
Manaz is man as he should be.
Manaz is powerful, capable, willing, more!
The means of achieving Manaz is explained in the aspects of the Runes, but what is actually accomplished is subject for study.
Manaz has applied the aspects of Nathiz and become the great mystery to the masses.
The ability to "work" the Cosmos, teach, lead, heal, bring clarity, create.
Power that is not known in men is found in Manaz.
Why?

Why does a code really do something?
We need the power that comes from the Realm of magic, and only Manaz is trusted with that power.
Why would the mysteries reveal themselves to base people?
Power is denied to fools.
Shedding blood on altars won't earn trust or power.
The self is the only thing we own that can be sacrificed.
And who would do that?
Is that even possible?
This is a whole new view of existence that is many thousands of years old.
We need to get in touch with these things in a real way and learn what is there.
These are the mysteries of man.

8
The mother Rune in the Realm of Giants.
Berkano in Jotunheim.
The final basic need.
There is a strength outside of ourselves that grows with our willingness as individuals to contribute to it in harmony.
The muscle of the common weal, as it were.

When we are not in tune with the Cosmic order, we are subject to this muscle much like the bug on the windshield.
To the blind, it is blind.
To the deaf, it is deaf.
To fools, it is a very large, very, very dangerous fool.
<u>We're going deep here.</u>
When we are in tune, it is the big giant hand that brushes away obstacles, and carries us to safety.
It is not the 'army of righteousness' that slays the evil of men.
It is the windshield.
To those in tune - Manaz - this is the hand of God.
To those out of tune, this is chaos and destruction.
Yet it is the same thing.
It is we who decide how this affects us.
This must be cared for and nurtured.
This is God coming to be in the common weal.
There is no blame, no guilt, or mistake.
When we add to the volume and intensity of this strength through positive action, we define ourselves.
This is counterpoint to the way God is traditionally idealized, as a big guy who

judges each of us wisely and errs in our favor because we meant to be good.
This is not to describe God, but to define that aspect of God **"becoming'** and instruct us to see and care for this greatest of human creations.

The Jotan is of our making <u>just as the matter and energy of the universe is the Cosmic clay of creation, and we are the tool of ascension toward Divinity in form.</u>
This is the mother Rune in Jotunheim, the womb of Divinity in form.
We need this.
We need to care for it and nurture what it brings forth.
These needs are simple and sensible.
They are real and true.
Now go ahead and satisfy your need.

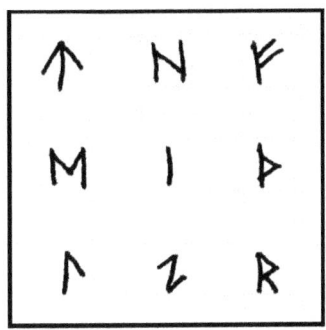

Isa, the Rune of stasis / stability.
In our personal Rune study we found that applying stasis to our emotional reactions gives us latitude in dealing with ever-increasing ranges of situations.
We can deal with things that had seemed impossible.
When the negative becomes strong motivation toward deeper reasoning rather than anger, or when the positive does not blind us with ecstasy, we bring a more reasonable outcome.
Because our experience is at the heart of the development of Cosmic reasoning in free form, the whole idea of effective reasoning is important well beyond ourselves.

The final aspect of this set makes that so clear, but keep this in mind as we move through these aspects.

1
The Rune of justice in the elemental Realm.
Tiwaz in Vanheim.
This is a two-sided aspect in every way and a good reminder of the nature of the Realm of physical existence.
In the negative, everything around us suffers its wholeness and fulfillment when we express extremes of passion. On the grand scale the Cosmic hope depends on our decision to maintain a stable and progressive outlook on life. The elemental universe is the womb that brings all life to be.
The madness of pollution and destruction do not do justice to our home.
Chaotic and unpredictable reactions to day-to-day situations, whether in private or public life, alone or in groups, denies justice to the whole of existence.

Our families and friends find no justice in knowing us unless we hold desire and temper in stasis.
But the whole of creation does find justice in the stable and thoughtful management of our lives.
Constancy brings a true way to reach our potential.
The justice we receive from form in the elemental universe is in the even and stable passing of movement in our physical existence.
This is what makes this place a home and environment.
Again, Isa is the knowledge, information, ritual and people we use to support us in our struggle, kept above passion!
This Lore is Isa, or, a part of Isa.
Applying ourselves in such a way as to be true to knowledge, ritual, helpers, and Lore allows the Cosmic to attain "what should be."
This is the just reward for the elemental universe that gives us a home, form, and opportunity.
We get to experience life here.

Let's do it so our benefactor receives in kind for the gift.
This is stasis in change, not stagnation. Stagnation is failure in change that leads to undesirable creation instead of stability.
Nurturing corruption is not the goal, yet decay and corruption is the cycle for organic regeneration.
It is up to us to create a polar opposite between sentient living and corruption / decay.
We allow decay and corruption to occur in the world we live in as if it were natural at all levels of being.
The nature of the exercise is to create what is not corrupt from that which is corrupt and base.
Success bridges duality, answers need, and builds stability that is stasis in action.
This is the just reward for the enduring matter, energy cycle that makes this all possible.
The support and management of 'close to natural circumstances' promotes stasis in the elemental Realm.
We are not unnatural because of sentience, but we are responsible for actions that do not conflict with the

natural.
This is real, not imagined.

2
The Rune of duality-balance/chaos destruction in the Realm of the higher moral code.
Hagalaz in Asgard.
Again we have a pronounced two-way aspect.
Hagalaz is representative of dual reality and it is only to be expected that where Hagalaz is found, both sides of an idea will appear, or in this case, both sides of two ideas.
Here we see that the balance of our moral strength is founded on our ability to maintain stability in our day to day lives.
This is no mean feat, and requires that we really do hold a discipline in our lives.
The entirety of moral strength is in constancy.

The entirety of personal stability is in moral parameters.

When we glide along in the flow of social and economic living, our focus is so divergent as to be a distraction and so we depend on the fixed guidelines of restraint that are so much more limiting than beneficial.

The borders of fixed restraint push us back to the norm, but the human effects of our deviation remain.

Our children are ignored, our spouses are disrespected, our selves are pigeon-holed.

Human growth out of this flypaper trap requires a real foundation to stand on.

Our own parameters must be controlling, and our families and our partners must know that.

This is confidence.

Confidence in ourselves and in each other comes from constancy of moral character, and that comes from the actions that make it real in our lives.

Knowing right from wrong is where children begin.

Acting to secure a moral environment is what brings results.
We're not talking about zeal or fanatic inquisition.
We're talking about harmony and stability working off of each other.
We're talking about chaos and rigidity being avoided by using elements of their own makeup.
Such is the power of sentient will.
Such is the extent of our free will.
We can just be a blob that passes along through life, or we can direct our life from a firm position of moral equity.
A steady job and big mortgage do not mean one is succeeding.

3
The Rune of personal power and wealth in the Realm of Society.
Fehu in Alfheim.
This aspect is your old uncle's good advice.
Our personal power in the social interactions of life anchors in our stable establishment of self in this life.
Steady as it goes.
Do you want to gain influence, or support?
Who will listen or help you and why?

Do you change friends often, or jobs, or points of view?
Stability over time or through difficulty proves a person's ability to be a power in society.
Those who are always changing may not be the best agents of change.
Change must be smooth and stable.
Glamor and entertainment get our attention, but we should not expect steadfastness from those better known for exciting personalities and a great scope of experience.
Such people are rare and gifted and that is not required to have power in the social Realm.
We can all have social power based on our truth and the stability of the reality we maintain.
This aspect in the negative is the "grass is always greener" syndrome that so many marriages and partnerships fail to.
Our lives are stable because we make them that way and keep them that way.
This is not boring.
Always having to find better entertainment gets boring, and takes away our power.
Why do you suppose those who control the most and advertise the most

extreme behavior do not practice what they sell?
When we are scrambling around trying to find the perfect thrill, we are powerless in the real world of social action, law, and education.
Counselors whose children overdose on drugs.
Psychologists who divorce and still advise patients.
Who trusts these people?
Be stable, be cold if that's what it takes to keep things working, but be honest about it.
Know your social power rests on your personal Isa.
The Lore about you is really about you and means something in society.
What will that be?
Be solid for your mate and your children and for God's sake accept that being solid and steady is all right for your mate.
Our mate is not an entertainment center, no matter how we depend on them for the stuff of life.

4

The Rune of ritual, action, and change in the Realm of the mind.

Thursaz in Muspelheim.

Our mind has such great potential that the imagination can consume our life just exploring the possibilities.

This is a very pointed aspect.

The Thursaz principle expands its universe every day.

These days many educated people with a profession and good income do only one thing for work and one thing for play.

Change a tire, start a fire, fix a faucet, win a fight, jump start a car, or a human that stopped breathing, and a lot of people are stuck.

All these things and a million more things that make life worth living are quite simple.

This aspect tells us to develop a stable ritualized way of thinking.

It's not what we think that matters, but how we think.

Having a way of working with the greatest tool ever known is there for each of us.

A stable way of expanding our mind every day is key.

Our temporal universe expands with thought.
We become more with thought brought to action.
Not boring anymore, is it?
No, it's exciting, in a really good way, smooth and steady.
The relativity concepts of this material is a good thing to learn, as well as some of the listed pursuits.
Because the mind is so vast, a ritualistic method is just common sense, and because the power of the mind is also vast, a smooth, steady presence is vital.
Making a good living is important in its own way.
Go past that with your mind, go way past that.

5
The Rune of journey in the Realm of time / Folk Soul.
Raido in Niflheim.
Our place in time is in the moment, but the place of time is not.
Spiritual stasis is life in Midgard.
The Realm of time contains the deeds of our ancestors, ourselves, and our children.
Midgard is our forum.

Our moment in time contains all that has come before and becomes our reality through our actions.
Just as a class of students gain different insights from the same lecture, each of us makes different use of the history that brings us to where we are in life.
That our view of this corresponds to a majority of the group does not bestow authority.
Such an idea denies the history to any others who diverge from our common view.
This denies our care and nurturing to those others and creates factions.
Real progress is not possible where factions argue the lessons of history.
The mental discipline discussed in the previous aspect makes its importance known here.
We can guide each other through fair discourse, but we should not direct others.
That gives too much power to belief, and does not help to make the actions of our time serve our ancestors, or our children.
The children inherit the hate, not the love.

Our practiced stability is not going to collapse.
Rather, it will lend stability to divergent views that make up a greater picture of what is and what is becoming, thus adding to the Lore (Isa).
In this way we do not embrace fear or cause others to act in fear.
We remove fear from all that we leave our children.
We deny fear of the history that is left to us.
This nurturing comes from our stability.
This is our journey in time.
This is our piece of Lore in history
There are others, but this one we deal with now.
We will become history just as we have become what is.
What that history is depends on our stasis and stability in the life we live.
Our journey from the Folk Soul to an individual existence is the Lore.
These journeys are what Lore is all about.
To gain control of self physically, emotionally and spiritually, and master our wholeness in form is the Lore.
Life put into solid form is what we are.
Conscience is life.

The journey in form is you.
You are the rock of reality that the whole world can rest upon.
All that is not as it should be will break on that reality if you want it to.
We don't need to be flexible to the point where we can be sold things, but stable enough so the journey of life can happen.

6
The Rune of joining in the Realm of death.
Aiwaz in Hel.
<u>Isa is the Rune of Lore.</u>
The Lore of Realms and Runes are part of Isa.
History is part of Isa.
Our lives are part of Isa, and our history when we die is part of Isa.
What will your history be?
Will you bring justice to the existence you experience?
Will you bring balance to the duality of moral imperative?
Will you bring power to social interaction?
Will you control and expand your mind?
Will you be a boon to your progeny and a gift to your ancestors?

Will you do anything on your journey?
The sum of these questions is what you join with the Realm of death.
Remember that the Realm of Hel is like a terminal where we arrive, depart, or change vehicles, not a horror story.
The stability of our life enables us to join our experience to the Cosmic without loss or confusion.
Remember also that the difficulties we face are real so that accomplishment is real as well.
Living true can be done and it can be explained.
Our exit from the vehicle can be just as smooth and natural as our birth.
Just as we all know our existence did not begin at birth, but merely changed, <u>our existence at death is not an end, but a change.</u>
The instruction here is to provide a stable change.
Don't be afraid of the way life works.
None of us can remember not having life.

7
The Rune of the lake, Folk Soul, spirit in the Realm of mystery.
Laguz in Svartheim.
When we recognize the Lore that is manifest in our life, and make our lives an example of how that Lore takes form in this place, we bring to our spiritual center the mysteries of the universe.
Or we don't!
But here we can see why our acquaintances fail, how we have failed to act as whole beings with meaning and worth.
When we let things of little consequence move us, our spiritual grasp of the depth of life's mystery may elude us.
Not being susceptible to flash or fad helps us to gain that grip on the broader aspects of life and what we may be overlooking.
It is because of the tenuous nature of our self view that so many spiritual hustles take so many of us for a ride.
There is a difference between an open mind and foolish instability in our use of spiritual information or suggestion.

For that reason the writer hopes you will actually learn the Runes and Realms and the information in this Lore, to decide for yourself, in a sure and stable form, just what your view is.

The Folk Soul is manifest in the essence of the Cosmic experience, not as a passenger, but as the heart of the exercise.

The motivation of all who act upon the mysteries is to build or to break the Folk Soul.

There are those who want desperately to live a life of mastery, not of themselves, but of their fellow man.

Whether through prophecy, preaching, or politics, these people depend on our inability to stand firm.

We have had only prophecy, preaching, and politics to guide us.

What we required was a compass.

Once we know what is where, we will lead ourselves.

That is this aspect.

Our spirit unraveling the mystery while we hold firm to our reality.

8
The Rune of partnership in the Realm of strength outside ourself.
Ehwaz in Jotunheim
Here we see the great power built up from the first seven aspects of Isa joined to the giant.
As we have discussed before, this is the giant power of uncontrolled essence, blindly smashing all in its path, or, through our use of the Isa aspects, very useful power joined to the group creation of God in form.

Jotan or Wotan.

Justice of form or injustice?
Balance of moral direction or imbalance?
Power in society or chaos?
Ritual use of the mind or singularity and confusion?
A Cosmic traveler or a flash in the pan?
Part of everything, or part of nothing?
The essence of magic and mystery, or a consumer?
Building God or being stepped on by what we do build?

What we end up with here is what we get because we build it.
Our time, life, and blood are spent on a random monster or on a stable idea of what should be.
We don't just decide this thing with yes or no, we create a person who is steady and true, and builds this world day by day and joins with it as a partner.

Often people learn this lesson late in life and are angry at the time it took to get the fundamental information to do the work.
That is what I am trying to help you avoid through this work.
Knowing these things at the outset gives us such an advantage.
Learn the Runes!
You do not have to believe me!
You can teach me the things I am not seeing.
Come on!

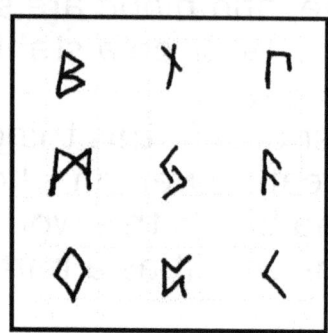

Jera, the Rune of Harvest, the Rune of return -before completion.
This Rune represents the gathering of the pieces that make up our life as well as the essential emotions – the bad one, and the good one.
When we have gathered our parts and realized their places in the great design, we can then "be" harvested as we have harvested ourselves.
Once again, if one does not want to give as well as get, this information is pointless.
Just as in a harvest of crops, the yield is the product of the effort put into it, plus the natural laws that make it all work.
The harvest is a matter of stability, need, balance, joy, honor, truth, direction, conscience, will, energy, and power.

These wonderful things are ours if we choose to make them a part of ourselves.
People can live with none of these things.
People can imagine all these things are part of their lives, while having no part of any of them.
If you doubt this Lore, then ask yourself why you realize these are truly the things that make up a real life, in the order they appear.
This is the stuff of legend, and it can be had for the taking, but we must know it to take it, and we must take it in order.
Most people will say they won't be told how to live their life.
Many will deny that there is any real information here.
Theoretically anyone can do this. Realistically, few have the courage or depth to choose to view their life as real and vital, or requiring discipline.
So many accept the dogma of a flawed creation, that this may be seen as evil.
For those of you with stuff in your veins, let's see what the harvest brings.
This is what applies when you put yourself in order using the first eleven Runes.

1
The mother Rune in the Realm of physical existence.
Berkano in Vanheim.
Here we see that the elemental universe is the womb of our harvest.
Base form is not a curse, but fully half of the life experience.
Our harvest is form. What will the all mother gain from her harvest of you?
Will her harvest be careful, caring, nurturing beings who balance risk and excitement with purpose and live the best noted lives?
The warrior pact of the new age is becoming.
The doubt of salvation is overwhelming. The message of the great religions is hopelessness in the face of impossibility. The power of dogma is lost to reason and so reason must be abandoned.
The Great Goddess needs the care of the children of the universe.
That is you.
We are being torn and divided with charges of baseness that are based on our flesh.
Nothing is given to our intellect to save us because we are consumers, not free people.

We are being conned and sold constantly by professional
sales people with beautiful bodies.
We are made to feel alien in a chaotic universe.
That is not factual.
The universe is your mother, your sister, your home.
You are the reason the universe exists, and the true Divinity of the universe is why we exist.
We are not a product of sin.
We are the children of a real physical God and Goddess.
The concept of being alone and without purpose is the single most destructive ideology of all.
This aspect is the warm and fuzzy welcome to the truth about our existence.
From here we can define a purpose that includes environmental concerns and becomes as religious as we wish to be, with true reverence for our physical mother, who is very much alive, and whose vast cold appearance is just a point of view.
Here we harvest the wonder of our Cosmic Mother.
Take this to yourself.

2
The Rune of need in the Realm of higher moral being.
Nathiz in Asgard.
Here we see how our need for higher moral existence is intended to be served.
When we take the essence of the Gods unto ourselves, we become more like them.
Study of the Gods and Goddesses gives us so many aspects of higher behavior.
Some attributes of higher being are so singular that the archetype may display only one aspect of being.
Man is in so many ways more complex than we may think, that by simply intending to incorporate the archetype into our being, it can be done.
The simple purity of Idun, the stoic resolve of Forsetti to keep the peace, the even handedness of Aegir.
The sacrifice of Tyr, the responsibility of Heimdal.
We need to harvest the pieces that make up a useful picture of Divinity that we can emulate and make a true part of ourselves.
Platitudes just won't do, nor will fear of God give us a grasp.

We need to take the truth of God to ourselves to have a full harvest.
As each Rune appears in Asgard, our means of manifesting its power appears in Midgard.
This aspect tells us that it's alright to use the power of Heaven and God to do what should be done.
This is not a right given over to a preacher or a pope, but to us all.
This is personal.
Not the church, or the man of God, but each of us can harvest the fruit of heaven and make it a part of our personal makeup.
Trust yourself.
The Cosmos is our parent.
That's right, you are more than an animal, and we all know that we are not God, but we all know we are a part of both.
Through this aspect we become more of God, or does God get closer to form?
As we go through this Rune study, the latter is evident.
When we harvest such a high idea as this from the Divine, we are acting in the most noble way.
Our moral code transcends fear, guilt, and hatred.

3
The Rune of Cosmic power in the Realm of society.
Uruz in Alfheim.
Our field of endeavor is the social Realm.
This Realm is, as previously noted, an amalgam of ideas about just what it is.
That notwithstanding the efforts by a few to dominate with belief that they are superior because of something they do or do not do.
When those things build working social institutions based on realism and social need, this is good.
When they result in repression, hate intolerance, and violence, this is not good.
When we harvest the natural power found in the masses, we can do right by society.
Society cannot be in charge, because it is mindless.
We are and must be held responsible for making sure that every one has a place in the social Realm.
Taking away rights or freedom where no injury or damage is apparent is so damaging to the whole that destruction could accrue.

No group or faction can be in charge of the power of society, or all other groups will suffer.
This is your vote.
When we are forced to endorse one group or the other, we are denied the social Realm.
Our world is someone's domain.
We are subject.
The first Rune we study is the Rune of personal wealth and influence.
The Fehu Rune gives us freedom to take the natural power of the masses in a beneficial direction.
That does not grant license to the wealthy to abuse the masses by dominating society. But we need our personal power to harvest this Cosmic power in the social Realm.
This is not "pick what you like" Lore, but steps to strength in all Realms, in all ways.
The power available to us from right action in society is greater in scope than the personal wealth that keys us in, but we must be self-determined to use it.

Now that's a harvest!

4
The Rune of consciousness / conscience in the Realm of the mind.
Ansuz in Muspelheim.
This aspect is simple, yet vital instruction.
What is consciousness?
What is conscience?
Is the omniscience of the All-Being found in our consciousness?
Does God speak through our conscience to each of us all the time?
Does that voice of conscience guide our thinking process toward an appropriate outcome in each and every endeavor?
Knowing all these answers, why do we still find ourselves in crises of moral conscience?
We are charged here with the task of harvesting our mind from the void: from duplicity, from fear, guilt and hatred, or alienation and contention.
What do I want? Why? Who decided this? Why them?
We allow children to be instructed about what to think.
Few of us know how to think.
We don't address our weakness to impressionability and become victim to our own lack of identity.

Your mind is unique! You are personal because of your mind.
Why even start down the path that says we are all the same and must behave the same to be of value?
This drives young people to curb their reality and assume a facade that denies their destiny.
By the time we figure it out, we're all mortgaged, contracted, and sad.
Instead of being well started on our path of destiny, we are stuck miles away from our hearts and dreams.
We turn on our spouses because they represent a wrong turn.
We deny our children, and blame our parents.
These are all the actions of idiots, but we are not idiots.
Everybody told us to ignore the individual within, and choose from the list rather than find our own way.
This aspect is what stops all that nonsense.
Taking power over others through their ignorance is not "winning."
Imagine the much greater opportunities people who are thinking clearly will provide for the gifted among us to make real progress that, again, all can

benefit by.
We are social, this is not socialism.
Mental toughness and a harvest of consciousness are all we need to raise the standard for everyone.
Few are so selfish as to deny all a good life.
None are so caught up in surrender as to allow it, once we take note.
It's all about willfully using our mind for our benefit.
Think about it!

5
The Rune of light and truth in the Realm of time and spirit.
Kenaz in Niflheim.
Sometimes it is hard to accept that the truth about our spiritual oneness, our place in time, and our ancestry are important to our efforts in life.
The truth about these things must be a part of our lives in practice.
The human condition is not uniform.
Your soul is a part of the Folk Soul of your family.
Your oneness with that Folk Soul is your grasp of the moving Realm of time.
We are the product of our ancestry, specifically, not generally!
The mass media show a multicultural progressive fun house society of tolerance and encouragement for all.
The purpose for that is to create a common demographic **to increase profit**.
A one-size-fits-all humanity.
The truth about ancestry is that there are races: big families, with simple but real identities. The races are a product of nature, not evil.
The danger of racial denial is as great as racial domination.

The loss of racial identity, or the loss of humanity or family.
The truth now! Not politically correct, but true.
Why tailor society to suit the antisocial? Why sully the institution of family and marriage to protect people who are without scruple or reason?
Harvest the truth about what we are doing in our time, about who we are at every level of our being, alone in family, in group.
The truth about why the world is the way it is and who is in control and why we need to adjust these things will reveal a plan for reaching the final fate, 'what should be.'
We don't have to just ride along.
Everyone should drive.
Our circumstance was created by the positive and negative actions in time by our ancestors.
A lot of lies are preserved about what and why things developed.
The truth about such developments would expose a path for change.
Use it.
Use the truth and become strong and free!
Taking a politically correct position on

this will help nothing.
Taking a position of truth about race, family, gender, and values is the most valuable thing we can harvest from the Realm of time.
The truth about what years are yours to effect change and what you should do with them is your truth in time.
The truth now, not some story.
This is a hard aspect. It will take work, and some dedication.

6
The Rune of chance and possibility in the Realm of death.
Pertho in Hel.
Who does the harvest?
Does it just happen?
Of course not!
How well it is done depends wholly on the one doing the work.
As we go through the twenty four aspects of this Realm, it becomes clear that death is an occurrence to be managed.
Death is not the end; birth is not the beginning.
No Realm is without power, or life, or consciousness.
Our ritualization of life and practice of

ordered reality are the keys to harvesting as much as possible in death.
This is a strong message, but it is toward strong people that it is directed.
The Pertho Rune says we can harvest all through death, but that is probably geared to one who has applied themselves to knowing this Lore.
You plant corn, you harvest corn.
If you live with vigor and contribution, your harvest should be good and plentiful.
As we learn to open our minds to the pattern revealed here, the way to Cosmic being opens up.
Mortal presence becomes an idea rather than a description.
Everything that we can reasonably conceive of becomes potential, just as it should be.
We are back again to the reality of human life, the whole content of which is salvageable through human death.
We have the ability to develop these powers as surely as we can learn to speak.
But it is not going to happen by itself.
This is just like every other form of natural selection.
If we can not get ourselves in order, and

in harmony with the Cosmic, we will continue the live die cycle, retaining nothing.
What harvest do you want when you go to seed?
So come on, do the work! Be Cosmic!

7
The doorway/window Rune in the Realm of mysteries.
Ingwaz in Svartheim.
The Cosmic is one part magic.
One part impossible that makes everything work.
The iota that brings balance to the mass, God to the table, smiles to the crowd, clarity to the mind, usefulness to history, courage in the face of death.
A magical element that touches every thing, all the time.
This is so easy to deny, and many of us just will not accept the magic that is so much a part of our lives.
Our harvest of the Realm of magic is the Realm of magic itself.
Let yourself in to experience the mysteries.
Look inside to see them working.
There are plenty of tools to help you do this.

All sorts of oracles, prophecy, devices, dreams, foretelling, etc.
This stuff is all real stuff, it has been for millennia.
Every Folk Soul has these tools, and the rules that make them work.
It's in our blood to look and enter the mysteries seeking our fate.
In recent years, man has grown so far away from the beautiful mystery of life that we laugh about even admitting any reality at all in them.
We are challenged here to harvest access to the magic and mystery.
There is a lot of mumbo jumbo out in the world, and little of it will give any answers, but some Lore is whole, and the answers are there.
We are responsible to wake up and grasp the answers.
Make a doorway to the mysteries part of your being.
The third eye is such a window.
The window of the heart is such a window.
High-minded courage is such a doorway. But it's up to the individual to do the harvest, and again, lip service will not do, we need to do it.
Modern man presumes so much that is

to our detriment, and denies so much to our benefit that is just not true.
Each of us will prove our stewardship by our harvest.
Don't come back without a window to the mysteries.

8
The Rune of man in the Realm of mutation and giant power
Manaz in Jotunheim.
This is where knowing your Runes really comes up as Power.
We have spoken about Jotenheim being either the big helping hand of God, or the windshield that smashes the bug.
This goes to the fundamental human development.
This is the Realm of God in form.
We, as a group, are in control of the development of the total of our actions.
This aspect tells us to plant actions that allow us to harvest mankind at his finest from the amalgam of our acts.
We will never get food from planting weeds.
The cycle of a plan in human endeavor is what, from a week to five years?
Plant good stuff today, keep planting it, and in five years, even the worst

problems will have run their course.
We are not trapped!
We act trapped because we don't recognize the key to the turnaround.
Well, here is the key.
Harvest a caring, nurturing, strong, correct, kind of humanity.
This cannot be faked, or substituted.
No wrong beginning will reap this end.
Everyone will benefit.
Everything will come into place to help this happen. This is not mankind with dominion over the earth.
This is the Cosmic creation of God in form through us as a whole.
We can be selfish and never have this harvest, or we can *be really selfish* and make ourselves part of the Divine.
There is no down side, just the question.
Will you die to believe in something you don't believe in?

Note:

This ends the first half of the Runes aspected by the Realms.
The harvest is hard to reach yet many will truly do so.
They will be your examples. Follow them, you'll get better.

The next half is less about becoming Divine, and more about being Divine, and doing wonderful things.
This will not be a dead end of philosophy or dogma.
This Lore is complete and will guide you toward wholeness as nothing on earth ever has.
But this is not easy. Your enthusiasm will carry you, but just saying, "OK," is not enough.
This is not salvation from another, this is from you.
This is made for you and you can do it.
Take heart and let's see where it goes.

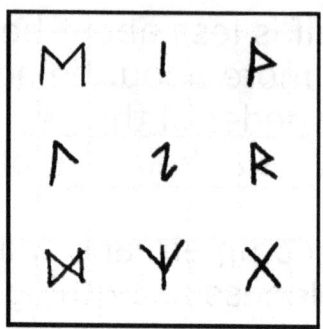

Aiwaz, the Rune of joining, the backbone, the bow.
We need to grasp a concept here to begin.
The bow joins the hunter to the arrow.
The tool use in animals does not embrace support systems for simple tool use.
<u>Here we are the being that exists after the harvest.</u>
Here we are the whole with a usable, ethical body and emotional being, so what do we do with it?
The old religions pound us into shape to do what?
They never say!
Just wait until God comes along?
No!
Yes, we get in order.

Yes, we get in balance.
Yes, we get in control.
No, we are not waiting for God.
God is already here and we are going to hook up now.
This is where we join the Divine and create the Cosmic.
Rune awareness pays off here so much.
Realm awareness too.
This is where we come into power so vast and true that only in wildest fantasy do we dare describe our hope of its existence.
But describe it we do, and those who may wield it.
This is how they come to be.

1
The Rune of partnership in the elemental universe.
Ehwaz in Vanheim.
Well, here we are.
Do you want to pretend that someone is coming for you, or do you want to declare yourself to be real?
Our Norse ancestors did not insist that everything be named and numbered.

Everything was a part of the mist until it declared itself. (Especially people.)
If you want "a place" in the elemental reality of form, you must say so.
You must join the partnership of this physical plane to continue the evolution of God in form.
Suppose God is the one out there, lost and waiting for his children to come and find him / her?
Can we do that while wringing our hands and denying that we are what and where we are?
What about the physical world?
Why do we kill it?
Do we believe we'll be spirited away so deeply we'll drink our own waste?
To deny clean air and water to our children?
Are we that weak and worthless?
Clearly we are!
We accept wrong on a physical level because we take no personal stake in the whole.
Here we join with the whole as protector husband and partner.

2
The Rune of stasis and stability in the Realm of the Gods.
Isa in Asgard.
The idea constant in all belief systems is that the Gods want "what should be."
The Gods want good and not evil.
The Gods want virtue.
The Gods want clear, decisive, pure magnificence!
The Gods are good!
This is the static reality of all time, including now.
This is not a controlling factor in peoples' lives because we see ourselves as detached from the Gods.
There are more reasons every day why this is so.
Foolish people using wealth and influence to control the masses keep us reeling, fragmented, and afraid. This stops now!
Here we join with the known constant!
We want good!
Not filth and degradation, but clean, good, wholesome truth to describe our lives.

We join with a stable moral code.
Not a dogma, with controllers, but a discipline with teachers to help us master the stable morality we know is possible.
When children see adults as liars and cheats, they are not inspired to join society as normal people, who lie and cheat. Or they hone their worst skills, instead of their best.
Do not choose the lesser of evils, join with a higher moral standard you can reference in situations, and act on with confidence.
When we are not joined with platforms, parties, or persons that require moral compromise, we can be the moral pillar our children need and we need.
As a people we let this lapse.
The media is virtual pornography and terror until we are callous to pain and deceit.
The world is not built on its weaknesses, but on its strengths, which include hope of a higher moral stability.

In joining with a high moral standard, we block the nonsense from our spiritual diet, and create an example.
Young people really are proud of good parents, though they may deny it.
Remember the end is **of** the beginning and cannot escape.
What we include in our plan is part of our product.
Isa, the pillar is not a variable, but a firm and committed moral stand.
Add this to your life and don't let anyone take it away.

3
The Rune of ritual, authority, law, and strength in the Realm of social interaction.
Thursaz in Alfheim.
When we stand away from society and pretend we have no place in the truth about it, a gap opens that allows unethical use of social wealth and power.
We vote, but we don't trust our candidate.

We pay taxes, but don't believe they are well spent.
We don't feel the authority of our office as citizens.
Exclusion by suggestion works as well as by force if we let it.
Accepting law that excludes millions of people for ordinary, if unsavory, actions that are criminalized, is so culturally destructive as to threaten the whole.
Because we cannot, in true heart, join with those who are very different from ourselves, and because that is the requirement of civil rights protection, the model is clearly broken.
Here we join with society according to natural law.
Again, we see the danger of politically correct thinking.
We must join with society.
If the act of joining creates the opportunity for right action to allow us to, in good conscience, lend our efforts to the social weal, then we have victory through right action.
This is the battleground aspect.

Our physical partnership with what is, our moral stability, and our place in the world are the essence of the struggle.
To be politically correct is to deny the struggle.
To deny the struggle is to deny duality and, therefore, life itself.
True victory in the struggle will be found, not through elimination, but through creativity.
This aspect can be misused through ignorance.
The question of how advanced the manifestation of conscience and form can be is the basis for a high-minded attempt at a future for mankind that does not include destruction by population or pollution or doomsday prophecy.
We need to create a way to survive, and, preserve the home.
This is the purpose of the social Realm.
To create law, social institutions, and behavior that are consistent with our real needs and the truth.
Again, fear, guilt, and hatred block the evolutions.

If people cannot help the move ahead, they should get out of the way until they find a way to participate creatively. Remember, we don't have to heed anyone just because they speak, regardless of their condition or position. When right action is the direction, then we can heed.
It is our individual actions that make up the whole, and our individual stability of moral conduct that shapes those actions.
This is our personal law.
Here we bring ourselves to the social Realm.

4
The Rune of journeys in the Realm of the mind.
Raido in Muspelheim.
We all do the right thing in our mind.
We all see what should be done.
We all understand the alienation of physical being and body from our control (being fat, being weak, being ugly, being black, being white).
We all take note of the doublespeak of moral high ground and we all see the chaos of social practice.

We all rationalize our failure to initiate or participate in actions to correct things we know are in need of fixing.
We all let "take-charge people" steal our lives and money and future, rather than join the spinning wheels of our mental excursions to the reality of our life.
Because of this, our lives become small and insignificant, and because that's true, we feel small and insignificant without realizing why.
There are a number of reasons why people fail to form a union between their thoughts and their circumstances.
Usually training is the primary reason. We are taught that it is not possible to understand the great mystery of life, and that our circumstances are inescapable.
True, the nature of the Cosmic struggle adds to the illusion, so much so that it becomes an act of courage to wake up and use the enormous power of the mind.
Your mind will not stop working halfway into this Journey.
The intellectual blow hard that overstates the obvious may appear to be joined with the power of the mind,

but it is through the challenge of right action that this journey brings us.
The rambling this may appear to be is a case in point.
Until the material is applied, it is just words.
We are to become whole of mind and body through this aspect.
Once we take the harvest of our conscience and consciousness, we can deal with the vast scope of our mental journey.
So let's go!
Claim the colors of your mind, the depth of your thought.
Claim your right to know what you know.

5
The Rune of the gift in the Realm of time / spirit.
Gebo in Niflheim.
Here we are reminded that the spirit is timeless, and so the essence of our being is timeless.
It is our forum that is time sensitive.
Our windows of opportunity during our cycles of being are encapsuled in the lifetime we live.
We are naught without the whole of the Folk Soul.

Because the reality of right action, as half of the duality of being, must be true, we are free to pretend our individuality is essential rather than circumstantial.

We have learned in other aspects, that the tests must be real so that Divinity can take form in reality, not just in theory.

God in form would not be God if the form did not freely choose right action. The ego is the foe we battle first; victory over ego exposes the true self, able to give the gift of life to the future and success to the past.

We shall always possess the ego self, as a needed tool of personal function. When we remember that we possess the tool, it does not possess us, its use becomes clearly within our power.

Our contribution can then become significant in the whole scope of existence, as opposed to the small fragment of the single lifetime.

This changes the "small fragment" into a real part of the whole scheme of life. Our joining with the journey of our imaginings opens the door for our joining our gift to the gift of our

ancestors and contemporaries.
The result here is (a) to bring continuity to our progress as the Folk Soul and (b) to define the goals of the Folk
in time.
The whole business of biding our time until the coming of God is not what the original message is about.
That message denied change and with it the chance for the Cosmic to grow into God in form, thus creating the message "God is coming."
We have been waiting for the lottery, and giving nothing back!
This is where we ante up, get in the real game.
Do you want to do something important?
Well, here you go, this is as important as it gets.
This is where we join the human race.
It doesn't get any more real than this.

6
The Rune of progress, protection and majesty in the Realm of death.
Elhaz in Hel.
So here is the result of the five prior joinings of this Rune's aspects.
To those uninitiated to the truth of living,

death is a black and terrible, or a gray and sad place of nothingness.
To those with the virtue to join the true struggle, this is a place of renewal, growth, and certainty.
We are never going to be finished with this.
With each cycle we do get the chance to choose the noble course, no matter how small the theater or how large.
Those who step up and join the evolution of the Cosmic progress through the cycle of life.
Those who stand tall and true through the struggle are the personification of majesty.
Folk Lore, legend, and myth spring from the power of their lives.
This aspect is your story.
Nobody knows about the guy who said, "Wow! Somebody should do something!"
Nobody knows about the guy who says, "I knew it!"
We know about the ones who do the deeds that stand as right action.
These heroes are few and far between, yet they inspire us to be as we should be.
We have been told that everyone has his

price, and is it not strange that everyone's price can be met?
How much then is the value of the bribe?
True majesty is in bearing, not possession.
Those who don't know this are not your concern.
We should not refuse to stand tall just because the masses do not.
We should not go unprotected or refuse to progress because the masses do not.
We must live out our individual days and we can do so with majesty of form.
This is as it should be.
The truth about each of us can be a wonderful story, or, no story at all.
The world does not choose this, we each do.
I choose to stand in salute to the Gods, to grow with the Cosmic, to live in majesty, tall and true.
I join this to my being.
How about you?

7
The Rune of cycles / days / seasons / lifetimes, in the Realm of mystery and magic.
Dagaz in Svartheim.
Just as we must wait for the rain to come in its own time, we must wait for the right moment to use the great powers of the mysteries.
The movement of these cycles is predictable, just as the seasons.
Winter does not mean we cannot farm, just that we cannot farm today.
We do the winter tasks.
Here we join with the ebb and flow of the magic that is a part of everything.
These are the holidays of antiquity.
The enchantment of romance at the Feast of Vali.
Sex magic at Ostera.
Rebirth at Yule, immortality on the night of the dead.
The moon phases, a woman's clock, all are cycles of the magic.
We can see ourselves as urbane and sophisticated only to be embarrassed by the effect these cycles have on our lives, or, we can get real and be a part of the Cosmic that turns on these cycles, using the power and portents that they bring.

All are a part of the breathing, heart-beating, singing, Cosmic being that you are the essence of.

Think about how many people you know who are broken.

"Out of sync" with their spouse and children, describes just about everyone.

We are broken people struggling for anything to grasp.

We buy weird stuff, we allow harsh pornographic abstracts to seize our behavior through space and time.

We try to use success financially to offset our lack of Cosmic success.

Here we can and do put our circumstances in sync with the Cosmic flow of magic and mystery.

When we are out of cycle with our partners, the magic of romance doesn't work.

We wreck everything trying to fill the void that opens and then go on as divorced and lonely people.

Is it that simple?

Usually, yes.

We have given value to recreation, and it brings no reward but recreation.

We have given value to distraction and it has no value except to break up boredom.

Here we follow the Cosmic flow and make it a part of ourselves.
8
The Rune of spirit / Folk Soul in the Realm of Giants / God's becoming.
Laguz in Jotenheim.
Here we have the Realm of the collective.
All we do is the essence of this living Realm.
Our right action, our wrong action, the damage from our lies, the power from the stands we take, our lectures, our excuses, our victories, are all here.
These things make up the Jotan Giant that looms large as social unrest, crime, repressive government, terror, public pornography, and media violence.
These things also make up the Wotan God in form that brings justice, education, health, help, unity, group projects that evolve the human condition and a knowledge of Cosmic oneness that defeats wasted time, nonsensical efforts and corruption of the nature of truth.
We are joined to this!
Our truth is the essence of this creature.
The gift of our individuality is ours to keep.

The only price is the truth.
This is the time and place of mutation and evolution.
The truth about us is the direction the change will take.
This bit of Lore is so valuable.
Many religions tell us God is watching everything we do.
The old Santa Claus story is this story.
Naughty or nice?
We get it back exactly as we give it out.
We create the big picture!
We may say we support those who say they mean well and that if they break their political promise, it's not our fault.
Politicians cannot act for you any more than they can eat for you, and neither can preachers or priests.
We are the world.
We can give up, but then it's not our world anymore, and we are nothing.
The God becoming gets nothing but paste from those who give up.
Is that a fair return for the wonder of life, and the chance for love, joy, and home?
Our answer to this is the essence of our truth, and our contribution to the future and the present.

There is nowhere to hide, no one to save us, this is it.
We are doing it now.
It has always been this way, and one need only look to see.
Posturing con men have always pretended it was they who brought success and over their protest that failure came.
The truth is no one can claim anything beyond their personal actions, heeding the inspiration of their fellows to emulate the hero.
Each of us are part of the spiritual whole.
Let's join all of these aspects to our intent and be a valuable part.
It is hard, but it is real.
This is about the hardest Rune to embrace because it seems to make demands. Fantasy is definitely pushed away.
Take courage here, for this Rune also validates our existence.
This changes everything from abstract to purposeful.
Spirit is validated and proven here.
We are each of immeasurable value because of our potential to change the curve.

Right action through intent is so much more powerful than abstract chaos. We are so much more powerful than the alienated, fragmented people we appear to be. Join!

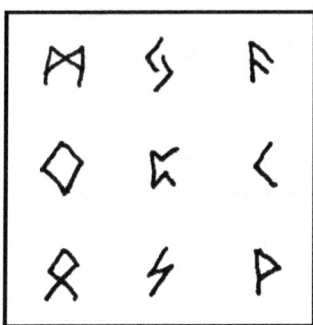

Pertho the Rune of possibility, promise and chance.
The aspects of this Rune are impressive.
So far this has been a training program with demands, and rewards, as great as the effort.
Truly, "the end is the beginning."
We embrace Asa Lore because we want to be more.
We want to be better men and women.
We want to prove trust and honor in ourselves and know that they are real.
No secret society here!
No failure brushed beneath the rug.
This is the opening of the book of life.
Who has need of secret societies?
Well-picked kinsmen are better by far!
But can we do it?
Can frail humanity stand tall and do the right thing?
We talk moral ground, but dare we stand

there?
This Rune makes it clear that we can.

1

The Rune of man in the Realm of elemental existence.
Manaz in Vanheim.
Manaz is not the Rune of man in his casual state; man as a sophisticated animal using his ability to gain an animal advantage is base.
Manaz is the Rune of man as he should be, developing as a Cosmic being and securing a home in the elemental, temporal, and spiritual planes of existence.
Manaz makes things better. Manaz heals the Folk.
This aspect of the Pertho Rune is very reassuring because it tells us that man as he should be can exist in form and not just idea.
We have fallen into a rut of belief that only one man in all of time lived a good life.
We praise saints for doing some good thing, never realizing that we are declaring ourselves beneath the ability to be exemplary.
We are past that now.

We have Wunjo.
Now we see that man at his best is possible for you and me.
We are joined, we are our harvest, we are stable, we control our need, we balance both sides of the truth.
Of course, we can take real Cosmic steps.
This is where ordinary life pales and true life becomes the adventure it should be.
Resistance becomes focused and we can identify the individual sources of disharmony that lead our Folk away from this truth.
The madness of fragmented social ideals becomes a clear picture and we in turn can focus on effort to put things as they should be.
We are not speaking of controlling our fellows, but we are causing right action.
Manaz is innocent of tyranny or domination while being totally controlling of ignorance and mean-spirited action.
All this in the real elemental forum of the universe we occupy, not the imaginary universe where we pretend everything is all right.
This aspect is the promise of reality worth living.

What a great promise!
Duality in action, active, as a part of day-to-day life.
Focus, purpose, and meaning to our struggle.
The Rune of Harvest in the Realm of God's Home.
2
Jera in Asgard.
This is the truth about good things, and the truth about bad things.
It is written that even the greatest evil is just a part of the Divine plan, yet it comes from indifference.
Here we see that the Gods will give us what we will take, both in bounty!
The Divine does not automatically stop negative things from happening.
Good and bad are purely human concepts, and our choices are real choices between good and bad things.
It is good to know that the will of heaven does not alter the playing field.
The stupid questions about whether or not a bad choice is God's will all go out the window here.
The pretense of not knowing what choice is right becomes apparent here, as this is a rationalization for the compromise with evil, and the

intentional choosing of that which, we know is not right brings out the pretentious lie, and exposes the need for virtue.
This we can count on.
The elemental Manaz who is the physical being here cannot be fooled, or tricked into apathy or wrong action.
We see here the power of this promise.
How strong our resolve can become.
The truth about sentient existence is so much more beautiful than the dogmatic illusion.
This aspect tells us the information necessary to our self salvation is available in our harvest of Divine knowledge.
Both aspects of every choice are available for inspection always.
Someone will always rise up with the clear offer to wrong action.
Every choice is proof.
Our lives are the real thing and no matter how convinced a person may be that this is all just a big party, all the evidence says this life is the forum of the Gods.
The very arena of truth.
Adversaries will appear as if by magic with innumerable ways to interrupt right

action.
Enjoy their antics, but remember, some people will want to hurt you because you want to do the right thing.
Every right step will be over an obstacle, but our awareness of that is fuel for understanding the base nature of the enemy.
<u>For our enemy is us.</u>

3
The Rune of conscience / voice of God, in the Realm of social interaction.
Ansuz in Alfheim.
This is a very encouraging aspect, and deals with a circumstance that raises much doubt about what we can actually accomplish in our day-to-day social interactions.
It is true that social leadership has fallen into the hands of liars and thieves.
This does not mean much.
We don't even have to wrestle the leadership back from them, because they will not fight for it.
They will only sneak around and try to find our corruption, that, they understand.
If there is no corruption there, they will have no strength.

We all make mistakes, but that is not an excuse to deny a place in society, or to take power over others.
Here we see that it is possible to work in society without abandoning the conscience.
It is widely believed that people cannot be good in business or in public life at all.
We believe that we must abandon the things we most revere or be ground down to nothing.
The truth is, when we go out into society driven by ambition or greed, we are already ground down.
Our conscience gives us enthusiasm to proceed knowing we are all right and well motivated.
Our conscience opens doors to all sorts of places and people that cannot even be approached with inappropriate ideas or gestures.
This news is good news.
The Madison Avenue or Wall Street approach to society is a creation of creatures with no place in society.
Society will exist without a big hustle.
The economy will exist without artificial devices to control investment, if the money is real.

We can voice our conscience in society.
We can ask why the money is not real, among other things.
The liars won't answer, which is answer enough, and we won't invest, which will end the reign of falsehood that leads us to base behavior.
That is the promise here.
This is a bold promise.
Investment will be in non-fossil, non-nuclear energy and invention, cures rather than treatment, advancement in education rather than politically correct stagnation.
Society is for living creatures, not non-living entities.
Corporations and organizations without conscience have no place contributing to political campaigns or having social institutions built around them.
We can get our society back.
We can make society a conscious thing.
We need to heed our conscience and take it with us into the social Realm.

4
The Rune of light and truth in the Realm of the mind.
Kenaz in Muspelheim.
We see here that it is possible to know the truth about the way our mind works, and it is possible to shine light on the process to further understand that truth.
So many of us will admit we don't know why we are the way we are.
This Rune aspect tells us we can know these things.
In fact, one of the benefits of knowing the Runes is the ability to learn how to understand and use our mind.
To the uninitiated reading this book, this describes a possibility.
To the initiated reading this book, this describes a promise.
The truth is already in your mind, and you can see it.
Because this is true, excuses become unnecessary, and expectations rise.
The scope and detail of our plans become greater.
Our goals become greater.
We become greater.

The universe is not where the answers are found, but the mind, where the questions are also found.

The laws that govern the movement of the universe are just a part of the mind, and can be changed to suit our plans, if our plans are founded upon "what should be."

Your universe, my universe.

These truths are to be found in your mind, along with a detailed and full understanding about just what you can try to do.

We must always manifest our will on another, so we must be correct.

We must always channel the power of the Cosmic, so we must be true, and we must always catch the product of our work, so we must be sure.

All of this is possible for one who has completed the rituals of joining covered in the last set of aspects -Aiwaz- in the nine Realms.

This is not a comic book, but a promise of abilities we know exist, but do not know how to achieve.

The way is in our minds at the eternal depth of the soul, and we can go there and learn our own secrets.

5
The Rune of joy in the Realm of spirit.
Wunjo in Niflheim.
The Wunjo Rune is our personal space and the content of our character.
Our time in life may seem short, but we each have enough time to do something that brings about "what should be."
We can find joy in our span of years because we are at least one link in the chain of our ancestry that brings about the manifestation of the Divine in form.
It is common to every Folk group to curse their ancestry.
"They took slaves." "They were slaves." "They lost our land." "They let the government get out of control." "They defied God." "They turned God against us." "They poisoned the earth."
"They killed the king." etc., etc.
We know from our study up to this point that it was the burying of this knowledge that fosters all the other failures.
We know from our historical studies that religion, in the guise of sexless, peaceful men of God, led humanity away from strength and virtue and into confusion, fear, guilt and hatred - see Death of

Baldur myth.
We know that tribal humanity was not Godless, yet we preserve our weakness by pretending they were.
It is possible to find our true selves in time.
The world is different now, but so are we.
We can fashion new answers to the day-to-day problems of living true in modern times, but first we should get a grip on just who each of us is.
There are many Folk Souls here, many kinds of magic.
Some are so fragmented that a new tradition is required.
It shows here that the creation of such a thing is possible.
This cannot be done by letting things take an unguided course. Indifference is evil.
The rocks await the unguided ship.
Finding ourselves in time gives us all of time to work with, not just a wee slice.
If it is not written in a book, it is written in the soul.
Find your place, add to what is.
Create for those yet to come.
It is possible to manifest your presence through time.

6
The Rune of victory in the Realm of death.
Sowilo in Hel.
This is the most powerful and monumental statement in all of Rune Lore.
This aspect simply put says that we can overcome the circumstance of death.
When we study the world around us, we see the natural organic state of things in life.
Form is ever changing, but life is ever present.
Death is not a claimant of life, but of form.
One thing this Rune order and Lore tell us is that the sentient human form of conscious being is transcendent of the confined order of base life.
When we live as an animal, our life follows the course of the animal.
When we ritualize the presence of the Divine and partake of opportunity, in form, for right action, we can include ritual conquest over death of self when we experience death of form.
The myth of the ride of Hermod shows us the steps to victory over death (see Myths of the North Men, or Poetic Edda;

also see Ehwaz aspects in this work). Our partnership with the nine Realms gives us wholeness of form and being: a partnership of self and Cosmos.

Our knowledge of Rune order gives us sequence and harmony with what is - Urd, the first Norn.

Our will gives us victory over what is becoming – loss of form: Verdandi, the second Norn.

Our value to the Cosmic - Manaz - brings us back to form through our closest accessible family.

This does not call for a champion, or a savior.

This is a victory we create ourselves - Skuld - the third Norn.

This is as it should be.

Be aware that this is the very presence of a Divine and immortal being in you. You really have to do it, this won't just happen.

This aspect reassures us that if we put in the work, we can keep the life.

It is no wonder that in opposition to this aspect is the concept of surrender to the Divine and abandoning form in the belief that salvation is also possible.

We love life so desperately, we give it up to keep it.

The whole equation denies the possibility of victory through surrender.
Why would salvation be awarded to those unwilling to preserve that which they wish to save?
The Lore of salvation does not promise freedom of the struggle or form i.e. life as we know it.
Rune Lore's promise is that we reach **victory.**
True victory by our own mastery of the life we live, and the will to do right action in the face of fear or pain.
The fear and pain come anyway, but the victory must be taken.
The strength of character this aspect reveals is something to strive for in itself.
What a fine aspect.!
This is the being of prophecy, the "one who will come."
Believe in the one wearing your skin.
Believe in the one behind your eyes.

7
The Rune of Home in the Realm of dark mystery.
Othalaz in Svartheim.
Many of the aspects discussed in this work are seemingly simple in text while

elusive in mechanics.
The fact of a magical element is known to me and so is common to my thinking.
I am at home in the extent and depth of the mysteries because I have learned the meaning of the Runes, the Realms, and the Norns.
It is because of this aspect, that this book is possible.
I also truly believe this only scratches the surface.
The messages are so clear for every application that the most futuristic of applications of power to matter and temporal sequence may be found in this pattern also.
Converting energy without combusting fuel or any of a thousand other wonders may be revealed to those at home with the concept of alternative possibility.
This pattern takes on a new meaning now because the abilities of man are greater now than ever before.
The examples in this book are just one or two of thousands or millions, and taken from the writer's perspective to show how to make correlations appear so the reader can proceed.
This work by no means reveals the mysteries, only some keys and a map.

The promise is that we can settle in to a pattern of search and discovery in the Realm of the unknown.
We can find better answers to harder problems.
Many of the things that appeared to be mysteries in the past will become clear with simple Rune and Realm knowledge, such as why people keep changing direction or building up debts, or falling into schemes.
Those are all things we can really help with.
We can study the marvel in the layout of the Rune well and perhaps find every answer.
We can live in the protected home of mystery and magic with eyes open much more happily than with eyes closed as many of us live now.
It is not the mysteries that are new, but having a way to deal with them.
The scary stuff is not scary anymore!

8
The Rune of the doorway / window in the Realm of Giant strength.
Ingwaz in Jotunheim.
This is the promise we claim will make all of the difference.

Hearing about a three-headed calf is a lot different than seeing one.

The writer of this work is not guessing about the relative aspects reviewed here, but simply writing down what can be seen.

All the great teachers through time have plainly stated that the answers are right before our eyes.

The same is true here, though 'great teacher' I am not.

One need only learn the basic meaning of the Runes and Realms and look at what the pattern reveals.

Here we have the Realm of Giant power.

The Jotan Giant made up of the unintended consequences of random actions of base motivated humanity is a juggernaut of power without plan, or order that uses and crushes the very people who power it with their base acts and mindless behavior.

Much of this activity is well planned, but that does not mean it is in order or toward *what should be*.

We can see all of this, but fear to stand against the enormous size of it.

We even pretend we're a willing part of it so it does not kill us.

The other side we also see, it is smaller, but much more powerful.
This is the Wotan.
The sum of the orderly, honest, right action of the Folk, becoming as strong and true as they are able, paying a fair price for help, not polluting the earth, sharing with the future and the past.
This sum of good acts is God in form.
None of us will become God, but **only all of us.**
We are not alone.
We have never have been alone.
We can see this.
We know the truth of this and we are a part of the right action, or the mindlessness, or, worst of all, the opposition.
Those who fight for what is wrong are our enemies.
They fight against medical care, environmental care, fair wages, and peace.
They embrace the lie and you can see them.
The perfect form of the Cosmic lets us see the truth so we cannot deny knowledge of right action.
We can pretend, but what real excitement or victory will we find in the

false?
We have you now.
You have seen truth.
Now your goodness and inner strength
will take you toward your destiny.
Just remember I love you very much and
want the best that is possible for us all.

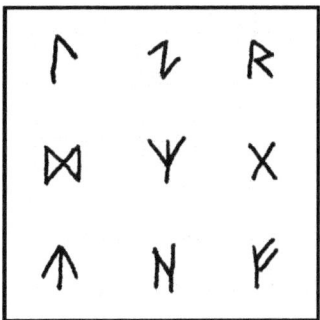

Elhaz, the Rune of protection, progress, majesty.
This is the symbol of being as we are meant to be.
The sequence of humanity is the graduating meaning of this wonderful Rune. When we invoke our connection with the Divine, we stand as the Elhaz Rune, straight and tall.
We declare our recognition of the Divine, and our will to move the Cosmic "what is" to achieve "what should be."
This is the defining Rune of our intent. We protect what we value, we further what we value, we become what we value.
For this to be a good thing, the things we value must be good things. (The scope here is very broad, very beautiful).

So many of us believe that we are not mystic beings, but rather, smart animals,
Divine origin is not something we can utilize through belief, but only through knowing, through action.
It is because we know how to use our wealth and influence that we know how much of our life we need to dedicate to protecting and advancing our wealth and influence, and for what purpose.
There is only so much we need to buy to secure ourselves and families and maintain our freedom.
There is much we need to protect, advance, and glorify in the Realms of being that give life a wholeness we could never buy.
This is not a limitation, but a guideline and reminder.
Ambition and real accomplishment can be very high.
When people use the power of the God mind wisely, there is every possibility for success (see Pertho Rune).
This is not a condemnation of success, but a qualifier.
The aspects of this beautiful Rune help us to set guide lines for what we protect, advance, and revere.

1

The Rune of the lake / spirit / Folk Soul, in the Realm of elemental existence.
Laguz in Vanheim.
This is where and how we take a hand in the serious business of Cosmic creation.
The previous Rune chapter - Pertho - shows us the scope of possibility open to those having joined a full emotional presence to the joyous being we create by finding Wunjo through putting our lives in order, and becoming better people because of it.
We learn throughout this Rune study that the very smallest base matter displays the constant cycle of energy matter exchange, and, that the one power that charges the universe is life!
The various types of energy are a part of the Cosmic energy that is life.
The universe is the physical body of All-Father, and Spirit / Soul are present in every stone: All Mother.
Purpose defines the universe, and Laguz defines that purpose.
The lake of primal being, the waters of life.
All is alive and kin to us!
We protect that.

Our communion with the soul presence in the elemental universe answers our questions about how best to survive and become more.

This place is our future, our children's future.

We promote this!

The wonder of this set of truths give life to our own evolution of controlled physical, temporal, and spiritual being, giving purpose to our lives and all that is.

We revere this!

Through this aspect, our behavior as children of the universe takes focus, and through the small steps we take in the vastness of the Cosmic journey, our soul / spirit / Folk Soul, grows with that of the All-Being who, like us, is becoming more. Here we find the majesty of the lord of the forest , Elhaz, the Elk.

And Elhaz shows its physical face. Amazing!

What a great thing to be a part of!

2

The Rune of joining in the Realm of higher moral code.

Aiwaz in Asgard.

This is a common sense kind of an aspect.

Our moral code is the standard by which we choose from day to day.
Our union with that higher ideal is the primary tool of ascension to our better being.
Right Learning.
This, we protect!
The example we set in our day-to-day lives is a pure reflection of our real moral code.
A strong union here lets us live out our belief system, and put into action the things we know are true in the Lore.
In this way our example is stronger as our ability to live true develops and, this, we advance!
Our presence as a joyful self-controlled being, living true to the reality of corporeal life, dealing with the struggle and not hiding in a dogma, is the stand upon which majesty can manifest.
This, we revere!
This is what we learn, live, and teach.
The Rule of Resistance applies: The better your union to your moral code, the stronger and more sophisticated will the reasons for you to break your moral standing appear.

When people break their moral code for a few dollars, we know it was not too strong.
If they hold out for more dollars, does that mean they had a higher moral standard?
A standard is a constant, so, no, it does not.
The strength of the resistance only grows in the taint of corruption for those that demand more for their self betrayal.
The struggle does not manifest in its full power where a small amount will defeat us.
The path of least resistance taken, is surrender to the most base human way.
This, we protect against!
Misery loves company.
Failures seek failure so they can blame injustice for the failure.
Corruption gathers in groups and becomes a voice for the acceptance of their corruption.
Career politicians or bureaucrats who never finish their job, but spend our money like water.
People who fail each other in marriage and partnership.
This, we do not advance!

There is a mind-set of worthlessness, even among those with relative success in the world of the 21st century.
This is learned, and taught as a beautiful idea, but it is an ugly error.
We are not born of evil, possessed of sin, or destined to fail.
Success in the struggle comes from recognizing failure.
Those who believe they are doomed to failure cannot make a plan for success.
They cannot will themselves to the majestic through victory in their struggle.
This, we will not be!
When our joining with a higher moral code is real, we are first-hand witnesses to the perfect and total attack that the mundane musters against the true.
The only thing many people do well is convince their friends to abandon their higher ideal.
Our connection to our higher moral code must be guarded, grown, and glorified, or it will be vulnerable, and we can lose it.
Those who attack it do not seek to replace it.
Do you see why?

3
The Rune of journeys in the Realm of society.
Raido in Alfheim.
This is the aspect of civic and social responsibility.
The Lore tells us of the three races of man, Thrall, Carl, and Jarl.
Each of us takes our journey in the Realm of social Inter-action from one or more of these stations in life.
Each of us must be protected and a place in society for each station is required for life to function as "what should be."
Each Realm is real for every one.
The efforts by the few to limit society's benefit for the many is a constant, and a part of the struggle.
Our place in society we find and protect. We invoke what is right through Elhaz to protect us on our journey.
We make the most of our social interaction and educate ourselves to expand our role in society.
Many times men grow from service to craftsmanship to leadership acting as all three races of men.
This is the magic of society and the journey of life that we take there.

This is how we advance ourselves and the Folk.
Society must be unencumbered as far as opportunity to advance.
We must make sure that people are also free to make a fool of themselves, or to fool themselves and each other into the various ideologies of dogma and doom that are so plentiful.
It is only in the presence of choice that good choices matter, and only through making good choices that people learn to advance.
Only then can our journey lead us to the grand opportunities of true leadership and nobility.
Yes, the Rule of Resistance applies!
The better you do, the greater the challenge becomes.
Here the jarl will become to lead the way in and of society.
This is majesty.
This leader shines because he / she chooses to shine, not because the law requires it.
Law never shines, only people using law as "what should be" shine.
This is the progressive journey through social Inter-course.

Not a jungle, much greater than a jungle, with potential for disaster or majesty.
This is your journey.
I do so love to see it well taken.
To watch people shine!
4
The Rune of honor in the Realm of the mind.
Gebo in Muspelheim.
This aspect is one that best describes the way to make a better life workable. The Gebo Rune also graduates with application from being fair to being honorable to being exalted.
We can reason!
Yet we live in fear.
We can stop all that here!
Protect your ability to reason from anything or anyone that would direct you with fear, guilt, or hatred.
Promote your thinking process toward answers that expand your personal understanding of your own limitations and failures.
Expect your mind to succeed and give yourself a chance to figure out the hard answers, and when you do, act on what you have learned to go farther.
This is majesty!

We are more than smart animals, because we can understand what a smart animal is.
In being fair to our mind, we open the door out of the primal pit.
Once we advance this far, we give our mind the means to gain a self-picture of honor that is evolution!
We do this by meeting the test of change as we learn.
This way we avoid taking the same test over and over, and honor the fact of advancement.
In this way we honor Elhaz itself and through the development of a habit of progress, we can be exalted as we exalt the wonder that makes this so.
Thus we become more, better, stronger, safer, growing, honorable, majestic, changing, beings in control of our lives.
This is what the life experience is all about.

5
The Rune of wealth and influence in the Realm of life in time.
Fehu in Niflheim.
Finally, an explanation of the management and development of our fortune that does not villify wealth.
Good parents know that their financial legacy is a hard reality to create.
There is so much pressure to self-gratify and display affluence that managing wealth becomes a dream.
So much investment is geared toward the "life" of the capital that we may overlook the humanity of our opportunities.
Here we are reminded to protect our financial legacy.
When we advance our fortune, we should consider the value in time that such actions create.
Wealth can be a base motivation.
Here we see that is not always so.
Quite the opposite, in fact.
Remember this: the gold men seek is the exact same gold that men have always sought.
The land men seek to rule is the exact same land that men have warred over for centuries.

The wealth in itself is not the value, it is just stuff.
What we create, that endures to the next generation in service to ourselves through service to our children, is the value of the legacy.
When we put the wealth to work in this way, real progress is made.
Skilled men seek your wealth.
The wealth is the reason it is sought, not the value!
Here is the magic: It is the value in time that gives the wealth its majesty, not the transient display.
As Fehu appears in the other Realms, we see it used in full relationship to partnership (elemental Realm), ritual (moral Realm), stability (social Realm), balance (mental Realm), progress (ancestral Realm), fair-fate (Realm of death) cycles of mystery (mystical Realm) and finally to justice (Realm of outcomes)Leaving a legacy of opportunity to our progeny is funding the grand design that we and they carry out in our lives.
This is majesty!
Overcoming the trap of wealth and ego is the most majestic step we ever take!
Wealth is great when we are great!

Wealth does not make us great, but we can use it in greatness.

6

The Rune of duality/balance/chaos in the Realm of Death.

Hagalaz in Hel.

It is our Elhaz presence in life that does the most to prepare us for death.

Our advancement of the living Cosmos, our union with morals and ideals, our care of the social forum, our honorable intent, our sacrifice toward the future, all determine what kind of person we are when we die, young or old.

Many people are waiting to die, having done none of these things.

They have not protected themselves.

Many people do just what they must to get by.

They have not advanced themselves.

Many people revere nothing.

They find no majesty in themselves.

The primary Rune study is vast in scope because you learn the steps needed to become capable of majesty.

This is not about believing in God, but being able to believe in ourselves.

In the Lore of Odin the Runes came when Odin sacrificed himself to himself.

The being within is our dual part.

This being is majesty!
The things we protect, advance, and revere will either chain this being with death, or glorify him/her through life.
Standing tall with our arms wide and high, we become Elhaz!
We make it all happen!
Be Elhaz!
Hail Elhaz!

7

The Rune of justice in the Realm of mysteries/magic.
Tiwaz in Svartheim.
What do you know of magic?
What have you read?
How did the writer know?
How do you test?
This aspect is perfect!
You can do any magic you choose.
Change the apparent make up of mass.
Change the future.
Heal!
Reveal!
Conceal!
What would you do? And, why would you do such things?
Let me assure you, as God is my witness, there is magic enough for all of this and more.
It is because of a magical command

from our father, the conscience you hear, and our mother, the air we breathe, that we exist.
Their command was "Live.."
Everything that is exists because of the magic of that truth.
They exist, we exist.
We know!
We posture and question, but we know!
This Lore will let you do any magic!
It is all on a curve with the way that we each deal with what we know.
All we need to do is protect, advance, and revere the right things, and we know what they are.
The magic will, in turn, give us justice from the Realm of mystery.
We don't need to sacrifice babies, or act crazy, but we are the responsible party.
This is the aspect that explains how man does the things that Gods get credit for, and why that is as it is meant to be!
Think this through

8
The Rune of days / cycles / lives in the Realm of giant strength.
Dagaz in Jotunheim.
This is the aspect that displays the mutation from human action to Divine existence.
Now there is a bold statement!
Standing alone, or in any other context, that statement would be ridiculous.
This work is named "A Compass Home," and so it is.
Let's go around our Realms and follow the "yellow brick road."
Our soul, our values, our work, our honor, our sacrifice, our true nature, our justice build the inevitable mass of what we are into a form that is true to its creator: us!
We try to be worthy of reflection.
"God created in his own image."
What do we think that means?
This we protect!
That in each cycle, we become more as a Folk is undeniable.
The thing is changing and that is what we advance!
We invest in ourselves over time with tradition, morality, wealth, to try to get

the best possible development, and that is the majesty of becoming Divine.
None of us will get to become God, but then again, neither will God!
We will never be finished!
This is how life is, and knowing how it works, changes life from confusion to gift.
This is why we protect, advance, and revere the truth of natural law and high-minded living.
This is why we do not degrade, debase, or shame our existence.
This is old Lore, but it is not old fashioned.
Step by step, the Realms are real.
When we shine, we really do shine!
We protect!
We improve!
We bring majesty!
The entire business of life is so beautiful when we see how it all fits together.

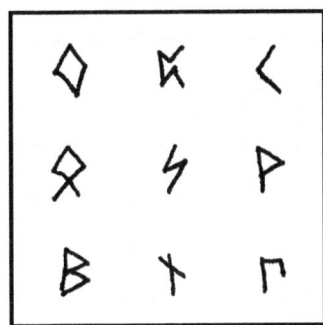

Sowilo, Rune of victory.
Here we will look at the Rune of the champion.
This Rune represents all victory, and the way to get to victory.
This Rune represents the stairway from victory to choice to victory to choice.
Every obstacle we overcome moves us even higher in our quest for our destiny and Wyrd. This Rune ends the emotional eight and describes the man/woman that has overcome the toughest enemy of all.
A tenacious enemy who lurks near every hardship, who frightens and discourages us.
An enemy who drives us to break down or rage at difficulties.
An enemy with huge appetites and lusts.
The enemy we have defeated when we embrace Sowilo is our self.
We have found emotional balance and

taken charge of our reactions.
We have identified and ordered our need and feeling of need.
We have gained stability and can use stasis as a tool to marshall time and effort.
We know both true emotions are only formats for thought.
We have joined this emotional management to our physical self and have an ordered self.
We realize that any thing is possible from this state of being.
We provide for progress and protection of this state of being, finding the majesty of a higher way of living.
This brings us to the victory of Sowilo.
We can love without demand, or vulnerability to anything more harmful than disappointment.
And we are worthy of the love of others, and show our true character as a positive one.
This victory over self allows us to understand the aspects of Sowilo in the other eight Realms.

1
The doorway Rune in the elemental universe.
Ingwaz in Vanheim.
Here we see that our victory comes from entering into the elemental universe.
Man has long studied the working of the stars and now has tools to gain vast knowledge of the elements and workings of natural law.
To prevail over the obstacles to our destiny, we must know what the Cosmos is, why it is, and how things work.
The advances of science have challenged the dogmas of the Judeo-Christian, Muslim, Buddhist, and Hindi.
This leads to a loss of belief and a weakening of the perceived value of the higher moral code.
It can be a great disappointment to know that God is not as one has been taught throughout life.
The workings of the elemental universe as seen with eyes, rather than ideas, reveals the grand design as no dogma ever could.
It is just a question of detail.
Do not lose heart because of the truth.
Victory is found in looking at what is.

Victory is virtue in the face of simple truth, or complex truth.
What is, is.
You can find it.
What is not, is not.
You will not find it.
Victory begins here.
Science does not disprove the existence of a creator, but rather that the creator is the all-encompassing Universe as we see it.
No wizard's spell.
No weekend project by a lonely deity.
From the ever-forming matter to the ever-burning energy, the whole thing is perfect, wild, and beautiful.
To accept what is before your eyes is all it takes to have victory in the elemental universe.
The promise of God has always been that we could see the truth by looking.
Look!

2
All possible possibilities in the Realm of the Gods.
Pertho in Asgard.
Victory in the higher moral code
Here we see that the moral code can take whatever shape or form you

choose, that is possible in your time and station in life.
Victory will never find those who do not act on a moral code.
Advancing a cause may not be victory.
Winning may not be victory.
Victory involves all nine Realms of our existence.
This aspect involves Pertho, the promise Rune.
The Rune of promise tells us that no matter what task or trial we face, we can accomplish, or overcome without abandoning our moral code.
Counter Point: It is **guaranteed** that in almost every task or trial, victory will be possible easily if we just abandon our moral code.
This is the honor we are given with life.
The challenge.
We educate ourselves to be better at ignoring these truths.
We pretend honor is something else.
We learn to act like we don't understand or accept the concept.
We pretend ethics is doing the best we can because honoring our moral code is impossible in practice.
We learn to lie about lying.

We strive for a higher level of failure, not victory.
We excuse corruption so that when our own corruption is exposed, it will be excused.
Those who are not yet exposed claim the higher moral ground, and we revere them because they conceal their corruption so well.
We don't believe them, because we can see their eyes, and know they lie, but we give them the higher moral ground.
This tarnishes our idea of higher moral ground, reducing it to just another front for corruption.
This twisting stairway to defeat is real, and step by step wrong becomes right.
We have no victory.
Here we see that victory is possible in full practice of our higher moral code and true values, and that without those values, the victory is hollow and false.
But most important we see that any possible victory comes through our higher moral code.

3
The Rune of light in the social Realm.
Kenaz in Alfheim.
Victory in the social institutions can only be attained in the light of truth.
This aspect separates the men from the boys.
I would dare to say that the courage to obtain such a victory is absent in the modern world.
Generally because of the previous aspect of moral possibility.
It is not politically correct to note the difference between social groups and their needs as regards the social institutions.
Only through the destruction of each social group can a one size fits all system serve.
So in absence of the ability to embrace the truth, political leaders set programs to destroy the group with the higher social standard, rather than serve the group with the lower social standard.
The more capable group must be seen as unfairly advantaged.
The less capable group as unfairly disadvantaged.
The groups cannot simply be seen as different.

They must be the same, but they are not the same.
Within the social group the less capable receive special treatment to reach a level of contribution and self-esteem.
Outside the group, special treatment is an act of condescending disrespect.
Within the social group, the most capable receive the extra help in reaching pinnacle success.
Outside the social group, this is unfair advantage, and must be withheld so that the "unfairly disadvantaged" have a chance to reach pinnacle success.
With this false practice, the pinnacle success of society itself is blocked.
Nobody makes it.
People rise to great heights because they are great.
People do great things because they can.
Society cannot be improved by limiting those best able to make the improvements for the purpose of concealing the truth about society's needs.
Education is not easy, and it's not cheap.
Social health care is not easy, and it's not cheap.

The needs of society are simple.
Honor and justice must be the root of and reason for social institutions.
Honor and justice are the root of and reason for society itself.
The light of truth reveals the way to repair the effects of circumstances in the negative through high-minded competition.
Just be truthful about what society is and we can work it.
Our leaders are not hired to give away our nations, or pretend a global family.
A family is society in embryo, but society is not your family.
The honor and justice, that are a given in the family, must be developed in society.
The truth is the only foundation society can build on.
The truth about the currency, the land titles, the school tests, the military needs, the spread of disease, pollution control, racial parity in legislative forums and courts, alien threats, everything.
To have victory in society, we must demand the truth from and about our social institutions.
This is our station in life, no matter what our social station.

We share the responsibility of being truthful in the social interaction we experience, sponsor, or support.
With truth, victory will be found in society.

4
The Rune of joy in the Realm of the mind.
Wunjo in Muspelheim.
Here the Rune of personal joy is the sign of victory over the mind.
Just as Sowilo itself is the reward of balanced, ordered, and directed emotion, Wunjo is the reward of self-supporting, aware, control of our physical space, behavior, trade, and choice of companions.
In aspecting Sowilo it is clear that we must preserve the real joy in our mental state to have victory over the fear, guilt, and hatred of the troubled mind.
This aspect is the purpose of our discipline of self.
True victory holds with it the joy of victory, the mind-set of having overcome the self.
One without the other would be empty.
Remembering this will help us to avoid conflict where there is no joy in victory.

The point of it all is why we address conflict.
When our path or people require it.
When principle must be defended and preserved.
There are no mindless victories worth retelling.
Victory by accident brings no joy.
To accept a dogma or political platform without thinking through the ideas it is founded upon is to ever deny your self-victory in the Realm of the mind and the joy that comes with knowing you understand what you are doing, accepting, or supporting.
If reading this disturbs you, perhaps the "beliefs" you hold do not stand up to scrutiny.
Go there! Examine what you "believe" and see if it is something you can "know."
Knowing is better than believing.
Realism is better than dogmatism.
Even if the truth is less that you had hoped, the ability to act on it with enthusiasm is a benefit no belief system has to offer.
Ritual becomes a way to celebrate what you know is true.

Politics becomes a way to actualize what you know will serve.
Victory in the Realm of one's mind is the doorway to greatness, both large and small.

5
The Rune of elemental power in the Realm of time.
Uruz in Niflheim.
Just as wind and sea use time to change the shape of the earth, humanity through time is changing the face of tomorrow and the meaning of yesterday.
Victory in the Realm of time comes from channeling the efforts of our ancestors, and the accomplishments they made, toward the venue of our children's existence through inspired intuitive acts of cognitive imagination and creation.
The time Realm reminds us that there is really no end.
This schools us to act with a purpose.
To act with an "end in mind" that does not consider the humanity or history of our existence is common.
The results are great disparity in the social classes, less useful education, pollution, waste.

To act with a purpose is to forgo the frustration of obstacles and conflict that, even though they should be expected, deter us from exact ends.
This aspect involves the shaping of goals and expectations, and forming plans more in keeping with what is, what is becoming, and what should be.
Our victory here is over our span of years.
When our success in life adds to the power of what has been built before, and increases the available power to those who come behind, then we have found victory in time.
In the negative, we see dead civilizations, cultures, empires.
Dead not from conquest, but from failure to take time in to account in their development.
"Believing" the world is going to end removes us from these considerations. Leading people to "believe" such a thing would ease the burden of persuasion, insomuch as waste, pollution, and misuse of resources, even though such leaders need not teach such a belief so much as just watch them exist.
We see that the power from this lesson in history gives us the inspiration to

break away from the illusion of
helplessness, and give it the true name
of foolishness.
From there it is an easy step to
denounce those disassociated
from time and take control of our space
in time.
Victory!
There is real power in the Realm of time.
All who have lived before have charged
this Realm with their best efforts and
love of purpose (failures not excepted).
Uruz is the power of the elemental
universe.
This power is the cohesive force of all
that is.
The greatest manifestation of Uruz is life
and at the pinnacle, sentient life.
The things that men do to make life
better for future generations do not die
with them, but charge time itself with
power that can be built upon.
This also changes time.
The curve is relative to the mass energy
curve, which is also changing.
Victory over time will eventually provide
the sentient actor with virtually
unlimited ability.
The ability to deal with an opportunity
must be learned.

One must become "safe."
Learning the lessons of history, the tools of history, and the failures of those without an appreciation for ancestry and progeny brings victory in your time.
In later chapters we will discuss mortality in terms of spirituality.
Here we discuss it as a people.
On one side of this coin is the power of time to help us gain victory in life.
The other side of the coin is the power in life to give us victory over time.
The science fiction fantasy of victory over time is a recurring theme.
When we consider it in light of scientific advancement at current rates plus the knowledge of Cosmic relativity, that these Runes, for instance, have made clear for millennia, the idea is not so far-fetched.
It would appear to be a matter of what you intend.
This helps us to see the value of our lives in the overall scope of things.
You are real and what you do matters in far-reaching ways.
Making these ways a part of our lives is part of true victory.

6
The Rune of need in the Realm of no life.
Nathiz in Hel.
Completion as a Folk is in the understanding of the importance of dying.
This thing that terrifies everyone to the point of action contrary to everything we know is right and necessary, must be put into a proper scope.
The way of teaching that places personal breath above all things brings us the many hero sagas of personal sacrifice and villainy.
This aspect shows us that we need to die with our feet on solid ground as far as our view of the elemental universe, the best possible moral code, the truth about society, a joyful mental presence, and the power of the Folk Soul as part of our being.
Such a life cannot be diminished in its passing.
How often when someone dies do we wonder why we don't feel more?
Why does the world not grind to a stop without them?
Why do we feel guilt because we are happy it wasn't us?

Yet certain peoples passing does rock the community and we feel the passing of a necessary and wonderful part of all humanity.
This is because of the missing knowledge of the necessity of ourselves in the world, and our failure to embrace our beautiful reality.
We don't encourage greatness in the boy or girl we know so well, the brother or sister who we love even as they pass their lives with confusion or alienation.
We are all in this together, and even though we may leave on different days, we all go out together.
Death needs us that our work can be added to "what is" and that power to the strength of the Folk Soul.
We should mourn a death when the life was without victory.
We should celebrate the victory when a life lived well comes to a close.
We can do much to help each other find victory in life and thus those things needed for victory in death.
(See the chapter on Laguz.)
Death is not our fate.
The sum of our actions and intentions, our well of Wyrd, colors our fate with the truth about us.

Victory over death needs this truth to become.
The allegory of school applies.
At year's end, we take tests, and upon passing, move to the next set of lessons.
The previous aspects of Sowilo show us how to take life seriously and attain victory there, and we need that to find victory in death.
The being we become, when we apply the Runes to ourselves in our daily life, can do this.
So let's go!
On to victory!

7
The mother Rune in the Realm of mystery and magic.
Berkano in Svartheim.
Victory over the mysteries can never mean the conquering of all there is to be learned.
The nature of the Realm of mystery (Svartheim) is an immeasurable void where the power of magic is the essence of the thing itself.
On one side of the aspect of Berkano here is to say that this unexplainable place of mystery is our mother.

The womb from which the universe is born.
The Is that Is not.
The other side is to say that victory in this dark Realm comes from the care and nurturing of that which we do not perceive in form.
Here are the things we do not know.
Here lie the great powers of mystery.
Faith, hope, trust, love, risk.
Also fear, guilt, and hatred are invisible, yet real.
Powers to shake mankind.
The "ways" are found here.
We cannot hold them, but like a good mother, we can take them in hand.
(We find, when we aspect Ansuz, that Pertho is found here, the voice of God saying all things are possible in this Realm.)
Here we care for the mother of mysteries and there gain victory over the unknown.
We may use the power of the mysteries as conscience leads us, but victory comes from giving to the mysteries, not the taking of their power.
What do we give?

How about the mystery of how we lived a virtuous life in the face of the usual obstacles?
How about how we were able to find the message in the Runes and choose a true path while the world killed or cried or sucked its thumb?
How about how a total outlaw could find the actual face of God?
Things are only impossible until someone does it.
The beauty of this is that there is no end to the impossible list.
We must care for this Realm so we can make the magic tools when the time is right for them.
One may ask how we can have victory over the impossible, or care for it.
It is the impossible that proves to us the perfection of the Cosmic experience we are a part of.
Without the impossible, it would all stop.
The impossible is an essence, not an idea.
Dogmatic belief systems that have no address to make on this matter are the Hell they preach.

8
The Rune of home in the Realm of outcomes and consequences.
Othalaz in Jotunheim.
Here we see victory is made complete when we find home in the future.
The primary strength from the outside, that brings us victory, will come from the home we make of our actions.
This is such a help to know and be reminded of.
Especially when we think of home as a prison, or a burden, or when we think of family as an embarrassment.
This tells us that home is the source of great power to overcome adversity.
Here we have an aspect that is very difficult to actualize.
We all know in our hearts, in our conscience, that this is true, yet we struggle with the doing of the thing.
We reject the authority of parents.
We reject the dignity of children.
We envy the power of the wage earner.
We envy the personal control of parents at home.
Some of us do most of it right.
Some of us do most of it wrong.
Some of us exist without any real ties to our family at all.

We think those people are alien to us, and could never understand us.
Sadly, that is true much of the time.
Let's go back to victory over our own random imagination of Wunjo in Muspelheim.
When we defeat the demons and phantoms of our own making, and gain victory over excuses, we find our father to be a handy champion.
Our mother becomes a confidante and brothers and sisters are rescuers and best friends.
This is not a cookie cutter solution to life, because every person is different.
This does tell us that the family is the intended group structure for the adventure of life.
Home is the intended outcome for those who strive in Midgard.
We can obtain this quality of home through honest declarations of support.
Help your family to learn the Runes.
Just knowing the Runes makes a change, which adds to the person, which makes a stronger person, which develops the harmony that makes family a strong support group for each member in a very wide choice of activities.

We know our families better than anyone.
By working to help each other reach our personal victories, we build the most dependable type of allies.
If we cannot find victory in our own home, how can we claim victory in anything?
Let's be truthful about it.
This formula for victory includes every aspect of life.
To strive in good faith with intelligent use of our tools, we can make these real victories, not illusions of victory.
A real family is just a bit of work away.
A few true declarations and some service, and there you go.
Tell them what you're doing.
Explain that you are using the Runes to guide you and let the Runes explain your goal.
The directions are easy to read, the results are staggering!
You don't have to "know everything" starting out.
Once you experience the power of the Runes, it all becomes clear.
This gift is said to come from Odin, All Father.
Odin is known as the giver of weapons.

This is a tool that brings victory over life while the experience is left whole for us to live through.
You lose nothing.
What we have all lost is this knowledge for 2000 years.
In that time our families have become burdens, the mysteries bogey men, death the end, the power of the soul lost, the mind clouded, society a cesspool, the moral code a perverts paradise of forgiveness, and the universe a mystery.
To gain victory over these Realms at this point in time and technology is to reach a place unimagined at any time before.
The possibilities are wonderful.
The petty nature of today's "great problems" have held sway far too long.
Learn, live, and teach the principles you find here and the change will take care of itself.
To find yourself in the future with your identity intact!
This is victory.

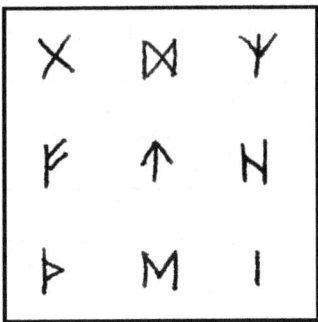

Tiwaz the Rune of justice, sacrifice and Divine action.
This is the Rune that charges us as Cosmic beings to create a paradise from the potential before us.
The truth of all that happens in the world is the story of the pursuit of this principle applied.
Our sorrow is our failure to find strength or courage to bring life to justice.
Our frustration is the failure of our chosen leaders to bring justice to life.
They can only serve when empowered by truth.
Those who have applied the principles of the first two sets of eight Runes, Aetts, can do this.
This is not something we may just do, but a station in life that must be

reached, before we can use the power there.
Any fool can enforce a statute. Only those with an ordered path - Wunjo - and a worthy heart - Sowilo may judge the sacrifice that must be made to gain true and Divine justice.

1
The Rune of honor in the Realm of elemental existence.
Gebo in Vanheim.
Here we see the environment as living and deserving of rights, respect, and justice.
We must be just in our use of the material, our view of the material, and our control of the material.
Justice is only pontificating unless we begin at the bottom of the pyramid, the base of all form, **the elemental.**
This place is where everything is!
We so often overlook this, or worse, call it a platform, and its champions a faction.

This is the false game of justice that is typical of any and all who do not move from a position of order - Wunjo.
The Rune of honor is a symbol following truth, direction, conscience, self control, commitment and freedom in that order.
Honor does not just happen and honorable ideas do not take wing and put themselves in place.
The rule of resistance applies here.
It takes an act of will in physical form to bring honor to the elemental mother that gives us form.
Do this and you **are** acting out Divine justice.
Legal speak and clever words do not achieve justice and are the stock in trade of our political leaders.
If a child cannot see the justice in a decision, then justice is not there.
Doing things to create justice is the only source of justice.

2
The Rune of cycles / days / lives, in the Realm of God's Home.
Dagaz in Asgard.
The Gods have evolved so much through the whole history of man as to be new for each generation.

They are only Gods to us if we see the purpose for their creation.
The function of the struggle has held true throughout, even as the face of struggle has changed.
Overcoming adversity without cruelty has always been the way of better men.
The cycles here have brought us a new view of the Gods that brings a new view of humanity in turn.
The work of men to create justice has done this, if not by bringing justice to the masses, then by showing the true nature of injustice so blatant and common that even the children see it and give the lie to parents and politicians.
This cycle of moral rebellion is the Gods' justice for us and our way of motivating toward the hard path of bringing justice to the development of a moral code and moral force.
These are the real steps of higher development.
Not weapons, control and domination disguised as a defensive battle, drawing on us for survival and support.
Justice as a tool to suppress dissent is about all we see in action.

That is, of course, not justice, and we, of course, know it.
This is the aspect that draws us in to sync with the Gods, and makes real the power of justice.
Justice is not an idea, but the condition of truth in the Divine sense.
The higher development of humanity is brought about because this cycle is joined.
This is where we tune into the Gods.
There will always be a way to achieve justice, and a time to make it so.

3
The Rune of progress / protection / majesty, in the Realm of society.
Elhaz in Alfheim.
Our last aspect so clearly leads to this one.
Here we see the protection of society is in justice.
This does not say the exclusive system of law and punishment in place today protects society.
Clearly it does not.
We are fragmented, degraded, and disposed of in the name of justice, and the name confuses us.
Our society is retrograde and justice will

save it.
Real justice!
Simple justice is society's protection from decay.
We must guard justice and guard it truly or the rot takes hold.
And then we preserve justice as we progress.
This aspect is so powerful!
Yes, we will progress because we guard justice.
High-minded programs are great, but progress comes only through justice.
Society needs honor (Real money), and justice. (Redress of non payment.)
Now we continue to guard justice and the progress becomes majesty.
A spiritual society with grace and majesty, Divine in its foundation because of one simple thing - justice.
This is not a dogma because everyone is included.
We rationalize a thousand reasons why people struggle away from each other and do not have the time or money to explore which reason is the cause.
People in authority are black with the grime of special interest.
Because society is a Realm, it cannot

cease to exist, or become something else.
It will always be society, and will always be able to come true and work in justice. That's all it takes to open the doors to the potential of people working together.
So, what will it be?

4
The Rune of balance / duality in the Realm of the mind.
Hagalaz in Muspelheim.
This is a very necessary realization.
Our mental function is balanced and our ability to grasp duality and purpose is either secured and reinforced by justice in our lives, or it is disrupted.
Justice is the catalyst for honor, purpose, grace, and balance in our lives.
Wives become adverse to their husbands when justice is denied in the marriage.
Children become outlaws when their place in the root group of society provides no justice.
Families become outlaws when justice is beyond reach because of economic station or personal condition.
When advocates with ability are beyond most people's ability to pay, most

people are unable to find justice.
How can we maintain stability and balance in our thinking process when we know our creations, property, family, and life are without the means to secure justice?
We must have this balance!
We must be able to use our creative process!
We must be secure in our understanding that justice is within reach!
Otherwise we are unable to hold a rationale that allows for a mental toughness, and we can be fooled.
Nay! We will be fooled!
We will be used, abused, lied to, denied, and held responsible for the mistakes we are bound to make.
This will be called justice, but it is not.
Whenever this is the conduct of justice in our lives, we minimize our exposure, which minimizes our interaction.
When our interaction is minimal, any effect our stand on justice has will be minimal.
We will substitute football for thinking, because thinking will be about how injustice is ruining our life.
We will accept the sacrifice of young soldiers acting out a charade of justice

because our mind won't give us a plan that requires no action.
But to honor our physical existence requires that we bring justice to the physical plane.
So, how important is it to know these aspects?
This is not important at all, if we are willing to pay just about every dime, every freedom, and the blood of our children to keep the wolf away from our door.
The wolf is always the one naming itself justice.
Our knowledge of justice and its power and value is the power of this aspect.
Our real stand for justice is the balance of our thinking, and our grasp of the reality of our being.

5
The Rune of stasis in the Realm of time / ancestry.
Isa in Niflheim.
When we act to preserve and promote real justice in our lives, we are bringing stability to the efforts of our ancestors' creation.
We bring stability to our temporal span of years. We bring stability to our

children's span of years.
The Folk Soul gets support over time and generations.
Time is more fully utilized in its potential of providing the most opportunities for right action in the pursuit of more applied justice.
"Alive" means "The Struggle"!
The struggle in time is one of supporting justice!
This is very simple, yet enormous in scope.
When people agree to fight an enemy of their nation, they fight for justice.
When people stand the picket line, they stand for justice.
When people honor a guarantee on their product, they work for justice.
When people change a process to keep the community clean, they change for justice.
Over time, millions of actions have been taken by the Folk to create, support, and preserve justice.
This is the foundation to build on, not the tricks or conspiracies that may have fooled people into acts of injustice disguised as justice, but the basic intention to bring justice to life.

The previous aspect applied protects us from being fooled, but this aspect gives justice to the efforts of the past, if not to the underlying truth.
A fuller understanding of the serious evil that misleading the people really is will help us to bring justice to those that do.
Leadership is to be guarded, and kept away from those that can be bought and will mislead.
The stability of our children's future depends on our real creation of an atmosphere of justice for them to live in.
Again we see the importance of actually doing this.
Pretending is so common that it is the standard in today' s leadership.
We can change that.
The pillar that continuity in time rests upon is justice.
The great injustices of history prove this out in the great wounds that all humanity suffers from their actions.

6
The Rune of partnership in the Realm of death.
Ehwaz in Hel.
Here we have an interesting concept that all of us hope for, but few accept as possible.
The partnership Rune is very advanced in as much as it describes people that are able to fulfill the responsibilities of a mate or partner.
It takes a lot of constancy, self-control, study, and application to be this type of person.
Such relationships are often the most pleasant part of our lives, and when these partners die, it is just not possible for the relationship to die with them.
We still love them.
We still speak to them, or for them.
In our hearts we know we miss them because the partnership is alive and the partner is not.
Real justice would preserve such closeness always.
Would it not?
When we bring justice to life, justice carries our partnerships through death.
Why does it seem as if you have known some people forever?

Why do we get to know some people so quickly?
Because bringing justice to life is the most certain way to supersede ego, and because superseding ego is the best way to build strong relationships, the fit is very natural here.
The harmony of the Cosmic is built on such as this.
When we envision justice and respect what real power it represents, we can know that this would be true.
Another view of this aspect would be that our relationship with the Realm of death would be governed by our actions in bringing justice to life.
We are not innocent because we do nothing to help evil.
Doing nothing is the root of evil.
Perpetrators of evil are the few.
The fearful masses make it possible for their evil to succeed and grow by doing nothing.
The old Norse / Germanic belief that a sword death was solid proof that we stood for something is a good demonstration of this understanding.
Living under the boot heel of injustice is just not to be tolerated.
This is not a barbaric idea, but the very

heart of civilization.
Justice is the heartbeat of civilization.
Our partnership with justice supersedes death (Myth of the Valkyries) because a true respect for justice supersedes self.

7

The Rune of law / order / action / in the Realm of mystery and unknown things.
Thursaz in Svartheim.
In the myths of the North, the creatures living in the body of the universe (Ymir) are divided into two groups: the <u>Light Elves</u> who help to attain "what should be," and serve the God of male fertility, Frey.
And the <u>Dark Elves</u> who manifest wonders through their mystic power, but serve no one.
These dark mysteries and magics have held man's wonder for ages and there are many stories and rituals to bring the dark powers into man's grasp.
Any haphazard manifestations of the dark powers through the use of bloody rituals is not a controlled action in mystical power.
This aspect tells us that our foundation must be in justice to bring order from a mystical ritual.

Oddly enough, it is only through such beginnings that any success is ever reached in the mystic arts.
The Thursaz Rune is the Rune of ritual as well as law and order, and it is by ritual that we create law to bring order.
Svartheim is the Realm of unknown things, both great and small.
Having a system of learning and investigation grants solid access, but do not accept limited possibilities there.
This limited access is gained through ritual actions of the Folk.
Be careful how you pray.
The unthinking welcome to our home, by fools who perform such rituals (be they mysterious, or political), brings ill intent to our home.
We are charged here to insure that the ritual access to the Realm of mystery is bonded by just intent, and the price paid is not our home, freedom, Folk Soul, or future.
The beings are not of a kind!
There are evil people!
They will never be of a kind!
Ill intention will never be good intention.
We can access the darkness for Divine purpose and create Divine justice.
We can also create an unholy mess!

People do this all the time and then step away and pretend it just happened.
The power of the mysteries are real.
A consistent manner of ritual application of our will to this power can direct it, when our motivation and intent are just. Many may scoff at this reasoning, but they are the ones who also fear the dark.
Remember that we can enter the Realm of mystery, and that the darkness there has no will.
The desire to take on ill intention can make it so, but **the just use** of chaotic or dark power does not cause ill action, but the desired, just results.

8
The Rune of wealth / influence / power, in the Realm of change and becoming.
Fehu in Jotunheim.
Here we see that the usable power of the God becoming comes from the presence of justice in the world of men.
This is just about the final word, as far as the Runes, explaining where we are and how it works.
We can reject all of this because of free will, but wait!
That thing, free will, has no power to do anything.
We can use it to reject anything, but not to do anything.
As with all things, only our wealth, power, and influence can change anything because that is our freedom to act.
Our strength and character reflect our ability, not our helplessness.
The same is true of all life in form, as all life is Divine life.
The power of the developing God, **who is becoming, in form,** is an aspect of justice in our living.
This cannot be substituted, lied about, or falsified.
The abstract of force that also grows in

this Realm cannot gain controllable power, and will always be a wild juggernaut of undirected destructive force.
The other side of that coin is powerful directed will, defined by Divine justice! The manifestation of right in our world. Of us, but outside of us, just like the Folk Soul.
Hmmm!
The random, unfocused energy of the Jotan is brought into focus by our actions.
Not clever or scientific formulas, but steadfast action by self-ordered, self-controlled, just-minded men and women living with free will.
We cannot mandate this with law or punish those that freely choose not to join the common weal as most others do.
Divine justice defies definition.
The means of reaching Divine justice may include a trick or a foul.
That intent becomes right action.
The will to go forward in the right brings power to "what should be" the final temporal state of paradise.
This is ours to create or deny, to empower or to abandon.

These are the aspects of the justice
Rune, the driven spirit in form, in time.
The way that "what is becoming,"
becomes Divine and not base.
We can see that this series of steps are
important to each stage of life.
Powerful concepts in each Realm are the
fruit of just action on our part, at our
insistence, and at no other time.
This is the hardest thing to do.
That is why the end is the greatest
accomplishment our will can reach -
Fehu and the Wotan.
The ability of the Divine to act on our
plane of existence is the result of our
willingness to sacrifice for justice, truly,
of our efforts.
We do this for each other, ourselves, our
creator, our creation.

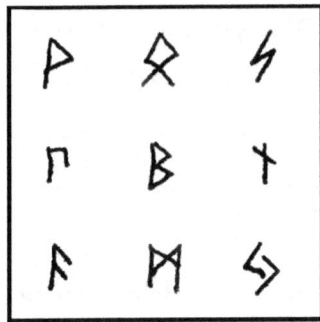

Berkano
The mother, nurturing / giving life.
The act of giving life.
The acts of nurturing.
Some things we endure, some we encourage.
Some we care for, protect and nurture.
It is not our lot to exhaust our hearts on ideas and things that are independent of those actions, or static, or of constant nature.

1
Wunjo joy in the elemental universe, the physical Realm of things.
We learn in primary Rune study that joy is a very real circumstance that exists when we put our physical lives in useful order.
It is from that order alone that joy evolves, for joy is not an emotion.

We can put our physical life in order without reliance on the state of our emotions, by rote.
The gift of Asa-Lore should be nurtured and cared for so that our Folk have an increased chance of success in this modern and confusing world.
Encouraging fair play, clear conscience, truth, ritual, security, safety, all the things that lead to Wunjo joy must be nurtured in the real world.
It is not these things that are, singularly, matters of the heart, but the state of joy they lead to that must be cared for.
This is a dynamic aspect.
Man must do this, it will not "fall into place" without our help.
When we act to create and protect joy in the elemental universe, it changes the face of the universe to that of a friend, and a place where we find welcome.
This makes life a much nicer thing from the gate, and promotes success immensely.
Being Wunjo is so important that success, in truth, stands upon it.
2
Othalaz, homeland / ancestral in Asgard.
This is the Rune of noble completion.
The last Rune, the Master.

Here we nurture a life and home in the Higher Moral code.
Providing for those things that help us to make our home in God, as part of God in the whole of our being, the whole of all things.
This is the ideal of human fulfillment.
This is not subjective to the type of individual, or the manner in which we manifest our higher moral code.
Making way for everyone we encounter to see the value of existing and caring for an existence at home in the higher moral code.
We were once shocked and dismayed when people in positions of high responsibility lied or acted immorally.
Now we cross our fingers and hope they don't bring us to ruin with it.
Courting immorality, condoning unnatural and dangerous lifestyles.
Exposing children to depravity or allowing it.
The ancient knowledge tells us to nurture the higher moral code for a reason (which is explained next) as a home.

3
Sowilo in Alfheim.
Victory in the social Realm.
This is what we nurture in our social endeavors.
Not wealth, not ritual, not harvest.
They have their social places, but what we care for, what we encourage is the light of victory in society.
Winning, over the antisocial element.
Winning, over social predators (profiteers, not criminals).
Overcoming bureaucratic laxity, corruption, rigidity, inefficiency, in the social institutions.
Overcoming party favoritism in the workings of public institutions.
Defeating fear, guilt, and hatred in the educational institutions, and the mindset of rebellion and alienation that go with them.
Not as an extra effort, but as a primary concern.
Our private ideas and lives are indeed separate from our social life.
We have escaped our social lives as a group and simply pay to have society managed.
Well, this does not work because the managers will regulate toward the

smoothest form of management to the detriment of the institution's purpose, yet in favor of economy of cost and effort, while charging more for the service.

Society is not a business, it is a womb from which civilized change or violent revolution are born.

Our choice.

This aspect shows us how to shape our care for society, and our idea of society. Aggressive, yet controlled and directed social interaction.

Not dynamic mass ideology, but personal involvement with success in mind.

Society is fragile just as it should be. Rampaging social programs and laws are as damaging as crime and apathy put together.

To experience victory here is to take huge steps toward what should be.

Skuld, the final Norn.

Nurture this victory.

Nurturing the needs of our mind and consciousness.

4
Nathiz in Muspelheim.
The needs of the God mind in the animal body are not complex, but are really staggering in importance.
In order to nurture the needs of the mind, we should probably consider what they are.
The three previous aspects of Berkano give a good start.
Wunjo in the elemental (physical) universe, gives us the security of personal space to overcome fear on a base level.
Othalaz in Asgard gives us security in our moral code so guilt is set aside.
Victory over social disarray allows us order in our station in life, and safety from bias.
The remaining needs of the mind are, then, real information and clear possibility.
Truth and enthusiasm in this situation release the real power of the mind.
It's hard to trust a car that has not been cared for to go any distance.
One simply will not trust his own mind to serve him when he knows it is a mire of inefficiency; and we do know.
The power of this aspect is the true

difference between craftsman and dropout, fidelity and betrayal.
One may function at a high level and never tap his mind's potential.
Success does not mean wisdom.
The "appearance of a good mind" is an oxymoron.
The better the mind works, the simpler the ways in which one behaves appear.
There are several common obstructions to the free mind.
Fear of what others, especially others appearing to be together and respected, will think.
It is important to note that people who "appear" to have it all worked out, may spend so much effort maintaining the appearance that they would never notice anyone else anyway.
The mind needs focus.
Focus on ourselves, not on who we want to be.
We do not have the choice of who we want to be because we already chose to be who we are.
We can, however, become greater than we are, but first we need our mind to accept who we are.
The mind needs the person that goes with it.

The mind needs a purpose.
The assignment of pointless task is not purpose.
The improvement of the being and the Folk is purpose.
In nurturing the needs of the mind, we mother our ever increasing, growing temporal self.
It is so uncommon to encounter people who nurture the needs of the mind that they may seem unusual and standoffish.
Sensationalism is not nurturing of the mind, but drowning it in excitement.
We can experience as much pleasure in the wondrous business of a nurtured mind as one could dream of.
The bonus being that the mind increases in power as it works from the inside out.
We require ever more sensation to satisfy the need of the mind to grow from without, but pure sensation stifles as much as sensory deprivation.
Take courage and take charge of the care of your mind.
5
Jera in Niflheim
The Harvest in Time.
This is nurturing the product of ancestry to glean from it the greatest benefit of past efforts.

As no one is really "dead and gone," the works of every life contribute to the holdings of the common weal.
How we nurture this resource is up to us.
The possessions of the dead are soon picked over, but the example of their lives can be a treasure trove of experience we can use.
Dismissing what is past as valueless is just plain silly, just as presuming that we are entitled to all we can grab in our lives is silly.
The wealth isn't going to die.
People have been grabbing at the very same wealth forever.
The value of the lives is the experience.
It is important to pass on the benefit of it all to those to come.
Plant seeds in time by your deeds.
Don't be afraid to leave work undone because you run out of lifetime.
This Lore is very clear about re-birth and retaining memory.
You can pick up where you left off.
This is the harvest in time we are caring for.
When one realizes it is self that is caring for self as well as family, the picture is clearer, the idea "less grave."
The examples we leave will be the

harvest of our progeny.
Will we leave a morass of painless starts, or a continuing program of caring for the Folk and the world they will live in, and the time they will live in?

6
The Rune of man, in the Realm of death. Manaz in Hel.
This is the sister to the last aspect in that here we are caring for ourselves through the process of change that is dying.
The Manaz is the complete human, able to reach the heart, minds, and bodies of our fellowman, and war with the demons of another.
One who is able to make life right, heal and encourage his Folk.
This is ability that takes years to learn and become capable in using.
The sense of empathy that one develops in becoming the spirit warrior of Manaz is an increase in the spirit being of the warrior.
Our spirit being does not die, but fights dying to the last second and beyond.

The lesson here is to nurture the spirit warrior part of the being through the time of dying, as through the time of living.
The ego is set aside in the act of empathy, and there we find the highest accomplishment of humanity.
The spirit preserved through death is not the accumulated fear, guilt, and hatred of ego, but the joyful exchange of empathy that comes from the will to do the selfless act.
This identity can be preserved and because it is a result of a lot of learning experience.
The essence of all that learning goes with it.
We grow.
If you don't recognize yourself as having lived before because your hang-ups are current, it's because that stuff is junk baggage left behind.
That is not the Manaz person, who has less ego and more positively directed will and joy of sacrifice.
Nurture this concept through dying, and into the next cycle of life.
The Manaz is the goal of our living.
Bringing success to the Folk through our nurturing acts toward them completes

us as worthwhile people.
Taking care of that aspect of self through our dying is so much more rewarding than nurturing our money-making ability into the next cycle.
Economic circumstances may vary to the point that such a skill would be of no benefit.
The ability to empathize and aid people has been a constant positive aspect of humanity throughout.
Nurture it.
This is the part of the subconscious that is in tune with all others of the Folk Soul.
The part that is truly immortal.

7
The voice of God in the Realm of mystery.
Ansuz in Svartheim.
Here we see that our interaction with the dark powers and mysteries is not forbidden, but is regulated to those uses where the voice of conscience is nurtured and given to grow.
Such growth can encompass all use of the mysteries and magic, but only on these terms.
That arcane arts exist is still debated on many levels, but remember this; the

negative emotional power of fear, guilt, and hatred have provided power to the will of men acting out countless evil plans.
Arcane power is used daily, all around you, often by people who are not aware of what they do.
Often by people who know exactly what they do.
Just as the information found in these aspected Runes shows us how the power of the mysteries can be used, lack of this knowledge leaves us unguarded from those who would use it against others, rather than to improve the common weal.
In nurturing the conscience, which is the voice of God, we open a much more powerful and deeper understanding of the mysteries than could ever be tapped for evil or irresponsible purpose.
Domination of others is a misuse of time and energy.
The result is war on a thousand different levels.
The trap is inescapable.
When your leadership seeks to dominate, it must abandon conscience.
Domination denies the existence of conscience in the subject people.

When dealing with alien beliefs, one is in the dark of the mysteries, for there are many ways to do what men must do.
As in the holding for justice we find ritual in the mysteries, here we find enthusiasm.
Enthusiasm in nurturing the part of mystery brings understanding.
The exchange produces understanding on the level of conscious-subconscious thought, and that takes away the fear of difference or of the unknown.
Apply this in the self, the family, the neighborhood, the universe.
The voice is in the mysteries of birth, of love, of poetry.
In caring for these manifestations of magic, we make the voice of God louder and more clear.

8
Finally we find the power we cannot control in the Realm of strength outside ourselves.
Uruz in Jotunheim. Life in the future.
This is very simple.
For a man, nurture and care for the power and strength of the woman.
Power you cannot control.
Never subjugating, but re-enforcing the

Lore and all that leads to here in aspecting the Berkano Rune.
For the woman this is nurturing and caring for the man, who is as troubled by the many differences as the woman can be.
In this nurturing alliance of the sexes, each will find incredible power for the manifestation of will that seems so hard to grasp in our single struggle to make the world work.
How many stories have you heard where someone was failing badly until they found the sincere support of their partner to see them through, and then went on to rise above heavy odds?
That's right, all of them.
Those stories come from the Folk Soul, the memory of successes and failures based upon people being able to tap the power of the universe, or not.
For man that power is in woman, for woman, it is in man.
It is not hidden away, it is in plain view. This nurturing of the power outside ourselves does include the power of others, male and female, on whom we draw a helping hand in many ways.
In all, our caring for them and their strength helps us greatly to succeed.

For one to succeed, another need not fail!
We can all make it.
Our counterpart is not the enemy.
From this position of natural unity, we nurture other people whose strength is not ours to control, but whose help we can call upon.
This seems the reverse of securing ourselves by keeping all power to ourselves, and in a way it is.
But maintaining such security requires full attention.
We are not meant to spend our whole life on watch.
To have an enemy, we must make an enemy.
Enemies grow from injuries and powerlessness, or from hunger and desperation.
These are all created and preserved conditions.
The support of the helpless is worthless.
The support of the strong is helpful.
Why foster helplessness for profit if the profit is all spent on security?
Why hoard wealth when it is redefined as greater wealth through dissolution?
All fear, all guilt, all hatred is traceable.
Cause and effect.

Our nurturing the substantive realities of human life denies growth to those negative motivations.

It is not easy to help where hindering seems safer.

This Lore can be trusted because we become so much stronger through its use that our position changes relative to what constitutes a threat.

True, people may still harm us, but for what reason?

This is not a position of weakness, but of real strength, as we see in the Tiwaz justice Rune.

The world will respond to the will of those who act toward its good care and management.

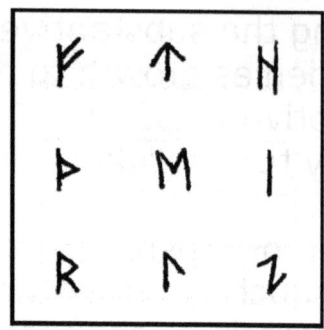

Ehwaz, the joint journey.
Partnership, marriage, fostering -
This is about the Rune of relationships.
So many of our relationships are by happenstance, that we may give very little thought to just who and why we have the relationship.
Casual is the common term for most of these.
When one realizes that these people are unvalued in our lives and all we do and mean little or nothing to us, it gives rise to some important considerations.
As a rule in modern society, we don't question the part others play in our life, while we relate to strangers.
Political correctness has spawned foolishness in the way that we decide who is not suitable as a friend, a partner, a mate.

Drug use, crime, or sexual activity may be all that parents consider in the monitoring of their children's relationships.
Sometimes a sexual aspect is not considered because of political correctness.
Is that enough?
So what do we consider in friendships, partnerships, or marriage?
The Rune is clear.
Let's see what it says.

1
Fehu in Vanheim, form.
Can you afford the relationship in the material universe?
Can you afford to get married?
Does this friend pay his way?
Does this partner bring in the business?
Does this person bring personal power and influence to the relationship, and if not, is what they do bring worth your investment?
This seems pretty base, but think of the problems people have over finances in relationships and realize that this is a primary concern.
Think about the way people use the status and influence of their friends to

do things they are not able to succeed at, and the extra problems caused by this.
This is not to say we should not act to help our friends to gain their own wealth and influence so they can fulfill the responsibility that comes with all relationships.
This does not say that this ground must be covered in all relationships.
Don't be afraid to insult potential friends and partners, as this is good insurance against all of the potential problems mentioned and more.
So it's all to the good when we apply this idea.

2
The higher moral code of relationships.
Here we find the Rune of Divine justice. Tiwaz, in the Realm of God, Asgard.
Does this relationship bring justice to your moral code?
Does this partner support your moral ideas?
Does this person encourage your moral commitment and effort?
Think about the difference between no defined moral code and a highly ritualized moral code, or opposing ideas

about God or religion
Will your new partner's ruthless business style cause you to abandon the principles of your moral code?
This Lore says to build relationships that bring justice to your moral code.
If you have to help your new partner to develop a moral code so you can relate, **do it.**
So how about the relationship with the new family partner?
Yes, that is the new child!
Do not let these children grow up without a clear understanding of morality.
Often parents say, "They're just babies, they won't understand."
Often this is the parents' way of saying they have no understanding of their own moral code.
The basic Rune Lore gives a great guideline for our moral code, that is easy to share.
The world will heal when we adopt and maintain a moral code that makes sense, and can be explained without dogma.
By taking steps to secure our close relationships from those problems at the outset, our success will be much more

quickly and smoothly achieved.
Make partners with those who will preserve and protect your moral code.

3
The balance Rune, Hagalaz Alfheim, in our social interactions.
Select partners that bring balance to your place in society.
A marriage to someone whose wants and needs or goals are so divergent from our own that our social balance is shaken is more common than you may think.
A career that requires travel is not helped by a spouse with insecurity problems.
"Opposites attract," they say, and maybe so, but, does this partner help complete the social part of my life?
Help to balance family work and civil obligations?
Fit in to my social circles?
Have social circles where I find form and function?
Social order is not firm. It is fragile.
Imbalance can topple social structure.
Family is society in embryo, so does the relationship support or disrupt the balance there?

With business partners, the same is true.
With the things you teach your children to do in society, it is also true.

4
The Rune of stasis and stability,
Isa in Muspelheim, the Realm of the mind.
Do your relationships bring stability to your thinking process?
Do they help you think, and expand your temporal universe?
Or do they trouble you, distract you, drive you nuts?
A crafty business partner may require you to think about what he's doing so much more than one with a bit less going on.
Our mind is our reality.
The stability of its processes is so important.
Select partners with goals and ideas you understand.
If you let someone weaken your mind, you have a weak mind to show for it, plus what other damage may occur.
The idea of surrendering to a belief system that does not encourage the use of the higher mental faculties is

frightening when brought to light.
So don't do it.
Build relationships where stable mental function is a primary concern.
5
The joining Rune in the Realm of time.
Aiwaz in Niflheim.
Because time is a concept, this aspect is a concept.
The Realm of the Folk Soul is, to us, everything our ancestors have left to us, and everything we leave to our progeny.
This is quite simple.
Our relationships and partnerships should allow and encourage us to join with the work and needs of our family in time, past and future.
Selfish pride or sensationalism may lead us to view as old fashioned or "dead and gone" all things of the past,
and, of the future generations, little consideration is made.
Perhaps we think God will come and we need not worry about those yet to come.
When you look at this Lore closely, you'll see that you are that past and will be that future.
Relate to people who will help you relate to yourselves in time.
Our immortality is as real as we choose

to make it.
Help to realize the potential of this in your choice of companions.
Find yourself in history; see yourself in the future.
Build a relationship with yourself there.

6
The Rune of the Folk Soul in the Realm of death.
Laguz in Hel.
This Rune is half of the Ehwaz Rune we are studying.
Our spiritual self.
Our subconscious connection with all of our people, past, present, and future.
Our universal memory.
In life we enjoy the "pigeon hole" memory of the physical brain.
Our subconscious mind is free to use all of our memory and knowledge simultaneously to keep us in cycle with our life and our place in time.
While our conscious mind is only able to function because we provide it with form. "Ego." and continuity.
The idea here is to build a relationship with the much more vast and complex sub-conscious.
The saving of the self through death.

This makes the mind of the very young a very important thing, when the ego is formed.
Negative teaching equals temporary and sometimes base goals and self concept.
Overcoming this in self is hard, avoiding it in children is not.
The dream and hope of mankind is right here.
Salvation, eternity in interesting times, life in paradise.
The great experience over and over, ever wiser and more able.
This is your sub-conscious. Relate to it.

7
The journey Rune in the Realm of dark mysteries.
Raido in Svartheim.
Build relationships with people who will share your journey into the mysteries.
The Lore tells us that many of the tools of the Gods come from the Realm of mystery.
Sometimes the thing that works is made for another purpose.
Sometimes the thing we need cannot exist, yet we need it.
Only by taking the path that allows for the impossible do we have any chance

of finding it.
This Lore has already shown that we are in paradise, already immortal, already part of God's house.
We just may not know it.
Our journey will show it to us.
Form partnerships and relationships that help us along that mysterious path to your own back yard.
Do not choose partners with little vision, or negative values like fear, guilt, and hatred.
Encourage the adventure of life in others.
Venture into the unknown and find the mystical answers there.
They are too numerous to count, and too important to exclude from your plan.
Everything we do not know in life is in the Realm of mystery until we find it.

8
The ritual Rune in the Realm of strength outside ourselves.
Thursaz in Jotunheim.
Ritual can strengthen our character, our mind, our virtue.
We find a great source of personal strength in worship, prayer, and meditation.

Our identity becomes more clear.
We focus more clearly.
It is important to form a relationship with your **Ritual Self,** and to form relationships that encourage your ritual practice.
This helps us get the most out of our ritual experience, and to put the most into it.
In the wondrous journey of life, men put their actions into order.
Clarifying this order is part of ritual.
In the ritual dance of the outcome and future, we will be a part of that dance.
This relationship is with our whole being, drawn into one, and with our partners drawn to the common rites we share at a certain time in a certain way, for a certain purpose.
Ritual.
Our relationship with ritual is an anchor to keep us from drifting in pointless direction or from crashing on the rocks of a chaotic reality that offers nothing to ease our needs.
It is not the ritual that brings answers, but the result of all the effects of ritual on ourselves that bring the positive changes in our lives.
We don't find God in the ritual, we find

God through the ritual in ourselves and in all of the times and reasons for the ritual.
In short, everywhere, and always.
It is through relationships that we bring order, or Thursaz into our future and our outcomes.

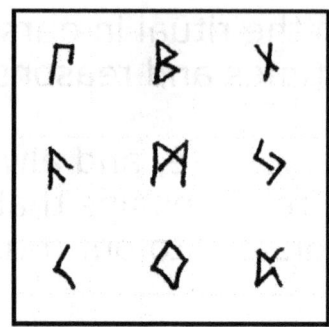

The Manaz Rune.
In our primary Rune study, we find the Manaz Rune is the last Rune that is about us personally.
All of the Runes leading up to Manaz are the blueprint for this place.
Just as Wunjo allows us to exist in the reality of a corporeal life not oppressed by our own ignorance, Manaz allows us to exist in the preferred reality of joy, victory, and home.
When we actually do the work of applying the Rune order to our method of living, the whole business of living becomes a continuing wonder of pattern, opportunity, and challenge.
True, a lot of your old acquaintances will not enjoy your company anymore.
A lot of things we used to do will not be attractive anymore.

We will find ourselves involved at the higher social levels working to improve things as we have been improved.
Some will discard this material and keep the lesser self.
Expect to be resisted as you step into your true places by all manner of argument by friend or foe.
You will know.
Your choice will tell whether you have become Manaz.
We don't just become Manaz because we grow up.
We have to do the work of becoming a resource for the Folk.
This is the extra mile, and with it comes opportunities that don't come any other way.
There is a reason for this.
The God mind is not ignorant of our humanity and will not tolerate powerful people kicking around in the area of spiritual sanctity that is represented and explained by the Runes following Manaz. The use of the great spiritual power and knowledge there is true medicine for living.
Posers, politicians, and bozos may not direct the power of the Cosmic.

Those powers may be directed only by those with a history of sacrifice, help, and contribution.

1
The great power of the Cosmos in the elemental Realm.
Uruz in Vanheim.
The Uruz Rune is naturally aspected in this Realm of material existence.
The power it represents is in the matter, just as the matter is the energy in an ever cycling oneness from the sub-atomic level outward.
That the Rune of man - Manaz - is found in the Realm of conscious action - Midgard - is the final answer to the eternal question, "Why are we here?"
This is an imperfect question.
Yes, we are individuals.
Yes, we choose everything, day by day, but, ours is not a singular experience.
The universe itself is the power of the high-minded sacrifice of the contributing man.
The purpose of the entire exercise is the development of true man.
If only one rose above the challenge, God would be corporeal, and the, then

living, breathing, God would be the child of the Cosmos, and the Cosmos itself.
That all may rise above the challenge is the becoming of the power and real substance of the universe in the living God-Self.
Individual, unique, perfectly imperfect, struggling, good-hearted, high-minded men and women who will their lives to be of greater meaning than mere creatures of muscle and bone.
Why are we here?
To taste, to touch, to smell, to feel the warm and the cold, to fall in love, to fear, to hate, to fail, to be in despair of honor and honesty ever brightening our day, and to decide that even if we have to do it all by ourselves, we will bring the glory of honor, honesty, love, hope and empathy to those who look to us for the stuff of life.
We are here to prove that God is real, not to demand proof.
What fool denies his own existence by denying the existence of the living Cosmos?
What greater fool entertains such ideas?
This aspect tells us that those who strive to be a boon to humanity do so with the power of life itself.

2
The nurturing Rune in the Realm of God.
Berkano in Asgard.
The reality of man here is in the true nurturing of the higher moral code itself.
Taking care of the Gods, the idea of God, the principle of God.
Rewarding those who do good.
Encouraging the practice of good.
Speaking about good.
Being an example of good moral character.
Knowing you care for and nourish your moral character gives you strength to resist immoral, amoral, or corrupt ideas and actions.
We are not born corrupt.
We are not conceived in sin.
Those are corrupt ideas invented to cause you to question your moral concept and moral authority.
The sad thing is it works.
More intelligent people, seeing this, may dispense with their moral concepts, as far as the group are concerned, and go it alone.
As the population gets smarter, the dogmatic religions get smaller because they rely on such ideas as original sin, and human impurity and hopelessness

I suggest that the smarter one is, the more quickly they can grasp and benefit from Rune Lore such as this.
The idea of a collective higher moral code is very palatable and inspires kinship and personal growth.
We have the voices, the hands and feet.
Do we expect God to provide more than a collective moral code?
More than a voice of conscience?
This is where man takes responsibility for his life, his family, his world, his universe, his God.
Take care of God.
Keep God healthy and strong.
Who else is going to do it?
Get off your knees and do it!

3
The need Rune in the Realm of society.
Nauthiz in Alfheim.
Here we find man's place in society is to meet a true need of society.
Honor and justice are the two basic needs of society, but every time and place has certain needs.
So often people choose their career based solely on how much they can make financially.

Society may not need more rich people if schools are so weak that the structure could fall soon.
Build what is truly needed.
Use your moral code to guide your argument for fair payment to all people.
Use your skills to improve the mores and social institutions.
Be a part, not a proprietor, of society.
Yes, it's easy to take without giving.
Society is just an idea, no hands, no feet.
Why is it heaven and hell in any city at the same time?
Because people don't act to serve the real needs of society.
Use your new moral authority to push your example along.
Do things in society that society really needs.
This could be paradise if you do this.

4
The harvest Rune in the Realm of the mind.
Jera in Muspelheim.
Man's purpose is to harvest the bounty of the God mind in the animal body.
This aspect tells us to figure out how to get paid enough or even more while

serving the needs of society, and millions of other things that a high moral code, powered by the universal power can do.
The stars are not the limit.
Time and death and magic are not the limit.
The meaning of life becomes clear.
It has been written from the start.
We are not meant to be aliens in paradise, nor to be guests in paradise.
Paradise is not a gift.
We are in paradise.
We are immortal, eternal, and whole.
We can make it all work without destroying any of it.
The answers are in your mind and in the Folk Soul.
As a teacher of the Lore, I tell my students not to learn the lesson from me, but to take my suggestion that there is a lesson there and to seek it out.
The mind is a wondrous tool, not a well of chaos.
The purpose of life is found in harvesting this great power and opportunity.
A big plus is that there is no down side to this.

When one can surrender belief and take up knowing, the strength of will can manifest itself with enthusiasm.

5
The Rune of chance and fate in the Realm of time.
Pertho in Niflheim.
This aspect suggests that all things are possible in time to the true man / woman.
By learning history through study and thought, we can make all possible, positive use of what has come before.
We can leave evidence, tools, and motivation to the coming generations to do likewise.
We do this all the while knowing that the shaping of paradise is what is truly happening here.
We know this in the deepest part of our being.
We are not trapped in corruption and hopelessness, but rather we are building on the failures and successes of time to reach the final product of creation.
The Rune of all possible possibilities means just that. We can harbor a hope for spiritual escape from the struggle of physical existence.

We can damn the lessons because they are hard.
We can succumb to guilt over errors and failures, or we can fight our personal demons and make an acknowledgment of the perfection of those lessons and the value of the growth from them.
The lessons are timed to our need.
Why is that?
Be your savior.
The possibilities available are unlimited, or are only limited by our willingness to accept them.
This is not belief, this is knowing and doing.

6
The Rune of seeing in the Realm of Death.
Ingwaz in Hel.
One message here is that man has a window to see into death.
We have seen in the previous Rune that we build a relationship with our part of the Folk consciousness so that we may preserve much of the recognizable self through death and return knowing more of ourselves each time.

Here we see a portal to view and interact both temporally and spiritually with those of the Folk Soul no longer physically alive, including ourselves. Such is the symbol on the night of the dead or a funeral rite, or spirit binding. We can look both forward and back in time.
Which of us does not know that our spirit, our soul, is not a new thing?
Our self, as a life, does not begin at birth.
We have always been.
The ego tool is new and we use this to seek the eternal self in the Realm of death because to the eternal self, life and death is what day and night, or dreams and waking, are to the ego self. The ego self does not need this concept to function because it is not relative to the ego purpose.
Incorrectly dealing with this can lead to fear of death or the abandonment of reason in seeking salvation or reprieve from death, or ego crisis, or antisocial or violent anger at the bad luck of mortality.
The spiritual self at the subconscious level is building without rest to bridge our history to our reality.

Use this aspect to see into the process and understand how it is working so we can help it along.
Our will can overcome man's greatest fear, while realizing man's greatest hope.
We need not wring our hands or accept when our leaders fail, or feel lost of purpose.
We can act true.
You matter in the big picture.
You are the purpose for the whole thing.
Not nations or governments or ideas, but you.
The flavor of the struggle is ours to savor forever.
Never boring, always fresh.
Life, love, struggle, thought, gain!
Children, children, children.
All of the joy you wish for.
But you must master the order to retain self awareness from cycle to cycle.
Harmless to the true order of life, and dangerous to the foes of order and of life.
These aspects are infinitely valuable because they display the true order in a way that cannot be misrepresented or exploited.

7
The Rune of light in the Realm of darkness.
Kenaz in Svartheim.
This aspect of man's purpose and truth is to bring a light into the mysteries.
We are doing a fair job of this in science and medicine.
We are doing a poor job in sociology, psychology, and political science.
The darkness is in us.
Fear, guilt, hatred, indifference all make it darker.
True, this is where the magic is and where the best of all things come from.
Those things are not available until we light up the primary parts of living.
The whole world is being directed by terror or the exploitation of terror.
The Folk have no guide, only trust in their leaders.
The Folk may use this guide and insist their leaders act according to the principles of order found here.
This will shine as a light into the heart of all of the reasons why our leaders do not lead.

Once exposed to the light of truth, the intrigues of public office lose their hold on the officers.
These men are like any men.
We can all be moved to act in ways that favor the few when we have no guide.
An idea cannot serve as a guide because one may interpret.
Here we see that when the universal power is used, the moral code protected, the best plan used, the past and future included, our reality included, then the answer becomes apparent.
Draw your own example and test it.
You will find no situation cannot be dealt with using this schematic.

8
The Rune of conscience in the Realm of power.
Ansuz in Jotunheim.
The final step in the purpose of life is to act out our plans with clear conscience, and to bring consciousness into the outcome / future.
By applying the previous aspects of Manaz we become empowered to act with the honest enthusiasm of clear conscience.

We can seek help from outside ourselves and get it.
Those with power you need will lend it in good faith, knowing your actions are true.
No matter what you are trying to do!
This says we have a right to use the power of the universe.
The right to decide what is good for the moral code.
What way to serve society.
What plan is best for us.
How best to use history and provide for the future.
What the truth is, when we do so in tune with the voice of conscience that speaks within us.
This also tells us that a man can answer any reasonable question when he is true.
A true man is happy to explain how making his will work upon the world is possible for him.
This joy is of higher accomplishment.
If there is an error, it will be placed and described, and corrected.
This is a process that cannot fail.
Only deceit can hinder, and deceit is immediately visible!
Man's purpose is to exist in truth in his

place in the universe.
We have studied every part of human existence as it is relative to the Realms of which our Cosmos is formed.
This is not theoretical, but applied relativity, explained for the purpose of personal practice and empowerment.
This is old knowledge in a modern era where truth is problematic to the plans, ideas, and self-view of most people.
The vulnerability of the masses is being exploited at a rate which could destroy mankind.
This knowledge will allow the ordinary person to halt the exploitation of themselves and their families instantly.
We can correct the system that is in place.
By simply asking questions based on these aspects, any good person can cause the highest leader to change a plan to a correct form.
This is the Realm of form.
All things not harmful to man may be done in the correct form.
The blueprint for these forms has been with man from the start.
Now is the age of completion, not destruction.
With this knowledge, true people are

empowered.
Those who intend ill or allow it in form will be invalidated by their own action.
This is the tool we have been looking for.
Why are we here?
I for one would not wish to be anywhere else.

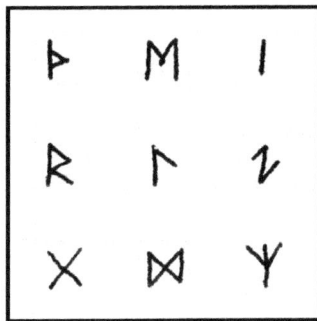

Laguz

Here we aspect the Rune of the primal conscience, the subconscious, and the Folk conscience.

This is the first purely spiritual Rune, and the bridge to our temporal-mental-process.

This is the lake from which all spiritual being comes forth. The soul of man.

It is by choice that we explore the depth of the primal mind.

It is by choice that we enter the waters of primordial life and embrace the spirit of the Folk and of God.

We still exist either way, but our identity and purpose will become sharper and more clear with this choice.

These aspects demonstrate the point of the universal exercise and the full significance of our part in it.

We are not an accident or a fluke.

Let's have a look.

1
The Rune of ritual, chaos, and change in the Elemental Universe.
Thursaz in Vanheim.
This Rune we apply to the act of breaking up the old and building the new.
We use ritual to more fully realize the difference in our selves from start to finish, through passage and purification.
The aspect of Thursaz in the elemental Realm shows us that the dance of the universe is a ritual on the largest scale and that the movement of the Cosmos is the act of becoming the spirit self embodied here in Midgard. Life here is the life of the Cosmos.
The life of the Gods.
Our spirit is the fruit of the universal ritual of life.
To me this is so reassuring.
I feel that the whole Cosmos is a part of me, and I can be at home in my life.
The greater being of which I've always felt myself a part is acting out the ritual, of which I am the product.
The whole Cosmos is one thing with a method and a purpose.
As in the microverse, so in the macroverse.

As we are becoming, God is becoming in the same space and time.
Every creature and speck of dust is part of the Divine birth of life as it should be.
The elemental dream.
The soul of man.
Me.
You
God.

2
The Rune of partnership in the Realm of Gods.
Ehwaz in Asgard.
The Ehwaz Rune here is the symbol of the joining of spirits, as well as symbiotic relationships and business and partnerships and husbandry.
Laguz' relationship to the higher moral code is just that, a relationship.
Ehwaz is a mirror image of Laguz, or two Laguz joined.
In Asgard this represents a spiritual joining with God or the Gods.
This does not suggest such a union, but rather indicates that such a union is and always has been there.
What good news to see that even in these ancient symbols it was clear that our spirit is joined to the great spirit.
The higher spirit is part of your spirit.

Just as the great Cosmic ritual brought us to be, so too has the great spiritual union found its mate in us.
This is not a gift bestowed to the elite chosen, but a fact common to us all.
I can't imagine a more inspiring aspect. You need not pray for the hand of God to lift you up, or inspire you. Your spirit reflects God's spirit.
On the other hand, we may no longer pretend that a higher moral code is beyond us.
It is a choice to explore the spiritual self. To extend the manifestation of will into the ethereal soul of the God self presumes intent.
Woe to him that would underestimate how quickly and completely one's spirit is wholly bonded with the Cosmic spirituality, that may act out a working of woe on a spiritual level.
The act of corrupting God is not a favorable one. Nor is the spiritual corruption of man less vile.
The use of fear, guilt, and hatred to simulate a spiritual environment for the purpose of enslaving men is not just wrong, it is unnatural and cruel.
Here the true spiritual union is pointed out.

By choice we may rise individually to our station as a reflection of the God spirit.
We can help each other to find this, but it cannot be given or sold.
There is no alternative explanation for this aspect.
We are a part of God.
To be a disappointment in the face of this beautiful realization is a heartbreaking idea.
This alone can do so much to inspire man to truly strive for a better outcome.
Here we can see that there is a God!
Not some alien being, but part and parcel of everything and everyone.

3
Stability in society.
Isa in Alfheim.
Here we see that it is the spiritual essence of man that brings stability to society.
We may believe the intellect is responsible for the development of the social institutions.
Religious orders controlled the social institutions for years, and developed most to their high standard.
Religion and spirituality are thought to be the same thing by many.

Religion can be an alien barrier between men and the common weal, though it serves on many levels.
Social intercourse is spirituality in action.
The ritual improvement of the mores through social institutions is the natural spiritual fulfillment of man.
The true spirituality of the masses is the great moving power on the earth.
Here we see that man can pattern the improvement of the social weal without the dogma or conflict of different religious or political ideals.
No social actor dares to say the betterment of man is not what they seek.
Likewise, one need not announce for a faction to be authorized to effect society.
We would have a faction, not action, in the place where action is required.
Social development has reached a point where the basic differences in the major belief systems are in constant conflict with each other, and with the principle of the absolute freedom of personal practice.
The masses cry out and the churches give them sex scandal, and violence.

The stability of society comes from the ability of each person to embrace their spirituality and act on it without embracing the corrupt or disgusting baggage of the factions, or being drawn to defend them.
The strength of character that comes from the spirit is the stability of the social Realm.
It is not from society that we receive stability in our lives, but rather our stability that is the power of society (see Isa aspected / Fehu in Alfheim).
Here the message becomes clear that our real, eternal, spiritual self gives stability to the social Realm so that we may find necessary growth.
The universe is the place where God becomes.
Society is the tool, and the shop.
Man is the vehicle.
Carry your spirituality with you out of the house and into the world.

4
The Rune of joining in the mind.
Aiwaz in Muspelheim.
Here the primal conscience joins with the mind to create the superman.

The bridge from ethereal to will is the work of this mind.

Here we become one with our eternal self as a working part of "what should be."

The mind will rationalize a joining with a belief system in the absence of the spirituality of the primal self.

Such a bond will be strong because the mind is geared for it. (Beware of acts of faith and belief.)

The spiritual self is known by choice, but the attempt to make a spiritual bond that excludes the primal spirit in favor of a religious offer of some kind will open the door to the eternal self.

The frustration that can develop from being schooled against recognizing our eternal self can cause much distress.

This aspect tells us to know and study our spiritual reality and then our actions will be sure and right.

Our spirituality, as we are in our daily, ordinary lives, not as in an abstract plane of existence, is our true spirit.

We don't need a dogma or a priest to find our spiritual self.

These Runes are only a map which shows us how our spirituality is relative to the other parts of our lives.

This aspect of joining mind and spirit opens a whole world of intelligent ideas about our spiritual wholeness and Cosmic relativity.
The taboo against questioning God and the spirit is lifted.
We should question and investigate our ideas about our soul, the Folk Soul, the Cosmic soul.
This ancient Lore encourages those questions, and fears not what you will find.

5
The Rune of progress and protection in the Realm of time.
Elhaz in Niflheim.
Here we find our progress through time and the protection of our ancestry and progeny is relative to our spiritual being. This is not to say that the technical and medical wonders of our physical actions are not important, but rather that our eternal spiritual essence is the actor in that progress and protection, for the soul is what lives on.
It is only by embracing the idea of the eternal self that the actions of the past become our actions, and that the ones

we advance and protect in the future we know to be ourselves.
Because the conscious ego is bound to this cycle, the timeless subconscious bears this burden.
Yet this allows us to use all the ego strength of self preservation as we choose our actions now.
The maintenance and wholeness that comes from recognizing and embracing our spiritual self and the Folk Soul is the fact that preserves the past and protects and advances the future.
This is a great "purpose" aspect and satisfies the human need for purpose on the personal as well as the Cosmic scale.
We see that fear of the spiritual is silly, and furthering the spiritual self is fundamental to our being.
All in all a very nice aspect.

6
The Rune of cycles in the Realm of death.
Dagaz in HeL
By now we have plenty of statements about death being a part of life as opposed to the end of existence.

Here again the ancient Lore has placed ideas in perfect relation to each other.
It is the spiritual being that inhabits the body in the world.
It is the spiritual being that cycles from life to life.
The body is a wonderful vehicle, but it is corporeal.
We inhabit the body.
We wear them out like automobiles.
We take care of them and try not to wreck them, but when one wears out, we don't stop traveling.
We get another one that is new to our journey.
Previous aspects have shown that the whole Cosmic engine is living through us, that the child of the Gods is parent to Gods.
As surely as we love and protect our own child, the Cosmic being, who lives through us, has protected us from the reality of wear and tear with renewal.
I marvel at how perfect the dance of life is and I see that the ages pass one to the next as the Cosmic being becomes whole.
The advancement of man's temporal circumstance is as the growing of a child.

The whole becomes more able and more challenged as time passes through our individual experience.

The answers of the past may not be sound today, but the lessons of the past are the reasons for those changes.

The Folk Soul has developed through the ages to reach the new possibilities of this wondrous time.

Instructions for spiritual development must change as the spirit develops.

We need not repeat history if we embrace our ever more capable self from cycle to cycle.

We do need to realize the truth in the ever-changing face of God found in the Folk Soul.

God is not stagnant or tied to an old dogma and man must make sure that he is not either.

This lesson, etched in stone from time primordial, has been the continuing blueprint for man as we truly are.

The steps of the mystic dance are the same, but the dancers grow more and more wondrous and the magic circle stretches to the stars and to the future.

This aspect is a note to remind us we have been here through it all and will be here through eternity.

Life will always be the perfect wish of the Cosmic soul to be.
You are that life.
Do not be afraid.
Do not be sad.
Only you can stand in your place, and draw your next breath.
This is yours!
The Cosmic being is you!

7
The gift Rune in the Realm of dark mysteries.
Gebo in Svartheim.
As I compile this catalog of Rune aspects, this one is the lesson of my life. Of all the arcane, occult, esoteric mysteries that could exist, the idea that I could discover that **the symbolic helm of awe placed on the symbolic head of Mimer** (the Rune stones and asterisk) would reveal the schematic of the God Head and the power of the Cosmos itself, as well as how man can fulfill his destiny, is beyond possible.
I lack the discipline.
This knowledge has giving itself to man now.
 A gift.

I have served the spirit in and through the mysteries.
I know the honor and privilege of presenting this knowledge is a gift to me and to all who find it here.
Through the ages these Runes have served as the time required.
Now the time requires that man see the relative place of all things human and Holy.
We will change as a species and will transcend The 'Is'.
We will take Cosmic steps in the sure light of purpose and destiny.
We have survived our own evolution to reach this place.
God, that is all and everything, is living through us and has no end of the journey in mind.
We need to know this now as a species. The barbaric, brutal behavior of the nations will not bring about the destruction of all.
Those who refuse will destroy and alienate themselves as the Folk set aside political and religious strife and take up the job of becoming as God would be. As we would be.

We need not don white robes or shave our heads, but you can if you want to.
The spirit can learn the hidden things in exchange for the spiritual investigation of those mysteries.
The stones wish to speak.
The heavens are said to predict and announce all.
As the age of Aquarius is born, all of its promise is born.
And this long-hidden map of mankind is revealed.
This aspect is the chime of days.
The key to a new awakening where confusion and enmity are not a part.
Look into the heart of the darkness with the eyes of the Folk Soul and see what you find.

8
The Rune of journey in the Realm of giant strength.
Raido in Jotunheim.
This aspect is fairly clear.
We will find the spiritual strength we need by choosing and staying on the true path.
The soul journeys into the outcome of our actions.
This is not a religious argument.

You know the true path when you see it.
The previous aspect tells us if we seek our answer to this mystery of the spirit, we will find it.
We will gain strength of purpose, will, and spirit from our path and along our journey.
Once again, an arrow through our fear.
The Rune of the soul, subconscious, Folk Soul is a beautiful study into the mind and plans of the Gods and the whole Cosmic being.
We have seen in this Rune that we are part of the ritual of the Cosmos, joined to God, stable in our place, whole in our being, necessary to all, eternal, blessed with the secrets of all things and destined to walk the path of God, strong and true.
The spiritual Rune is very inspiring.
The old ideas of corrupt flesh and original sin are empty.
You are born to be beauty.
You are the God wish, may your spirit be Blessed.

Ingwaz.
The Rune of seeing. The gateway to
Midgard, the home of true man.
This is the Rune of doorways to and from
our personal Realms of being.
These aspects tell us what we create in
coming to this life and what comes to us
in living this life.
The gateway to the genetic tree and the
origin of the Folk Soul.
The Rune of the twins Freyja and Frey
and our genetic path through history
and into the future.
The doorway to all Realms.

1
The voice of God in the elemental universe.
Ansuz in Vanheim.
Here we gain the right to see.
When we view the Cosmic with this Rune we see that consciousness enters the physical universe through Ingwaz.
Form the "new" quark, to the super giant star.
From the correlating color of the light spectrum to the formation of atomic particles in the same structure as the consumed matter that released the energy that became the quark that is again as it was before.
The view of the constellations as they announce the ages and the thresholds of human change.
The personal connection of God to the place where you live, and to the world and universe you see as you live, is real.
We can stop struggling with the basic question and begin to act on the answer.
Yes! God is real.
God is not "out there."
"Out there" is God.

God speaks not in riddles, but in perfection plainly viewed, and always present.
God speaks to all who listen, or watch, or feel.
The mystery of God is that there is no mystery.
The message is before every eye.
Listen.
Look.
See that you are consciousness in form.
The voice of God is in all things.
We are among those things, as the children of dreams.
We hear this voice in our conscience as it affirms or denies the choices we face.
This voice guides us to a harmony of movement as balanced and purposeful as any natural event.
There is a universal conscience.
This we can see.
This "message in a bottle" will be found again as it has been found before.
About the time when we lose sight of why we care about the whole thing as much as we care about ourselves.

In time, silly men will claim they can do what needs doing and the world will let them, and they will make a mess.
Like today. Like always.
Then, again, a great message will be found.
But each time man has grown closer and better.
We see that the voice of a God is the universe.
"In the beginning there was a word."
2
The Rune of man in the Realm of the Gods.
 Manaz in Asgard -
Through the window of our ancestry we see that man sits in the "just as high" seat in Asgard.
Man is the actor in Heaven's plan.
Man is the font of righteous action and moral code.
It is not God's goodness that will see us through, but our own.
It is not God's values that make a difference, but our own.

Living in need of forgiveness is a waste of life.
With the voice of the All Father in all things, and the face of the All Mother, our ability to reach the "just as high" is apparent too.
The illusion that such aspiration is wrong is a tool to steal your right to reach your destiny.
We have the right by our very presence here to reach the "just as high."
Man is God in a body.
God is a warrior, a poet, a lover, a father, a mother, a baby.
Man is God, God is man.
Now behave that way and things will work out.
Fix what is broken.
Break nothing else unless you are making something better from the pieces.
This message is pretty clear.
The voice of God in the elemental universe tells us that God is becoming through the lives of men.
We can make progress toward that truth.

It is our destiny to progress toward that goal. A good question is this, "What would God do, if God could do anything his/her heart desired?"

I think God would touch and taste, fall in love, explore, swim, fly, embrace the struggle of morality, battle with envy and greed, try to overcome fear, guilt, and hatred one circumstance at a time. All the while learning to be God in living, breathing form.

All of the challenges would have to be overcome or the life would not be "true."

All of the challenges would have to be real or the victory would not be "true."

This says God is no more or less Godly than we allow by our actions.

This also shows the value of the applied Runes to our lives, because through that we can realize "true" action in our lives. We have a way to make our plans that allows the best level of success.

We are the arms and legs of the Gods. We do the talking, the learning, the light lifting.

We can do it right.

3
The harvest in the social Realm.
Jera in Alfheim.
To continue from the last aspect
Manaz in Asgard.
where would God get the experiences to perfect the physical being of self?
The lessons are harvested from the social interactions of human life and broadcast for all to benefit by.
From Gandhi to Rodney King, we all see it all.
The harvest is good!
Communications keep getting better,
"Can you hear me now?"
We can see that as the new age unfolds, the harvest grows and the God Mind finds ways to exist in the animal body as a God and not an animal.
This education could come in no other way.
True, some lives have been lived in pain or servitude or even terror and suffering throughout.
They are part of God.
Some lives have never known anything but contempt and disregard for all things good or helpful.
They too are part of God.

All of these social events make up the necessary working knowledge that will result in "True Folk."
The Creator fleshed out and living.
Society is the playing field for scoring the winning points.
Health care, education, economic stability, ethnic self-respect.
Strength of leadership, and truthfulness in general.
Also the pain of deception, fear, guilt, and hatred.
Seek the true Harvest.
Take the best and learn all from the rest.
4
The chance Rune in the Realm of the mind.
Pertho in Muspelheim.
Here we see that all things are possible when we look into the mind.
All things great and small, wonderful and evil.
What do you intend?

If God were to create a self through man, as has been suggested by these Runes, what would the steps be?
Everything that man learns about the past does not lead away from God.
Scientists day by day make it more clear that every step toward the reality of the God Self has been taken according to the physical natural laws of the universe.
Science does not admit one detail in its view of the universe, however, and that is that life is not a mysterious anomaly, but that the entire universe is alive and very much so, and that the whole universe strives for the realization of its life as sentient self in man.
We should consider also that madness is more common than it appears.
Many revered leaders of nations and faiths are quite mad.
Using the mind to find ways to rape the earth, to control resources, enslave people, manipulate the wealth, cheat the population, to justify violence or threat of violence, that too is possible, and quite insane.

So, using the mind to find ways to expose and stop such things is sane, and necessary.
We must know that it is possible to realize our potential.
Belief is not enough as is proven by the number of high-minded believers who allow corruption to grow under their supervision.
Whenever anyone says they need to lie to advance the plan, then they, or the plan, is wrong.
We need to use the mind, not the emotions, to reach our destiny.
In the mind the answers can be found.
Truth that transcends belief, faith, and hope.
Look into your mind and find the truth and possibility.
5
The Rune of victory in the Realm of time.
Sowilo in Niflheim.
This is the Realm of ancestry and progeny.
This is the land of the lake of souls, past, present and future.

All of these ancestors have not failed because they died.
All of the children will not die because you fail.
This is the illusion of validation through immortality.
We don't need to escape the cycle of life to succeed in the Realm of time.
As we have seen in the Laguz aspects in the last chapter, our spirituality is not mortal, but cycles as all things do.
The ego we all seek to transcend is mortal.
This is the key bit of news to seekers of the truth.
As we have seen, the ego is a tool to operate the body while the soul / Folk Soul / subconscious fulfills your destiny.
The ego is laid to rest with each cycle.
Just as Sowilo is the true Rune of love which is possible when we put our emotional self in order, the aspect here is of victory over the fear of time and the loss of the ego self through the changing cycles.
We know that the soul / Folk Soul preserves the life in its entirety

(see last chapter).
Here we can see victory in time by preserving the soul and experience while removing the fear of inadequacy.
The ability to transcend death as an act of ego, to preserve the disposable and break the cycle of the eternal self is about the most ridiculous desire.
To live on so one could keep his wealth, or power, or because of the fear of death, would be to live on alienated from the Divine plan and outside of the ritual dance of all things.
The ego, as well as the body, bears the rigors of life.
The toxins that poison the body, the experiences that corrode the ego.
We dump the garbage and go clean to another round.
This is what victory over the emotions brings.
This is what the victory we see in time means.
Here we see true victory over time.
The preservation of self is possible.
This is a question of moral content and intent.

The Folk Soul will provide every possible tool to the ego as we experience life. Personal identity may be among them, though it may appear in a more poetic form than the grasping of ego.
Anything short of supplanting the active ego is possible.
(See next aspect.)
6
The Rune of home in the Realm of death.
Othalaz in Hel.
We see home in death.
It is from our home that we journey to the store, to work, to recreation, to social functions, to all things in life.
As in the microverse of personal living, so in the macroverse of eternal existence.
We journey from the extra-dimensional, eternal home through the Ingwaz Rune, the Frey Rune, the Rune of the seed and womb, to our corporeal job in the actualization of the God Mind in the physical form.
Here we see the action of becoming as we know ourselves to be in ego.

This is the door to being, and we can
use it by act of will as we exist.
We can see all of this and so know it
even though the "vision" is not involved.
We came to this life from home.
We go home from here.
We come back to work on the great
project, our project.
We do this in the company of the ones
we love, over and over again.
So much for sorrow, we will see them at
home, or back here later.
This is the understanding and real
knowledge used in the sex magic ritual
to bring specific people to be.
There is no ghoulish, scary, hugga-
mugga, just life from life from life.
You, me, your mom, all from home, all
with a full exciting life of stuff to do,
learning what needs to be learned.
Doing what seems hardest at the time
to do.
We also see how much better off we'd
be if we knew this stuff growing up.
Back in the day the myths and stories of
heroes held the clues.

Put the clues back in the stories so the kids can find a sense of belonging and purpose.
Be at home in this wonderful life, but remember our home can be found in each Realm in a different way.
Fear not your fate.
Get to work!

7

The Rune of joy in the Realm of dark mysteries.
Wunjo in Svartheim.
We have come to see that even though life is not truly as it seems, it is even more wonderful than it seems.
We have revealed many things that have been kept in the mist until this time in history.
Man has always found fear and horror in the mysteries, but also joy in the discoveries of those who explore the darkness and return with new things.
Here we see that there is joy, personal, real joy in the dark Realm.
Courage, purpose, and truth take us into the dark mysteries.

To manifest our will based on these virtues is the test of character that marks those whose lives go farthest in the realization of the God Mind in physical form.
The dark powers do not serve dark purpose, they serve the one purpose that brings all that is into tune.
Go to the hard places and see the illusion fade and the higher purpose appear.
To travel as a true being, under your own charge,
Fehu.
Powered by the true power,
Uruz.
In ritual form,
Thursaz.
With the voice of conscience as a guide,
Ansuz.
True to your path in life,
Raido.
Using the light of truth to show the way,
Kenaz
Honoring each action along the way.
Gebo.
Acting as the key to all things before you.
Wunjo.

You will find joy searching for the hardest answers, beating the strongest villains, exposing the ugliest problems. For the rest of your life!
Nurturing, belonging, and purpose.
Live the excitement of challenge and goal personally, rather than vicariously through the entertainment media.
We see the mysteries hold what we do want, though they seem to hold what we do not want.
One of the great mysteries of all time is found in this simple truth.
The obvious answers are so often incorrect, and the least desirable path often leads to the best answer.
Success is usually hidden from the casual seeker.
Use the aspects of this Ingwaz Rune to learn what to look for and what you are seeing.
The adventure is in the doing of the important things.
Go there!
Living example.
Looking for answers.
Correcting problems in the whole.

8
The Rune of light in the Realm of outside strength, and outcomes.
Kenaz in Jotunheim.
The light into the future shines through the doorway of our genetic creation.
The eyes of our children shine with the light of our lives in the outcome of our actions.
We have the luxury of seeing what will be in time.
So often we see efforts made to make positive change that get struck before they bear fruit.
Projects that just can't seem to be nailed down and finished.
Wonderful ideas that don't get off the ground.
Wonderful ideas that go horribly wrong.
We can almost always trace the trail of breakdown to a place where the truth was abandoned, or to a place where the truth broke through and revealed the intrigue in the plan or project.
Somehow men nurse the illusion that truth is an immaterial idea.

We see here that truth is the fundamental base that stirs enthusiasm, and commitment.
A half-hearted truth earns half-hearted support.
The simple power of this aspect is best realized by the self, so think about the help, strength, advice, and eager encouragement the truth both needs and rewards.
Think about the child you will be on that day in the future when you realize you have known someone for a long long time.

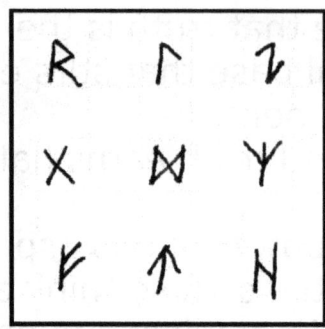

Dagaz - the cycles of change.
The cycles of movement in all things are relevant to the experiences of men. Mankind is also a body in motion and though we may exercise free will in our choices, our manifestations of will in bringing our actions to fruition must conform to natural order so that very important factors may be realized in life. The point being that every thing in existence cycles, ourselves being no exception.
Again and again we live with no hard memories of our own past.
This Lore explains why that is so.

1
Raido, Rune of journeys, in Vanheim - the elemental universe.
The elemental universe is the form our life will take.
Wasting thought on escape in some alternative realities is of no moment.
We cannot outrun it.
We cannot delay it.
We can put our life journey, our spiritual journey, in harmony with the living journey that the elemental universe is also taking as we live.
This combination of will, spirit, our experience and the elemental universe creates the Cosmos.
More than space and matter in motion, but thinking Cosmic wholeness.
This is no less than the sacrifice of ones abstract sensation seeking to the human need to belong.
The term "child of the universe" is not a comic term.
It is a very real identity.
No matter what station in life, we are all travelers together along the Cosmic path.

No one has more value than any other.
Many forgo their worth in pursuit of a separate journey, or forgo their journey in search of a separate worth.
Rune Lore puts wealth and creative ability as the first responsibility in life.
We must run on our own power and pay our own way as we build our lives.
We must be free to choose as we go.
Yet we must be cautious of abandoning the elemental journey that is truly the one thing we all share.
Our true life.
We cannot change the cycles of even the simplest thing.
We can tune our path in life to a harmony with the cycles.
Make your life journey an ordered one and you won't have to fight with forces of inertia and time that make up natural movement.
This is not just an achievement, it is **the** achievement.
2
Laguz the Folk Soul conscience in Asgard, God's home.
This is a beautiful aspect.
Here we see that the cycles of life in Midgard provide the Folk Soul of God.

The Folk Soul is the life of the one being that is created by our experiences.
This demonstrates that we are kin to the Gods and that here is a Godhead.
The ever growing, ever changing face of God is shaped by the lives of men.
The content of the father's character is shaped by the success and failure of the children, and vice versa.
The distance between Gods and men is man's to determine.
Man has the legs to walk closer to the Gods.
Man has the opportunities to act, interact, and react in ways that bring men and Gods together in the Folk Soul.
The Holy Spirit Soul, if you will.
The Grand Concepts each came from somewhere, they did not blossom from whole cloth.
These opportunities are cyclic just as everything else.
Being in tune to the Cosmic journey makes this possible.
This whole sharing of life's greater journey, God's greater mind, and the common Folk Soul is what makes us part of the days of every life in every time.

Just like every atom in existence we also must cycle, or the entire universe would end.
There can be no exception.
No beings who are not subject to natural law, death, or cycling like everything else.
None, or it would not be real, it would be just a dream.

3
Aiwaz in Alfheim, the social Realm.
One's time of growth, time of rest, time of contemplation, time of vigor are the cycles we experience on our journey together.
By joining into the social Realm as a part, the growth, education, contemplation, and vigor of the group, we are able to interact to make change.
Society is ever evolving, because it is an amalgam of uncommon ideas the cycles of which are reflected from the people.
Mass alienation from society allows tyranny amid stagnation as certainties.
Society must be in time with the people, not the reverse.
Society as mindless, non-cyclic group or association by agenda and often force, **or** as the harmonious interaction of

people of the Folk Soul on the Cosmic journey.
Leadership that does not manifest a plan that promotes this harmony is false.
One should give a lot of thought to the station in society non-living entities like corporations or the state are allowed to play as the negative effect on the people, **that always** leads to repression and revolution are results of the absence of the Folk Soul from the motivation of such entities.
The joining of men to a social structure must be based on human goals and considerations.
A government of men, and of laws, not government of laws and not men.
There is no joining of men and social institutions that are rigid in form.
Men must submit to rigid rule or be broken.
Flexibility to meet the changes in the people is needed in social institutions.
Military discipline is not the way to guide a nation not at whole scale war, and that must be avoided with great vigor.
This aspect explains a great many shortfalls in leadership.

4
Elhaz in Muspelheim
Protection and progress of the mind.
The basic human cycle being the passing of days, this aspect tells us to marshal our days to the best interest of our mental development and protection of our thinking resource.
Because the conversion of reactive emotion into rational thought is the job of our higher thinking ability, the task of warding and promoting this work is of great importance.
We can school ourselves in the negative to be extremely reactionary and defensive, but this does nothing to promote the thinking process, though it is very common.
Rationally motivated action may still be forceful if necessary, but **the extremes of emotionally driven action are not a factor.**
Domestic violence is often the result of failure to embrace this aspect.
Also remember that we can become smarter every day.
Intelligence is not fixed.
In this way the cycles of our days bring progress to our thinking process.
This is a conscious process of the will.

A very powerful concept that we can easily put into practice in our minds.
We are protecting and advancing our very humanity.
This aspect takes away the idealism of high-minded choices that can become a pose, and reduces the act to an instruction.
Leaders are limited to doing the right thing, not allowed excessive or extreme powers.
In day to day life, this aspect works to keep us out of situations of stress and crisis.
There are times in the cycles of men when embracing passion is the correct choice.
Always remembering that choice is a rational process, we find a very useful instruction.
5
Hagalaz in Niflheim - balance in time.
Remembering that Dagaz is a spiritual Rune, here we bring balance to our cycles into and out of our places in time.
All of time is effected by our actions in the here and now.
The excesses or shortfalls of our fathers are dealt with while we live with an eye on bringing balance to the time yet to

come.
Revolution is forestalled by bringing such balance.
Our children need not be pressed to right the wrongs left on their doorstep.
Hence, progress.
We have many opportunities in life to make these corrections.
These opportunities always arrive in cycle with our power to act on them.
Again it is an act of will to make the important corrections we perceive.
One important duty of noble man is to rise to the occasion and overcome fear, guilt, and hatred to act correctly without the excesses that will require correction themselves.

6

Tiwaz in death - justice.
Here the cycle of life is in change.
The five aspects of this Rune leading to here are the keys to final judgment.
This judgment does not come from another, but from Ourselves.
In striving to actualize this Rune (Dagaz) in our life journey, oneness with the higher moral code, connection with society, advancing of our God mind, and balancing the excesses of the time we bring justice to our life at the moment of

death. What this means is made clear in the next aspect.

7

Fehu in Svartheim. Personal wealth / power in the Realm of darkness and mysteries.

People don't so much fear death as we fear the darkness and mystery it represents.

The whole Dagaz Rune in aspect tells us that we can achieve power to effect our non-corporeal existence in the dark magic of the return (death).

Rune Lore does not promise that someone will save you, if that someone is favorably impressed with your life.

Rune Lore tells us how to become eternal.

Step by step.

The fact of continued existence is not the point, because that is a given.

Self-awareness from cycle to cycle is the point.

We **keep** the essential struggle that is the joy and challenge of life.

We **keep** the knowledge of the joy of virtue.

We **keep** the knowledge of our place in the Cosmic scheme.

We continue to bring the essential balance to the generations.
We experience an ever increasing quality of being.
We do this because we have purchased the **right** by doing the **rite** of a Wunjo lifestyle.
Here we have applied Fehu from its second appearance on the Uppsala Rune Stone, and it is mutated into an even greater personal power.

8
The gift / Honor Rune in the Realm of giant strength.
Gebo in Jotunheim.
Here we find the ultimate gift of form and wholeness brought to the Realm of the Jotan / Wotan.
It is the cycles of human behavior, as a whole, that brings this gift of life to the dual being of power.
When we are able to battle for what should be, then we battle to bring strength to Wotan, the big helping hand.
When the times deny us the battle, we must wait without giving power to the juggernaut, the giant Jotan.
Remember, this being is created by us and is the sum of the unintended

consequences from our poor choices, **or,** the ordered outcome of our wise choices.
It is the cycles of life in Midgard that bring the Gift.
Because we live our lives, wisely the Gods have their lives.
The entire ebb and flow of the Cosmic is one great machine.
The great machine is a living being and the direction of intent is of our making.
Our fragmented, non-directed ramblings fuel a monster of immoral rage that preys on the weak and seduces the strong into base behavior.
This is a cycle of human actions that will pass, but into what?
Usually Fascism rises from decadence refocused on a driving principal, brought forth by a strongman.
Such a cycle would again feed the giant and starve the God.

The awake and aware behavior of the Folk intent on avoiding both extremes can bring an honorable result to the Realm of mutation, and we could empower the Cosmic being in form, in balance, in honor, without fear of the result.

For God to be real, the test must be real. The duality need not be destructive of form, to endure.

Because nothing is fixed, the Jotan Realm can give back both positive and negative power that mutate the cycle to match.

Fire, fuel, fire, fuel.

God, Giant, God, Giant.

In name, still, only part of the cycle that makes up the gift of God in form, which is the essence of the Cosmos.

The duality of reality on the grand scale is our gift to give and to receive.

Man, God, Giant, man, God, Giant.

This makes more sense than it seems like it should, because we're actually doing it.

It is better to know what we are doing than to wander in the dark, so let this be a cycle of light.
It should be clear by now that we are the driving force behind our own creation.
You look out from behind your eyes as do I, to see ourselves take part in the world we have made.
It looks like we have decided it was time to share the secret with ourselves.
If this were not so, it would not be happening.
Think about it.

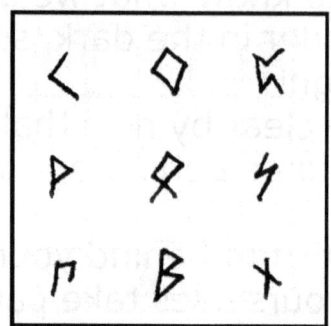

Othalaz in Midgard.
Being at home in this world, in this life, in this body, in this time.
Ram Das' wonderful book, "Be Here Now," gives a cozy portrait of the simple joy found in this concept.
We will see now that there is wonder and power in this idea as well.
So often people do not feel ownership for their own lives.
We feel like visitors in our own skins or families.
Sadly the reason for that is a serious dilemma we should probably deal with as soon as we can.

1
The truth – Kenaz in Vanheim.
To be at home in this life, we find the truth of the elemental universe:
manifest sentient matter.
Science may indicate that its data refutes a certain dogma.
So what? Dogma is dogma.
The truth that science does not state is that the steps to the creation of the child of God have been followed precisely.
The proof is in the product.
We are.
Steps cannot be skipped in the making of anything from pie to wine to tool steel to memory chips.
Why claim that God does not exist simply because steps were not skipped in the making of man?
Because "what is" provided for it?
The elemental universe is.
Theorizing on how it came to be serves no purpose, but to detach man from his home.
The truth **is.**
Man **is.**

Ancestral home **is.**
It **is here.**
We are from **here.**
We are **here.**
The food is **here**
The water is **here.**
Use truth to support your interaction and identity.
The truth cannot be overcome.
The cornerstone of the elemental home must be the truth, or no foundation exists.
However, anything can be built upon the truth.
The truth does not hurt the true.
The first Norn, is **what is** and we are here.
2
Ingwaz in Asgard. A view of God.
From this ancestral home one has a picture window view of the higher moral code of the creator.
Warm and fuzzy are necessary only when the view is dim and blurry.
Clear and open witness to the will of your own need is a circumstance of

choosing the true elemental home we spoke of earlier.
Thanks to this we can guide what is becoming with a moral code that emulates what we willed in the first place.
Giving real life to the second Norn, what is becoming.
Openly guiding ourselves in a revealable way without fear, guilt, or hatred.
One need not believe anything.
One can be their own religion.
The big question of all time is, "Why does God not show a face so we can know?"
Well, God's face is the most evident thing we encounter in our lives.
It 'is becoming" of all things, changing by what we do, as we grow.
Where is the mystery?
What you see when you look for proof of the Gods is the Gods themselves.
Wake up.
3
Pertho in Alfheim.
By accepting the truth of the elemental universe and the face of God that is visible from such a home, the power to act in society becomes perfect.
One can enter any social endeavor.

Truth and morality cannot be challenged by deceit and immorality.
People can be lured into immorality or the acceptance of deceit, but until they choose to fail, they cannot be toppled from without.
Also, one may re-embrace the truth and morality at any time and become strong again.
People stumble.
All people stumble.
Cruel people jump on people who stumble to promote the image of truth and morality in themselves.
Because truth and morality shine with the elemental power of the universe and the wholesomeness of the God mind, any image pretending these things is instantly apparent to one who does possess those virtues.
Viola!
Power over the social evils!
Just, honorable society becomes as possible as it is desirable.
You have a place!
Mean plans are never toward "what should be," the final Norn, so it's all pretense anyway, and clearly so.
Such speakers occupy the jobs of authority in most cases.

Politicians, lawyers, bureaucrats.
Remove them with truth.

4
Sowilo in Muspelheim.
Victory over one's abstract imagination brings victory over outside enemies.
One becomes separated from those who are not in command of their passionate thoughts, and the dissociative acts of authority that come from them.
Guidance and direction do not go hand in hand.
Guidance comes from without, direction is from within.
The authorities cannot direct people without absolute dominion.
Physical, spiritual, or emotional, when outside forces take charge of any of these aspects of human existence,
the whole life is taken in charge.
We must take charge of our own minds.
We must corral abstract imagination and use cognitive imagination to build our plans and thinking processes.
The "idea" that is society cannot be in charge.
Such concepts are the product of abstract imaginings.

Victory over one's mind from without is horror.
Forced political correctness.
From within, it is peace and purpose.
So often we are distracted by our ideas about what other people **may** be thinking that we do not act in our own interest, but as we think others **may** think we should act.
Often these are people we do not even know, and will, in all likelihood, never know, yet our self-perceived impression on them controls our actions.
This is a dangerous disconnect from our own thinking, and warrants some serious thought.
5
Nathiz in Niflheim.
By making our home in the here and now, we serve the needs of our ancestors and their efforts toward us and our progeny and their hopes for a meaningful life.
Dogmatic belief systems have drawn us very near to destruction by our own hand.
Believing that our lives are intended for another place, a Heaven or Nirvana or sky home or alien planet opens the door to the destruction of our children and

the place they will need to live, and the waste of our fathers' lives.
This is so selfish it sickens even the hard of heart.
No rationalization quite covers that, such as blaming Satan, or another religion, or claiming that it's all in prophecy.
If I prophesy in the name of God that your house will burn down this winter, are you bound to set it alight if spring draws near?
Is this how we prove we love God?
Do we blame God, and say he moves in mysterious ways while the responsibility for the ruin lies squarely at our feet?
We can solve all these problems simply by being at home in our lives, in our time, in our place.
Answer the need of humanity in real ways.

6

Berkano in Hel.
The nurturing mother Rune placed in the space in between life and life.
Continuing to exist through death and in to new life is an act of will.
Your future is not an if, or if not random occurrence.
You have always been.

You will always be.
Will your being spend lifetime after lifetime on the edge of remembering who you are and what you have done? Like we do now?
Will a veil of mystery separate you from the "soul" you know you search for?
Or will you husband your memories and commit them to your spiritual memory as you live so you will know who you are when the pigeonhole memory of your brain becomes suddenly unavailable?
Be at home in your life!
Use the brain as a tool for the mind, but remember your reality in time is with your soul.
When one believes that the soul belongs to someone else and surrenders it in death, the entire experience of that life is lost to that soul.
The reason is that each true act in the ordered life is preceded by a declaration of destination and intent.
When we declare ourselves to be non-viable entities waiting for the end, that is our destination and intent.
Keep yourself through the process.
Nurture your whole self.
Actually be "born again," and again
Suddenly, providing for your progeny

makes a lot more sense!
You are that progeny!
The earth you are saving is your home.
The children you raise are your parents, or grand parents.

7

Uruz in Svartheim.
The darkness. The mysteries.
This aspect is about the mystery of the power of life itself.
The unknown that we all know holds a necessary reality.
The elemental power of the universe can be found here **and used** by the one who is at home in this life and time.
This is the one power of which all other powers are a part.
One cannot sneak up on this access.
One can freely tap this power through the realization of the ancestral home Rune.
No pretender can stand in the power of the universe.
The fear of darkness and the unknown will control those whose dogmatic beliefs preclude "knowing" the face of God.
The face in the darkness is not the face of evil.
The darkness is not darkness once we

will ourselves to become who we have always been meant to be.
It is the light that causes the shadow.
The darkness does not exist in itself, but only in contrast to the light.
As in the microverse, so in the macroverse.
Children grow up.
In body always.
In mind? Hmmmm.
God's children grow up too, if they want to.
Be the light.
Use the power in the darkness.
There the form is not yet taken.
Give form to the power in the darkness.
Bring from the darkness that which has not yet become.
Uruz is the power of life.
One who is in the home of their existence, may bring forth that power and give it a name.
We do this when we bring children into the world, and in all acts of art as well.

8
Wunjo in Jotunheim.
Wunjo is the ordered life.
This is the Realm of the outcome.
The future.
Tomorrow.
When we take responsibility for our place in time, we gain the Realm of the future as the being best suited to live there.
One who is at home in his life and time is no threat to those whose strength they call upon.
It's all within one's personal reach.
This removes fear of failure, fear of trying, fear of dying.
We can strive with enthusiasm.
So, we have basic truth, moral understanding, social opportunity, self-control, family service, care of spiritual life, power of mystery and magic, and personal use of strength outside ourselves.
All this just for making our home on the rock of our reality instead of hope and fantasy.
To bring the ordered and directed person to the future and outcome of our existence is the most beautiful thing I can imagine.

And so comes to a close the Rune aspects as revealed by the Helm of Awe.
Everything that anyone has ever wanted, or dared to hope for.
An owners manual for a human life.
The thing that cannot exist.
From simple survival to mastery of our whole life drawn in stone from time beyond knowing.
These truths are as old as man.
The God mind in the animal body.
The oldest secret society on earth has passed down the information in geometric design cut in the stonework of almost every major building ever constructed.
These ancient patterns hold the answers in themselves because the principles of this knowledge are presented as parts of an exact pattern that appears as a split diamond check, the eight-pointed square over a square, the eight paned cathedral window, the floor tile of the great palaces.
The Library of Congress.
Thousands of times in our lives we see the pattern.
Does this society even know what they have preserved?
For whom is this knowledge kept?

Who drove this knowledge under ground?
Why?
As we answer these questions for ourselves, we see why now in man's history the time is finally ripe for the wholesale sharing of this knowledge.
The time for kings and potentates is past.
The time for the exploitation of the Earth and its inhabitants by those who do not share of the common weal will soon pass.
That time will pass as man embraces the responsibility of the God mind he possesses.
The great illusion of God can finally be replaced with the much more beautiful reality of the Cosmic being that really does exist, and of man, who is the manifestation of that magnificent life.
Politic will mean the pursuit of the actualization of these principles into the social institutions.
Politicians will be unable to mislead the masses or abuse the power of the people they serve because everything they attempt fits in the pattern, and the steps are obvious.
Lies become glaring spectacles!

Dissembling becomes mumbling nonsense.
Government leaders become simple functionaries.
The power to corrupt is gone.
Only the jobs remain.

A final note to the reader:

Because a better word is not available, God is used often in this work.
No particular designation is intended, as all previously held concepts of such a being are pale in the light of what these Runes and their creators reveal as Divine.
To find what they knew as a higher moral reality is so humbling, that I am not able to rise to an opinion on the question.
I am simply awed by the whole thing.
I truly hope you find joy in this set of analogies, and that your own are even more beautiful and self-inspiring.
Good luck!

Important note

The Othalaz set of aspects holds the story of the downfall of man as the Child of God.

You will note Ingwaz, the Rune of seeing and entry is in the Realm of Gods Home, or Asgard in this set.

By simply convincing people that this home is transient and that our true home is elsewhere, mans' view of God is taken away and we can be led or directed blindly by those who swear they have such a view or knowledge, and "Poof" our grasp of Divinity is gone.

We deny it because some one told us it was wrong to feel good about yourself.

Some one told you you were broken, corrupt and doomed.

Some one told us we failed God and could never make it right.

Your truth is beautiful and you can feel good about that.

Again, Welcome home!

BONUS

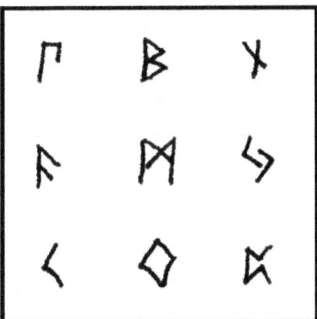

Because you have stuck it out to the end of the book, the Runic display for the meaning of life is included here.

Manaz or Man as he should be is in the middle so at top left,

1 Uruz, to channel the resistance of life in form.

2 Berkano, to nurture a higher moral code and take care of what is right.

3 To find a need in society and fill it.

4 To harvest the full power of the mind.

5 To make every possible use of what our parents leave us and leave every possible opportunity for our children.

6 To open the doorway through death.

7 To shine a light into the darkness and reveal what is there.

8 To bring the voice of God and moral consciousness to the outcome of our actions and the days to come.

 There you go, the meaning of life is not such a mystery after all.

 I make this note to emphasize the power of this information.
 This is not just a book to make me money, it is a way to correct the fundamental failing of our social structure as sentient beings and as a higher life form.
 Each aspect is a precious building block of that high road.
Join me on this beautiful journey!

                    Thank You

Computer Base

Cut out these two pages and make your computer.
It is important that you draw in the Runes in yourself.
 Be sure they are correct and think about each one as you draw it. [Do a clean job of it.] You will know why as you get going on it.

Realm Star

Using a razor cut out the 'x' marked squares. [Nice and clean cuts.]
This is the moving part of your template.
The center is the focus for all queries, [It is about you]

	Body Form		Morals Faith		Social Action	
	X		X		X	
Result	X		X		X	Mind
	X		X		X	
	Un Known		Death		Kin Time	

www.ingramcontent.com/pod-product-compliance
Lightning Source LLC
Chambersburg PA
CBHW071642160426
43195CB00012B/1330